The New York Times

REPORT
FROM
RED CHINA

The New York Times

REPORT ★ FROM RED CHINA

Tillman Durdin
James Reston
Seymour Topping

With Photographs and Additional Articles
by AUDREY TOPPING

Edited with an Introduction
by FRANK CHING

QUADRANGLE BOOKS

New York/Chicago
A New York Times Company

Contents

CHAPTER TWO
THE TRANSFORMATION OF CHINA   121

CHAPTER THREE
THE EVERYDAY LIFE OF 'MAOIST MAN'   181

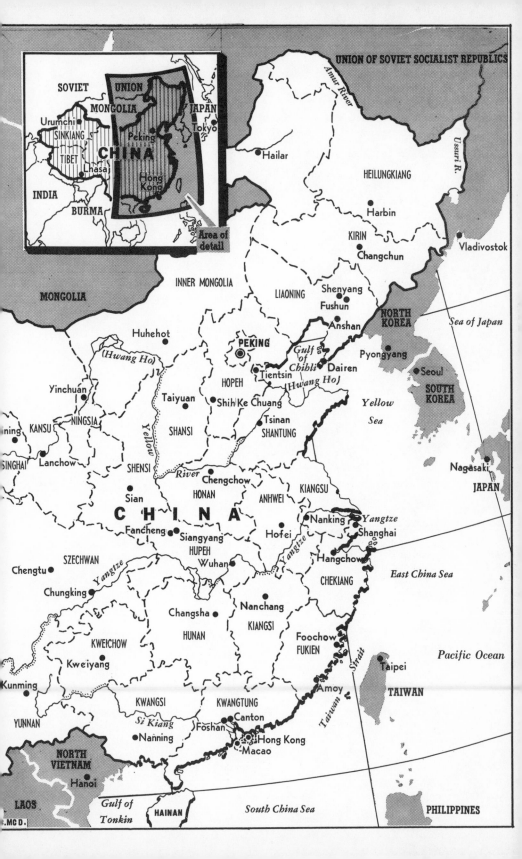

Introduction

by Frank Ching

RELATIONS BETWEEN THE UNITED STATES and Communist China, which have been marked by more than 20 years of unremitting hostility, took a dramatic turn with the invitation in April to the American table tennis team to visit China. This, the opening move of a phase in Chinese foreign policy, marked the end of a period of xenophobia and isolation that had characterized the China of the Cultural Revolution. As domestic tranquillity was gradually being restored and the Communist party structure rebuilt, Peking moved to mend its fences abroad.

Emerging from an isolation partly imposed and partly of their own choosing, the Chinese Communists have launched a diplomatic offensive that promises to outmaneuver both the United States and the Soviet Union. Beginning with the establishment of diplomatic relations with Canada late last year, Peking has pressed its new, outward-looking and more moderate stance and won the recognition of more and more nations until it has finally surpassed Taiwan in the number of countries with which it has diplomatic relations. The mere fact that for 21 years the People's Republic of China, with a population of 750 million, had diplomatic relations with fewer governments than the Chinese Nationalist Government, which rules over 14 million people, is a significant commentary on Peking's former diplomatic feebleness. Conversely, the increase in Peking's prestige signals an erosion of the Nationalists' international diplomatic position and coincides with a decline in United States influence.

For 21 years the United States has fought a losing battle to

1

keep Peking ostracized by the world community, and this isolation of Peking was starkly evident in its absence from the United Nations and other world bodies. The United States, through behind-the-scenes wire-pulling, succeeded in keeping Peking out of the world organization, first by not permitting the issue to be discussed and, in recent years, by pushing the so-called "important question" resolution whereby any change in Chinese representation required a two-thirds majority of the United Nations General Assembly.

This seemingly implacable United States position underwent subtle changes in the mid-1960's, but it was not until Richard Nixon assumed the Presidency and Washington took a series of small, undramatic steps, unilaterally relaxing trade and travel restrictions regarding China that the way was paved for the events of 1971. At the same time, the American people, by their acceptance of these changes, showed that seeking better relations with mainland China was no longer a political liability. The cold war mentality and the fear of an expansionist China eager to swallow her smaller neighbors and to spread her revolutionary message by force of arms had receded.

Understanding of China and Chinese politics deepened in the sixties, as the Government and private foundations invested huge sums for the development of academic specialists in Chinese affairs. The explosion in Asian studies spurred an intensive re-examination of China's traditional role in Asia and her present security and other needs. China was no longer seen simply as the aggressor in India and Korea who had to be contained, if not isolated, but, in many cases, as the victim of military and economic encirclement.

The education of the American people in general, a monumental task, was carried out by informed, dedicated individuals, such as those who worked through the National Committee on U.S.-China Relations. The reform in our school curricula, the media, and other institutions that mold public opinion is by no means complete, and a tremendous job of overhauling remains to be done. But the steady and constant pressure exerted by a number of people dedicated to formulating an enlightened and responsible China policy did much to clear the air of suspicion and hostility.

Simultaneous with the re-evaluation of United States attitudes toward China, Peking found itself confronting an increasingly threatening Soviet Union, which had massed up to a million troops along the Chinese border. It is natural that, finding itself without any major allies, China should, in its vulnerability, seek to improve its relations with the non-Communist world, at a time when many Western countries were eager for such ties. The first publicly reported Chinese-Soviet border clashes occurred in March, 1969. The following month, the Chinese Communists held their Ninth Party Congress, which marked an end to the violent and irrational phase of the Cultural Revolution. The Chinese discovered, after talks began in October, 1969, that the more powerful Russians were adamant in their refusal to settle border disputes if the Chinese demanded an acknowledgment that Czarist Russia had seized huge areas from China through unequal treaties in the 19th century. Peking evidently believed that the threat of a Soviet attack, possibly a nuclear one, was real indeed and began a frenzied program of war preparations, digging air-raid shelters across the land, in city and village, and storing up grain. There is evidence that, by late summer of 1970, Peking had arrived at a basic decision to shift tactics and break through what it saw as the encirclement by the two superpowers, the United States and the Soviet Union.

While the Soviet threat was perhaps China's major preoccupation, another country that Peking also saw as a menace was Japan. The increasing economic strength of Japan, coupled with what the Chinese regarded as a resurgence of militarism in that country, created concern over Tokyo's ambitions, especially with reference to Taiwan. The Chinese vividly remember Japan's invasion of China in the 1930's and 40's, and are keenly aware that Taiwan was a Japanese colony for 50 years and many Taiwanese retain warm memories of Japanese rule. In addition, Premier Eisaku Sato, in the Nixon-Sato communiqué of November, 1969, on the reversion of Okinawa, had stated that Taiwan was "a most important factor for the security of Japan." This was interpreted to mean that Japan felt her vital interests were involved in Taiwan and she was therefore not only opposed to any Chinese Communist attempt to "liberate" it but also harbored a secret desire to regain dominance over Taiwan.

Largely through the charm and skill of Premier Chou En-lai, the Chinese succeeded in developing warm relations with a number of East European countries and winning diplomatic recognition from more and more countries allied with the United States. It became obvious that Peking was attempting to turn the tables on Washington and Moscow, isolating these two superpowers from "small and medium-size countries."

Carrying this process one step further, Peking sought to isolate the Government of the United States from its citizens by fostering people-to-people relations with the American public in general. This is in line with its longstanding policy of isolating the Liberal-Democratic Government in Japan. The invitation to President Nixon marked an interruption of that policy.

Any lasting improvement in Washington-Peking relations has to be preceded by an understanding on Taiwan, the seat of the rival Nationalist Government, which has up to now been recognized by the United States as the legal government of China. The Chinese Communists have for 21 years reiterated their determination to "liberate" Taiwan, and they are unlikely now to give up this objective, which is close to being first on Peking's list of priorities.

The United States finds itself in a quandary. Not only does it have a mutual defense treaty with Taiwan but, in addition President Nixon, in announcing his trip to China, had pledged that his attempt to normalize relations with the People's Republic of China would not be made "at the expense of old friends"—a clear allusion to Taiwan. Yet, with Peking and Taipei at opposite poles, any move toward one inevitably means a move away from the other. And all the United States suggestions offered— such as the acceptance of "two Chinas," or "one China, one Taiwan"—have been rejected in no uncertain terms by Peking.

In this regard, it is undoubtedly in the United States' best long-term interests not to involve itself in what is basically an internal Chinese problem, though one that, over the years, has taken on international ramifications. But again, how to with- draw honorably, and with reasonable assurance that such a move will not be followed by a forcible take-over of Taiwan by the Communists, is an as yet unanswered question. The most desirable outcome is certainly an accommodation between Peking and Taipei, perhaps one that provides for a degree of autonomy for Taiwan. The possibility of a Nationalist-Commu- nist agreement should not be ruled out. The present existence of two Chinese governments is deplored by the overwhelming majority of Chinese, Communist or otherwise, who wish to see national unity and territorial integrity restored.

The frequent reports of secret talks between Nationalists and Communists ought not be discounted. Many of the high Na- tionalist officials who rule Taiwan would undoubtedly prefer a united China, with Taiwan under Communist rule, to an inde- pendent Taiwan cut off from China. As Nationalist China's in- ternational diplomatic position continues to erode, it will be- come ever more difficult for it to prevent a spirit of defeatism from spreading in Taiwan itself, leading to a loss of morale and internal instability.

As pressures mount, the Taipei Government may find itself forced to pick one of two courses: a reconciliation with the Communists or an accommodation with the Taiwan indepen- dence movement. Chou En-lai has voiced his Government's op- position to and concern over the Taiwan independence move- ment, and an independent Taiwan is likely to be as intolerable to Peking as a Nationalist China, perhaps even more so. Moreover, it is difficult to envisage an independent Taiwan being able to withstand Chinese Communist pressures, including perhaps open military operations, without the support of the United States or Japan. And considering the direction in which events are moving, the possibility that the United States or Japan might sponsor an independent Taiwan in the face of vociferous Chinese Communist opposition appears remote, though perhaps one not to be entirely discounted.

In the meantime, relations between the world's major powers have to be readjusted in the light of new realities. The Soviet Union has already shown itself to be much more amenable to coming to terms with the West, as is evident in the Berlin agreement and progress in arms talks. Japan has assumed a new, independent posture in its relationship with the United States, and Washington itself is on the threshold of a new era in its evolving relations with Peking. The Chinese Communists have benefited not only by having the Russians thrown temporarily off balance, but also in creating difficulties in relations between Washington and its allies in Tokyo and Taipei. It has also won new prestige, and the Nixon trip to Peking has cloaked the Communist Government with new respectability. All this affords the Chinese Communists new flexibility in their own foreign policy, providing them with opportunities for maneuver while world power alignments are in a state of flux.

It is significant that while the Chinese broke off the Warsaw talks with the United States after American troops were sent into Cambodia last year, an allied thrust into Laos last spring was followed weeks later by the Chinese invitation to the American table tennis team. Part of the explanation for this behavior undoubtedly lies in the fact that the Chinese have become reasonably convinced that the United States, under pressure of public opinion, has embarked on a withdrawal from Vietnam that is irreversible, and hence is no longer a major threat to either China or her ally, North Vietnam. Moreover, opponents of improvement in American-Chinese relations had been loud in pointing out that Peking had not responded in any way to the easing of American restrictions against trade and travel relations with mainland China. It is quite likely that elements within the Chinese leadership thought that the time had come to make a gesture to test the sincerity of American intentions. The table tennis team's visit, and permission for a select number of American newsmen to enter China, followed.

The Chinese Communists have been able to make their dramatic re-entry onto the world diplomatic scene only after having restored order in their own country. The Cultural Revolution, with its accompanying tumult, was an attempt by Mao Tse-tung to instill a new sense of purpose into the Chinese people, to revitalize a revolution that was rapidly approaching the smugness of middle age, and to rededicate the Chinese people to the goal of uniting the country and building it up into a great power.

The aging leadership in Peking is also clearly concerned over the development of a new generation of revolutionary successors, one that would carry on the goals of Mao. They are seeking to fashion a new, selfless man, described by Seymour Topping as a "Maoist Man." To what extent they will succeed remains problematical.

They have to overcome a heritage of several thousand years in which devotion to the family was put above loyalty to the state, indeed in which the vast area now known as China was often not considered not so much a unitary state as simply a cultural entity.

Beyond attempting to overcome China's past, the Communists are seeking to transcend human nature by eliminating all selfishness, individualism and material incentives. Of course, the Communists say that there is no such thing as a universal human nature, only class nature, and hence what is seen in the West as a transformation of human nature is but an elimination of all exploiting class natures.

The dispatches that follow show to what degree they have succeeded. There has already occurred a tremendous leveling in society, so that there no longer is the difference between the very rich and the very poor. Indeed, the leveling appears to have blurred distinctions not only between workers and those in authority, but also between the sexes. The great mass of Chinese, male and female, wear hardly distinguishable drab, shapeless clothes, with the women using no cosmetics at all.

The masses of peasants, it appears, are adequately fed and clothed and, though this is difficult to substantiate, appear to be reasonably happy with the Government, indeed some would say they are imbued with a sense of purpose to rebuild the motherland. The army is omnipresent but, it should be pointed out, the army in China has to a large extent been integrated into civilian life. It is characterized as not only a fighting force but also a political force and a work force.

Communist rule has resulted in the elimination of the old operas and traditional popular novels, with only a few ballets and operas judged ideologically sound being performed and only works by Mao and those in praise of him being read and sung.

Revolutionary committees were created as ruling bodies in all schools, factories and government units during the Cultural Revolution. They are described as "three-in-one combinations" because they consist of soldiers, party or government officials, and students or workers. But they are "three-in-one combinations" also in that they include the young, the old and the middle-aged. This attempt by the Chinese to bridge the generation gap is worthy of examination by Western society, beset by a widening gulf that impedes communications between young and old. The United States could conceivably benefit from a study of other features of Chinese society, such as the treatment of the aged, the provision of cheap medical care for the population at large and the maintaining of a balance between the satisfaction of individual ambition and society's needs, not to mention Chinese accomplishments in science and medicine.

These accomplishments, in the absence of aid from either the United States or the Soviet Union, have to a large extent been the result of mobilization of China's main asset—its huge and industrious population. The Chinese are constantly exhorted by the Government to be self-reliant or, as James Reston put it, to "move mountains with teaspoons" if necessary. One 30-mile canal, it is reported, was dug in 18 days by 50,000 laborers.

The transformation of China has inevitably affected family life. Late marriages are now the rule and the tradition of having many sons—a form of old-age insurance—is disappearing. The families are now smaller, with the children more independent. Filial piety is no longer regarded as a virtue and children are encouraged to "draw a class line" between themselves and their parents where necessary. The head of the household is no longer necessarily the father, but whoever is most ideologically progressive.

The emphasis on conformity to Maoist ideology, and the virtual adulation of Mao himself, are difficult for Westerners to accept or comprehend. Ascribing progress in all fields to "Mao Tse-tung Thought" appears to many to be anti-intellectual and to verge on idolatry. It is difficult to judge to what extent people in general accept Mao's thought as the answer to all of China's problems, and some of the dispatches in this volume hint that not everybody, especially the intellectual, feels comfortable with the practice, which originated with Lin Piao and the army before spreading to the population at large.

The stories told by the dispatches and pictures in this volume represent a distinct phase in Chinese-American relations. The articles, by Tillman Durdin, the first American newspaperman to report from mainland China, Seymour Topping, assistant managing editor of The New York Times, his wife, Audrey, and James Reston, a vice president and columnist of The Times, depict China as it is 21 years after the Communist revolution swept the Nationalists off the mainland to Taiwan. Both Mr. Durdin and Mr. Topping are old China hands, having reported extensively from China before the Communist take-over in 1949, and they draw upon their rich knowledge of the past in their assessment of the present.

Though circumscribed by limitations of time, language, geography and access to officials and the Chinese public in general, the articles, taken in their entirety, afford a fresh view of China, providing an immediacy that is denied to China experts working in Hong Kong, Tokyo or Washington.

The initial excitement of having American newsmen send dispatches under such datelines as Peking, Shanghai, Wuhan and Canton was exhilarating, after so long a period of estrangement. Despite the efforts of a dedicated corps of China watchers who labored at listening posts on China's periphery, mainland China itself had assumed an air of mystery, and American newsmen relished the opportunity at long last to see at first hand how the Chinese people lived and observe their relationship with their Government.

But the articles are important not only for what they say. They are perhaps more important for what they stand for: They represent a new chapter in Chinese-American relations; a reaching out by Peking to the outside world, including residents of the "imperialist" United States; a more active phase of people-to-people initiatives that was immediately dubbed "Ping-Pong diplomacy."

While relations between the United States and China are still far from normal, and no American newspaper as yet has a bureau in Peking, it is conceivable that this normality will come about in the not too distant future. And, when that time comes, the period captured in these dispatches will be seen as one of great historical significance, a period of transition in Chinese-American relations that may well affect world peace.

It was obvious from April 14, when Chou En-lai received the American table tennis team, that Americans would have access to China, which they have not had for 20 years. (Many American newsmen had made it a habit to apply for a visa every few months, without much hope of their requests being granted.) The trickle of American newsmen began after Premier Chou said that they would be permitted to enter China, "but they cannot all come at one time, they will have to come in batches."

But while the entry of American newsmen is to be welcomed without qualification, their present circumscribed scope of activities must be borne in mind. Many of the places visited were, undoubtedly, showplaces. As Tillman Durdin wrote:

"Whoever gets in will go only to places approved by his hosts and see and talk with Chinese under the surveillance or with the knowledge of officials. At present in China there is no such thing as a foreigner striking out on his own, entering offices or knocking on residential front doors and talking privately with anyone that he would not be dealing with—such as personnel of public service organizations and taxi drivers—as a necessary part of his travels.

"Signs on all main roads in the suburbs of cities say 'Foreigners not permitted beyond this point.' No foreigners can go anywhere without permission outside cities."

And while there "is no censorship of what he might write from the country, he would, under present procedures, be asked to leave if he wrote repeatedly in ways obnoxious to the regime."

It is hoped that this state of affairs is only temporary and, as relations between the two countries improve, American newsmen will be permitted greater freedom to travel and report in China.

Nearly all the pictures in this volume were taken by Mrs. Topping, a Canadian citizen who visited China with her father, the retired Canadian diplomat Chester Ronning.

Except for minor revisions, the articles here are reproduced in their entirety.

CHAPTER ONE
Peking's Foreign Policy

The First Step Into Communist China

by Tillman Durdin

CANTON, China, April 15—There was a slight hitch at the start of the venture into China.

To the chunky, stern-faced guard on the Chinese side of the Hong Kong border, the passport was offensive, not, it turned out, because it was American but because it contained a visa for travel to Taiwan and many entry stamps showing the visa had been used.

"This is an attempt to promote two Chinas," the guard said through an interpreter. "I protest against this."

"I see," I replied noncommittally. Then I stood waiting.

After a brief glare, the guard waved me on, and from then on all was smiles and good cheer on my first journey into the great continental mass of China since 1948.

Not an eyebrow was raised when I presented for exchange into yuan some United States dollar bills refused at the border currency counter on previous occasions.

At the customs counter, there was sharp and thorough questioning by a curt little woman in khaki uniform, but no inspection of luggage. The interpreter-guide for the two-hour train trip to Canton was a genial conversationalist who said he had improved his English at the language institute in Peking years ago by reading newspaper columns written by Cyrus L. Sulzberger and Walter Lippmann. When my passport was handed back to me just before I got on the train that runs from the border to Canton, I found that I had been given a visa marked for a direct air trip to Peking, flying beyond Shanghai where the

United States table tennis team spent today in the closing phases of its visit to China.

It looks as if I will have no contact with the team here. Forces with broader interests are obviously taking a hand.

My passport, it turned out, was objectionable to the Chinese, who did not choose to use it. Not only did it contain the offending visa, but I had never taken action to have effaced the stipulation on one page that it was not valid for travel in the Communist-controlled part of China. So my visa was stamped on a separate piece of cardboard.

The stretch of hills and valleys between Hong Kong and Canton is still a bit of old China, with some new touches.

The fields of green rice shoots, and the clumps of bamboo around clusters of tile-roofed village homes, look the same except that collectivization has obviously removed some boundary ridges, and the ancestral tombs that used to mark the countryside are for the most part gone, removed to make way for more cropland.

But along old stone paths through the paddy fields, men and women in faded blue still swing rhythmically under heavy burdens slung at each end of shoulder poles, and they still bend over in water-filled plots weeding and transplanting spring seedlings.

Not a mechanical implement was in sight except for an occasional bicycle steered precariously over narrow walkways or village roads.

And all that has been said about loudspeakers in China is true, I found. In station and train, their stridency never ends. The revolutionary songs, the hortatory news, overwhelm all else. And portraits of Chairman Mao Tse-tung and passages from his sayings are visible everywhere, from village walls to hillside placards.

Canton was drab and mist-covered, the streets filled mostly with pedestrians but with a few motorcars, the Tung Fang, or Eastern, Hotel huge and cavernous.

At an enormous banquet for 4,500 visiting businessmen and their hosts marking the semi-annual Canton trade fair, Chen Yu, chairman for the fair, made a ritualistic condemnation of "U.S. imperialism," but after this was applauded, a fair official sitting next to me raised a glass of sweet grape wine and proposed a toast to "friendship between the Chinese and American people."

Chou Attacks U.S. But on a Subdued Note

by Tillman Durdin

PEKING, April 25—Premier Chou En-lai struck a relatively mild note in a speech at a banquet held here tonight to mark the first anniversary of the summit conference of Vietnamese, Cambodian and Laotian regimes at war with the United States and its allies in Indochina.

The host for the occasion was Prince Norodom Sihanouk, who still upholds the status in Peking of head of state of Cambodia. Other principals for the occasion besides Premier Chou were Kaysone Phomvihan, vice chairman of the Lao Patriotic Front; Hyon Jun Guk, Ambassador of North Korea; Nam Tranh Binh, chargé d'affaires of the Communist-led provisional revolutionary government for South Vietnam, and Ngo Thuyen, Ambassador of North Vietnam.

The Indochina spokesmen denounced the United States presence in Indochina, pledged mutual support and affirmed continuation of their fight until victory and the expulsion of the United States from the Peninsula.

Premier Chou stressed the support of the People's Republic of China for these aims and said, "The Chinese Government and people firmly oppose the U.S. imperialist frenzied aggression against the three countries of Indochina and firmly support and assist the heroic peoples of Vietnam, Laos and Cambodia in their war against U.S. aggression and for national salvation."

He said, "The U.S. aggressor troops and their vassal troops must withdraw completely from Indochina so that the three Indochinese peoples may respectively settle their problems by themselves."

The Premier voiced support for North Korea, opposition to what he termed the revival of Japanese militarism and backing for national liberation struggles of Asian, African, Latin American, North American, European and Oceanian peoples, and for "the American people in their just struggle against the U.S. Government's policies of aggression and war and racial discrimination."

But these statements of time-honored positions were not accompanied by any harsh invective against the United States and there was no reference in the Premier's speech or any of the other speeches to the United States role in Taiwan, usually made on such occasions. Backing for China's stand on Taiwan by the Indochina countries and North Korea was a prominent feature of joint statements at the time of the summit meeting of Indochina last April.

Tonight's banquet for several hundred guests of countries that have recognized the Peking-based Cambodian Government under Prince Sihanouk was attended by a stellar list of Chinese officials. Besides Premier Chou, others present included Huang

Yung-sheng, Chief of Staff of the armed forces; Yeh Chien-ying, Chang Chun-chiao, Yao Wen-yuan, Li Hsien-nien, Li Tso-peng and Chiu Hui-tso, all members of the Politburo, and Kuo Mo-jo, prominent in foreign relations.

The banquet was held in the huge social hall of the National People's Congress building. Premier Chou, looking fit despite his 73 years, exchanged banter with foreign photographers who circulated freely around the head table to take pictures.

He and Prince Sihanouk invited newsmen to come to Pnompenh when it has been occupied by the forces fighting the Government of Premier Lon Nol.

Premier Reminisces With an 'Old Friend'

by Audrey Topping

PEKING, May 1—Strains of music and noises from half a million people assembled for a May Day celebration in Tienanmen Square drifted in through the open doors of the Great Hall of the People as Premier Chou En-lai welcomed an "old friend."

Premier Chou met his "lao peng yu" ("old friend") Chester A. Ronning just inside the hall, which looks out on the square, and ushered him into a spacious reception room for photographs, tea and reminiscences.

The two had first met in Chungking, China, in 1945, and they renewed their friendship in the years 1949 to 1951, when Mr. Ronning was chargé d'affaires of the Canadian Embassy.

The conversation turned to the 1954 Geneva conference on Korea, at which Mr. Chou headed the Chinese delegation and Mr. Ronning was acting head of the Canadian delegation.

It was recalled how Mr. Chou had opposed the permanent closing of the conference when it became deadlocked. Instead, he proposed that it be adjourned sine die, to be recalled when the time seemed more appropriate to replace the Korean armistice of July, 1953, with a peace treaty.

"If we had accepted your proposal at the Korean conference," Mr. Ronning said, "we could have had a peace treaty."

The Chinese Premier nodded in agreement, laughed a little and waved his arm.

"I still remember how Mr. Smith waved his arm at me and closed the conference," he said. He was referring to Gen. Walter Bedell Smith, who headed the United States delegation.

The conversation also touched on the problem of water and earth pollution, over which Mr. Chou expressed concern.

"The greatest pollution has taken place in the most advanced industrial countries," he said. "Developing countries, like China, which are not as far advanced industrially can benefit from the experiences of these countries to avoid similar problems."

The Premier, wearing a gray tunic suit and smoking a Central Flowery Kingdom cigarette, was in a jovial mood and looked much younger than his 73 years. He asked why Mr. Ronning had retired "so early."

"I did not retire early," Mr. Ronning replied. "I remained in the foreign service until I was 71. Canadians are supposed to retire at 65."

The Premier smiled broadly and replied: "Well, you and I are exceptions to the rule. Take me, now. Why should I retire?"

Also present during the conversation, which lasted half an hour, were Huang Hua, the Chinese Ambassador-designate to Canada and Wang Kuo-chuan, a leading member of the Chinese People's Association for Friendship with Foreign Countries. At its close, Mr. Chou invited Mr. Ronning to return for a more serious discussion of problems of mutual concern. Mr. Ronning is leaving next Saturday for a trip to his birthplace at Fancheng, in Hupeh Province in central China.

U.S.-China Thaw Is Mild So Far

by Tillman Durdin

SHANGHAI, May 4—The visits by American and other foreign table tennis players and journalists not only seem to have broken China's isolation from the capitalist world but have produced a widely favorable reaction in the United States and elsewhere.

The somewhat improved atmosphere may make it easier for Peking and Washington to consider their differences. But it does not appear to have caused the Chinese to modify any positions at the core of those differences.

Nor do statements by Peking give any indication that it believes that the United States has changed any fundamental views.

In spite of the thaw, then, a chasm still separates the two Governments, and the Chinese attitude seems to be that it is up to the United States to do most if not all in bridging it.

The Ping-Pong phase of Peking's recently inaugurated relaxation in foreign relations is itself about to come to an end. Following visits by American, British and African teams, only an Australian group remains, and it is on the point of leaving.

Coincident with its exit the foreign journalists who started entering the country a month ago on the premise that they would be covering the table tennis events will also be departing, except for a late arrival.

As for American-Chinese relations, Taiwan remains the principal focus of discord. The view in Peking is that as long as the island is kept from under the sovereign mantle of the People's Republic of China by United States military and political support of the Nationalist Government in Taipei, no broad agreement with Washington is possible.

The Chinese Communists insist not only that the United States cease its "military occupation" of Taiwan, although this in fact does not exist—and withdraw from the Taiwan Strait—a move the Americans carried out more than a year ago—but that the United States defense treaty with the Nationalists be dismantled. Also, no seat for the Nationalists in the United Nations would be countenanced under any pretext.

Thus Peking, sternly hostile to an American shift to a two-Chinas policy, rejects the position, stated last week by the State Department and long held by Britain, that the juridical status of Taiwan is unsettled.

The noncommittal silence with which the Communists greet the idea, also advanced by the State Department, of a direct settlement between Taipei and Peking indicates that they do not think much of the prospects for such a deal unless the United States makes it possible by withdrawing protection from the Nationalists.

The Chinese Communists seem less categorical about differences with the United States in Indochina. The impression is given that in view of the convincing evidence that President Nixon intends a sweeping military withdrawal, the issue would not in itself block a resolution of differences.

The Chinese Communists do not seem to be counting on any early breakthrough in relations with the United States and seem prepared to wait indefinitely to gain their ends. They feel that opinion is shifting their way and that Washington will ultimately meet their terms.

They are plainly gratified by the favorable reaction they have aroused in the United States and elsewhere at little material cost to themselves and without any concessions on basic issues, so they are making plans to continue people-to-people contacts.

Foreign Ministry officials are compiling lists of American journalists they are considering for admission and indicate that they will also admit some favorably disposed American political figures and scholars and possibly some businessmen of political orientation.

They will have no shortage of names to pick from. Baskets of applications have accumulated, they say.

Peking's more immediate objective appears to be a United Nations seat this year, but the officials give the impression that the seat itself is less important than scoring over the United States and denigrating the Nationalists in the process.

Another consideration in the friendly approach to Americans undoubtedly is a desire to worry the Russians; in this they appear to have succeeded. Diplomatic quarters report that the prime preoccupation of the big Soviet mission these days is trying to read the daily barometer of Chinese-American dealings.

Whether Peking will reopen the Warsaw talks as part of the new tactic is problematical. The officials give the impression that they are not much interested in view of the fact that nothing has been accomplished in years of meetings between the United States and Chinese Ambassadors.

There is speculation among foreign diplomats in Peking that Huang Hua, the new Chinese Communist Ambassador to Canada, may be in contact with American emissaries in what would amount to a shift of the Warsaw talks to Ottawa. If that occurs, Mr. Huang, who, as the Chinese representative, proved an expert at stonewalling at the Panmunjom talks that ended the Korean war, would be a tough proponent of "you play it my way and we can agree."

Chou, at Dinner, Talks of Rift With Soviet

by Audrey Topping

PEKING, May 5—Premier Chou En-lai said today that the split between Moscow and Peking developed because Nikita S. Khrushchev took the road of revisionism and peaceful coexistence rather than continuing vigorous revolution after he came to power in the nineteen-fifties.

Mr. Chou said that he had tried to dissuade Mr. Khrushchev and his successors but that the split had persisted and even deepened.

Those views were expressed at a small dinner party the Premier gave for Chester A. Ronning, a retired Canadian diplomat, and his daughters, Mrs. Sylvia Cassady and myself. Asked after dessert if he would mind if I wrote about our discussion, he replied, "That is your freedom."

The 12-course dinner, attended by 12 people in all, began with numerous toasts and an exchange of Chinese jokes and riddles. Then the conversation took a more serious tone.

In reply to a question whether he had ever imagined that China would accomplish what it has in the course of his lifetime, Mr. Chou, looking relaxed and very fit for his 73 years, smiled and said that the Chinese had not yet reached the goal by far. "We still have a long way to go," he said.

During his youth, he went on, he only imagined that the revolution would attain victory. At that time he thought that revolution was quite simple; it was only after suffering several setbacks that he learned how to make revolution from the teachings of the Communist party Chairman, Mao Tse-tung.

After the triumph of the revolution, according to Marxist-Leninist principles and Chairman Mao's thoughts, he said, the revolution must be carried on continuously to win complete victory over the reactionaries.

Discussing the circumstances that led to the Chinese-Soviet breach, which became public in 1961, the Premier said that China tried fruitlessly at a conference in Moscow in 1957 to dissuade Mr. Khrushchev from going too far along the path of revisionism—the Chinese Communists' term for the Soviet policy of coexistence with capitalist states and for what the Chinese view as a revival of capitalism in the Soviet Union.

Then in 1959, Mr. Chou said, Mr. Khrushchev tore up the agreements between the two countries on atomic energy cooperation. Moreover, he went to the United States and met with President Dwight D. Eisenhower to begin his exercise in flirtation with the United States that, Mr. Chou said, was the so-called spirit of Camp David.

When the Chinese-Indian border dispute broke out in 1962, Mr. Chou said, the Soviet Union went so far as to side with Prime Minister Jawaharlal Nehru and to condemn China. The Chinese leader also said that in 1960 the Soviet Union broke agreements and contracts for both industry and construction and all Soviet experts and technicians were withdrawn.

Nevertheless, Mr. Chou explained, in 1961 China sent a delegation headed by himself to the 22d Congress of the Soviet Communist party. It was at that conference that the Russians expelled the Albanian Communists and the public polemics began.

Mr. Chou recalled that Mr. Khrushchev was ousted in October, 1964. It was a coincidence, he added, that China's first atomic bomb was exploded the following day. His eyes sparkled when he remarked that some foreigners had said that the explosion was deliberately arranged as a sendoff for the Soviet leader.

With a bright smile, the Premier added that, after all, the ex-

plosion of the Chinese bomb was thanks to the Russians' behavior since Soviet experts had been withdrawn and the Chinese
were compelled to rely on their own strength.

Mr. Chou went on to relate that when Leonid I. Brezhnev
came to power in Moscow, China had hoped for a change in
policy and sent a delegation to Moscow in 1964 to celebrate the
anniversary of the October Revolution even though it was not a
five-year celebration. China also persuaded other reluctant Communist parties to attend, he said.

They discovered that the change in leadership in Moscow
was not a result of a change in party policy, Mr. Chou said, but
was motivated by a struggle for power in the leadership, which
was very disappointing to the Chinese.

The following February, Mr. Chou related, Chairman Mao
met the new Soviet Premier, Aleksei N. Kosygin, who was in
Peking. Mr. Mao told him that because China and the Soviet
Union had differences in principle, the polemics would go on
for 10,000 years.

Mr. Kosygin commented that it would be too long, Mr. Chou
said, and the Chairman replied that since the Soviet leader had
said so, 1,000 years was taken off, which would still leave 9,000
years for polemics.

Nevertheless, Mr. Chou went on, state relations between the
two countries could have been improved, but instead of doing so
the Soviet Union prepared to go to war with China and by 1969
had stationed over a million troops along the northern frontiers
of China and had even dispatched its troops into the Mongolian
People's Republic.

Faced with the situation, Premier Chou continued, China had
no alternative but to make preparations against war. (There
were exchanges of fire between border troops at the time.)

He went on to tell of the conference he had with Mr. Kosygin
in 1969, when the Soviet leader was on his way home from the
funeral of President Ho Chi Minh of North Vietnam. Mr. Kosygin had requested a meeting at the airport, to which China

agreed, and Mr. Chou talked with him there for three hours.

Mr. Kosygin agreed with Mr. Chou's view that in order to improve relations the two countries could start with boundary negotiations, Mr. Chou said, and the two leaders reached an understanding on certain questions:

¶The dispute on principle should not hamper the normalization of state relations.

¶The two countries would meet in Peking at the vice-ministerial level on the question of disputed boundaries in the Ussuri-Amur region.

¶The negotiations should be free of any threat. To this end, before the negotiations on the boundary alignment, the two sides should reach agreement on provisional measures to maintain the status quo and halt armed conflict.

The boundary negotiations began on Oct. 20, 1969, and are still going on.

In referring to the boundaries, Mr. Chou noted that a great area of China had been ceded to Czarist Russia as a result of unequal treaties. In spite of that, he said, China is still willing to take the old treaties as the basis for defining the boundary line.

Pointing out that maps of China and maps of the Soviet Union show a number of disputed areas, Mr. Chou noted that the Ussuri and Amur Rivers run for over 1,200 miles between the two countries. He explained that according to the international practice of defining river boundaries, the line should run along the center of the main channel.

Even the Bolshaya Encyclopedia published by the Soviet Union in the twenties conceded that the boundary line in that sector runs along the center of the channel, he said, but later the Russians would not agree to the criterion and insisted that some of the boundary lines were on the Chinese side.

The dinner party took place in the Kiangsu room of the Great Hall of the People, which stands on Tienanmen Square. The others present were Chiao Kuan-hua, Vice Foreign Minister;

Huang Hua, Ambassador-designate to Canada and his wife; Chang Wen-chin, director of the Foreign Ministry department in charge of Western European, North and Latin-American and Oceanic affairs; Chou Chiu-yeh, member of the Friendship Association, and his assistant, Chou Chiu-sheng; and two of Premier Chou's interpreters, Chi Chao-chu, a Harvard graduate, and Miss Tang Wen-sheng, who was born in New York.

Ceausescu Gets Big Peking Welcome

by Seymour Topping

PEKING, June 1—Premier Chou En-lai welcomed President Nicolae Ceausescu of Rumania to China on a state visit today and praised Rumania for "opposing big-power chauvinism," an allusion to the policies of the Soviet Union.

Premier Chou told a banquet audience in the gilded Great Hall of the People that Rumania had defied "brute force" in safeguarding her independence and sovereignty.

Earlier the people of Peking, ordinarily garbed in somber attire, shed their blue tunics and trousers and in gay costumes turned out to welcome the Rumanian Communist party and Government delegation. Nearly half a million people with drums beating and cymbals clanging lined an eight-mile section of the route from the airport into the city and through Tienanmen Square to the state guest house.

Hundreds of thousands of smiling school girls wearing brightly colored skirts danced and waved colored paper flowers and streamers, shouting "Welcome" in unison as they held aloft their little red books of Mao Tse-tung's quotations. The skirts were an unfamiliar sight in Peking.

The extravagant welcome appeared to have been organized by the Chinese to express appreciation for the stubborn stand of neutrality that the Rumanians have taken in regard to the ideological dispute between Moscow and Peking.

At the Soviet Communist party congress in April, President Ceausescu refused to join in the condemnation of the Chinese Communist party expressed by the Soviet party's General Secretary, Leonid I. Brezhnev. The Rumanians have insisted on maintaining cordial relations with the Chinese.

Praising the Rumanians for "keeping the initiative in their own hands," Premier Chou declared: "The Rumanian people have won important victories in their struggle of opposing big-power chauvinism and building socialism. They have withstood foreign pressure, foiled imperialist control, interference and threats of aggression, and courageously defended their national independence and sovereignty."

In his reply at the glittering banquet attended by more than 500 people including Prince Norodom Sihanouk, the exiled Cambodian leader, Mr. Ceausescu refrained from taking a militant line and pleaded for an end of the Chinese-Soviet conflict.

"Our party and state make every effort toward overcoming the difficulties existing at present in relations between socialist countries and between Communist parties and actively campaign for strengthening their cohesion in the fight against imperialism and reactionaries, for socialism and peace in the world," the Rumanian leader declared.

Premier Chou noted that Rumania had been one of the first

countries to extend diplomatic recognition to the Royal Government of National Union of Cambodia, the exile regime headed by Prince Sihanouk.

The Soviet Union has not recognized the Sihanouk government, which has some guerrilla forces fighting in Cambodia with the Vietnamese Communists.

Premier Chou also attacked what he termed "United States imperialism," which he said was "finding things tougher and tougher" throughout the world.

The Ceausescu party is scheduled to remain in China for about one week before continuing on to North Korea and then North Vietnam.

Air-Raid Shelters
In City and Village

by Seymour Topping

PEKING, June 3—On the streets of this capital as well as in rural villages, bricks are piled high and dust rises as a massive program of building air-raid shelters goes forward.

Chinese officials do not discuss the program, which has been under way at least since late 1969, except to insist that the shelters are purely a defense measure. They apparently are meant to be a safeguard in the first instance against Soviet nuclear attack and, second, precaution against United States action.

Traveling through the country, this reporter found no evidence of a propaganda campaign designed to stir war fever. Yet there is evident determination that China must prepare against any eventuality.

Premier Chou En-lai has told recent visitors that the shelter program was spurred by the 1969 clashes with the Soviet Union, when, it is said here, the Russians massed more than a million troops on China's border, threatening invasion.

Diplomatic sources said the Chinese were shocked during the crisis when hints were passed to them through the Australian Communist party and others that the Russians were considering a nuclear strike if China continued its stubborn stand along the disputed central Asian boundary.

While the crisis has passed, the Chinese have not forgotten how exposed they were.

China has detonated at least 11 nuclear test explosions, including hydrogen devices, and in May, 1970, it orbited a satellite, indicating that the development of its missile-delivery system was well advanced. However, it does not have a nuclear deterrent sufficient to stand up to the Soviet Union and the United States.

Until the mid-seventies, when United States experts expect that China will have developed a fairly substantial arsenal of missiles, it is depending for protection on the extensive system of air-raid shelters, which are being openly dug in urban areas under homes, shops and offices and in village locations. It is no secret that the new Peking subway, still closed to the public, was constructed to serve also as an underground bunker.

In rural communes, under the Maoist slogan "Prepare against war and natural calamities," large reserves of grain are being stored. At the Nan Yuen People's Commune south of Peking, a visitor was shown the reserves of the Huai Fang Agricultural Brigade. Officials said there were more than 300,000 pounds of rice for the 3,680 people of the brigade, each of whom, like most Chinese, consumes somewhat more than a pound a day. In excess of 700,000 pounds more are being held in state bins nearby, the officials added.

"These reserves are for use in case of drought, other calamities or war," a Communist party official said. "We also have air-raid shelters in the village in case aggression is imposed on us."

It seems that the current state of readiness would allow a substantial part of the population to go underground in case of nuclear attack.

The people appear highly organized and motivated, and everywhere they repeat the official line: "If war is imposed on us, the whole nation will stand up."

Internal propaganda against the Soviet Union as a potential aggressor has eased although ideological polemics go on. State relations have improved in the last year and Peking has agreed to increase trade, which had sharply dwindled.

On the other hand, there has been no resolution of the border dispute in the talks in progress in Peking since October, 1969.

Diplomatic sources say the Chinese have indicated readiness

to reach a settlement on the basis of the present line of control, with minor territorial rectifications, but on condition that the Russians admit that the czarist boundaries were imposed on China through "unequal treaties."

Moscow, which gained vast stretches of Chinese territory under 19th-century treaties, has been unwilling to make that admission, apparently fearing that it would lead to problems later.

The United States has apparently not aroused the same degree of fear in China, apart from the period of the escalation of the air war over North Vietnam in the mid-sixties and the recent South Vietnamese lunge in Laos.

With the advent of Ping-Pong diplomacy, Chinese propaganda has emphasized friendship for the American people as distinct from the Government—a line that has found the population responsive. The writer has encountered genuine, spontaneous expressions of friendship for Americans wherever he has traveled.

Senior Chinese officials, in public statements and the central press, continue sharp attacks on United States policy, particularly with regard to the Taiwan and Indochina issues.

Touring the communes and factories, one sees occasional posters depicting American workers demonstrating against the Nixon Administration and repeating the Maoist slogan, "People of the world, unite and defeat the U.S. aggressors and all their running dogs." However, the great bulk of the slogans and posters are given over to exhortations for improving production.

In Peking there is still apprehension over "collusion" between the United States and the Soviet Union against China. The United States is bitterly condemned for what is termed the fostering of a revival of Japanese militarism, which seems to be genuinely feared.

The real danger of a clash with the United States is believed to revolve around the Chinese Communists' determination to "liberate" Taiwan eventually despite the Chiang Kai-shek Government's security treaty with Washington and the Seventh Fleet's protection of the island.

On the wider scene, the Chinese have declined to enter into international disarmament talks except on the basis of an agreement to prohibit and destroy all nuclear weapons. They seem bent on developing a nuclear strike capability as a deterrent, as a world status symbol and as a means of enhancing their negotiating position.

Confronted by the overwhelming superiority of United States and Soviet forces, the Chinese have repeatedly pledged that they would never be the first to employ nuclear weapons.

Chou Asks Nations To Resist Superpowers

by Seymour Topping

PEKING, June 8—Premier Chou En-lai, warning that the danger of world war persists, called today upon small and medium-sized nations to unite and resist bullying by superpowers.

In an unusually militant attack on the Soviet Union and the United States, the Premier asserted that China had no intention of assuming the role of superpower "neither now nor ever in future."

"We will always stand together with oppressed countries and peoples in firmly opposing power politics of superpowers," Mr. Chou said.

The Premier made his remarks before a "friendship meeting" in the Great Hall of the People at the conclusion of a weeklong visit by President Nicolae Ceausescu of Rumania to China.

There were indications that the independent-minded Rumanian statesman, who has sought to remain neutral in the Chinese-Soviet ideological dispute, had encountered problems in his discussions with Chinese leaders.

The "friendship meeting" was delayed about two and a half hours, apparently because of a protracted final negotiating round between the Rumanian party and government delegation and a Chinese delegation headed by Premier Chou. About 10,000 people, including the diplomatic corps, waited in the auditorium for more than an hour. Then diplomats and newsmen were escorted into an adjoining room where they waited for another hour amid a buzz of speculation.

No explanation for the delay was offered when the Rumanian and Chinese delegations entered the auditorium and took their places on the dais.

President Ceausescu warmly praised Chinese achievements and said that views expressed during the Chinese-Rumanian discussions had been "identical or close."

The Rumanians joined the Chinese in taking a stand against Soviet interference in affairs of other Communist parties. Without mentioning Moscow directly, President Ceausescu declared that "each party must formulate independently its line and strategy" and that relations between parties must be on a basis of equality and noninterference.

The Rumanian President, who is also his country's Communist party leader, added that he was striving to eliminate differences among Communist parties and restore cooperation.

President Ceausescu denounced the United States role in Indochina and backed Peking's claim to Taiwan.

The Rumanian allusions to the Soviet Union and references to the United States were mild in comparison with the rhetoric employed by Premier Chou. The Chinese leader declared that the American people had "raised a revolutionary storm in opposition to the Nixon Government's policies of aggression and war and racial discrimination."

Later, at a banquet given by the Rumanian Embassy, Premier Chou returned to attack the Soviet Union and the United States. Praising the Rumanian Communist party for adopting an independent course within the international Communist movement, Premier Chou asserted: "Certain people vilify it as what they call 'nationalism.' As a matter of fact they are using this as camouflage in a wild attempt to carry out interference, control exploitation and plunder against other countries.

Warning against being deluded by those he termed imperialists, Mr. Chou said: "We must always keep a clear head about imperialists, neither fearing their bluster nor easily believing their 'nice words' and make all necessary preparations both mentally and materially and wage unremitting struggles against them. Only thus can we be invincible and only thus will it be possible to prevent a new world war."

President Ceausescu flies tomorrow to North Korea for a state visit and will then go to North Vietnam and Mongolia.

U.S. Defense
Of Taiwan
Is an Obstacle

by Seymour Topping

PEKING, June 21—Premier Chou En-lai said tonight that the security screen the United States had erected around the island of Taiwan, now ruled by the Government of Chiang Kai-shek, was a key obstacle to the establishment of diplomatic ties with the United States.

The Chinese leader, urging settlement of the Taiwan issue, said that no vengeful action would be taken against the people of Taiwan if the island yielded to Peking's control.

Premier Chou also said that he had received a Soviet proposal for a five-power disarmament conference and that his Government would discuss it, but he indicated personal reservations.

The 73-year-old leader made his remarks at a small dinner in

the Great Hall of the People for William Attwood, publisher of
Newsday; Robert L. Keatley, Washington reporter for The Wall
Street Journal, this correspondent, who is assistant managing
editor of The New York Times, and their wives.

Mr. Chou, in a jovial mood, noted that it was the first time in
25 years that he had had such a dinner meeting with American
newsmen. He added that reciprocal contacts would gradually
develop between the peoples of China and the United States and
that his Government would consider a request by American
businessmen to attend the semiannual Canton trade fair.

The dinner took place in the spacious Fukien Room of the
Great Hall, a reception room furnished in brown and cream.
The Premier and his aides and guests dined at a round table at
one end of the room, the other end of which was occupied by a
semicircle of conference chairs.

The room is dominated by a huge painting of a group bearing
fluttering red banners and standing atop a Kansu mountain peak
high above a cloud-shrouded valley.

Premier Chou, dressed in gray tunic and trousers and brown
sandals over black socks, was flanked by two interpreters, Chi
Chao-chu, a former Harvard student, and Miss Tang Wen-
sheng, who was born in New York. He demonstrated some grasp
of English as he discussed world issues and quipped about the
women's liberation movement in the United States and about
the moon shots, which he deplored as wasteful.

In the past the Chinese Communist leadership has declined
to discuss the future of the inhabitants of Taiwan in the event it
took over the island, saying the question was purely an internal
one. Some observers have warned that there might be reprisals
against the 12 million Taiwanese and against the more than two
million mainlanders who fled there in 1949 and who have governed since.

Tonight, in response to questions at the two-and-a-half-hour
dinner, Mr. Chou said the economic well-being of the people on
Taiwan would improve since they would receive the same in-

come, but without paying income tax. There is no personal income tax in Communist China.

If there are unemployed people from the mainland on the island, the Premier added, they "could go back to their home provinces and they will not be discriminated against."

"If Taiwan returns to the motherland, then its people would be making a contribution to the motherland for which we should give them a reward," he added. "Far from exacting revenge on them, we will reward them."

In what seemed to be an allusion to Peking's attitude toward members of President Chiang's Government, Mr. Chou recalled that high-ranking officers of the defeated Chinese Nationalist armies had been living in Peking since 1949 and "were well looked after."

"How Taiwan will be liberated is our internal affair," he said, adding, "It will not be all that difficult."

"Chiang Kai-shek is opposed to the so-called two Chinas and is also opposed to one China and one independent entity of Taiwan," he continued. "In the past we have been allied with Chiang Kai-shek, and we became hostile to him, but on this question we have our common point. There can be only one China. So a way can be found."

Premier Chou, remarking that "the world will change," said it would be glorious if United States forces were withdrawn from the Taiwan Strait. The United States Seventh Fleet conducts a token patrol of the strait under the 1955 security treaty with the Chinese Nationalist Government, guaranteeing the island against attack.

"Once this problem is solved, then all other problems can be solved," Mr. Chou said. "The People's Republic would then be able to establish diplomatic relations with the United States."

He did not insist on a declaration by the United States recognizing Peking's sovereignty over Taiwan. "If the United States Government withdraws all forces from Taiwan and the Taiwan Strait and no longer considers Chiang Kai-shek as the representative of China," he said, "then the logical result would be that Chiang Kai-shek and Taiwan would be matters internal to China. This would be recognition that the People's Republic of China is the only lawful government. There can be no possibility of two Chinas or one China and one Taiwan."

Sidestepping a question whether he would welcome a visit by President Nixon or his emissary, Mr. Chou said with a smile: "Such a big question! It was said by Nixon himself that he would like to visit China. Since he said that, he will know himself under what circumstances he would want to visit China."

Asked if Chinese would be going to the United States on reciprocal visits, he said: "I believe that day will surely come. Whether it comes slowly or quickly depends on efforts of both sides." He added that contacts between the peoples "can surely gradually increase."

"We will also go there," he added. "We must do some preparatory work. Our people did not realize beforehand that such contacts would develop so rapidly. The table tennis team is preparing to be the first to go. People of other circles have been invited but some preparations must be made."

He said that his Government might consider sending the Peking Opera Ballet to the United States.

Warming to the conversation, the Premier invited the men to doff their coats, commenting, "We men should also liberate ourselves." He draped his tunic over a chair and, sitting in a short-sleeved, open-necked white sports shirt, made these observations:

On the American Presidency—"It's a terrible thing to be President. He has to look after everything."

On his advancing years—"In spirit always young, but my material base is getting older and older." He said he was giving up drinking.

Jokingly, on the import market in the United States for mao tai, a clear 60-proof sorghum liquor—"We will not be able to supply so much mao tai."

On women's liberation—"Men and women should be equal, but there are still old habits that hinder complete equality. We must carry on the struggle. It may take 10 or 20 years."

On moon shots—"We have so many things to do on earth. Why go to the moon? It is a great waste and the people must pay for it."

On the American economy—"The American people will be able to overcome their problems."

With the remark that he could express only personal views about the Soviet proposal for a five-power disarmament parley because his Government had not yet discussed it, Mr. Chou said:

"First of all, we are not a big power although the extent of our territory is vast and we have a vast population. From the point of view of power we are rather weak and backward.

"Secondly, we are in an experimental stage of our testing of nuclear weapons. We cannot call ourselves a big nuclear power.

"Thirdly, every time we conduct a nuclear test, which is necessary in a limited way, we issue a statement as follows: 'We will not at any time and under any circumstances be the first to use nuclear weapons. Never! Secondly, we advocate that all countries of the world regardless of their size sit down together and agree on the complete prohibition and complete destruction of nuclear weapons.'"

By way of explanation of the nuclear tests, Premier Chou asserted: "We do it precisely for the purpose of breaking down the nuclear monopoly and blackmail and to bring about a complete solution to this problem."

Foreign Policy
Goal: United Front

by Seymour Topping

PEKING, June 22—Premier Chou En-lai, forcefully re-entering the diplomatic arena, is seeking a new coalition of nations that will inhibit the power of Washington and Moscow.

While Ping-Pong diplomacy has aroused the interest of the United States, the astute 73-year-old Premier has devoted more attention to consolidating relations with governments of varying political complexion in Europe, Latin America, Asia and Africa.

The stated aim is to create a "united front" of small and medium-size nations that will resist political, economic and military prerogatives exercised by the "superpowers," that is, the United States and the Soviet Union. Premier Chou has appealed to such disparate potential allies as members of the European Common Market, which resent United States fiscal hegemony, and independent-minded Communist states such as Rumania and Yugoslavia, which are fearful of Soviet intervention on the pattern of Czechoslovakia.

In the plush, carpeted halls of the Foreign Ministry compound, there is more traffic than at any time since 1955, when Premier Chou was frustrated in his effort to attract and lead non-aligned African and Asian nations.

Once again, Premier Chou has put a fresh pragmatic face on Peking's foreign policy. The strong emphasis on an overt interventionist policy to spur "national liberation movements," which existed in 1965 just before the Cultural Revolution closed China to the rest of the world for almost five years, is gone.

43

However, judging by internal propaganda, there remains an underlying dedication to close support of "liberation movements" and world Communist revolution with Peking as its center.

In pressing for a "united front" of Communist and non-Communist states, Premier Chou obviously hopes to gain tactical leverage in realizing key policy objectives vis-à-vis his two principal antagonists, the United States and the Soviet Union.

From conversations with Chinese officials, including Premier Chou, and foreign diplomats in the capital, the salient lines of Peking's strategy for dealing with the "superpowers" are as follows:

There is no prospect for a substantial improvement in government-to-government relations with the United States until the Taiwan issue is resolved. Peking insists that the United States must remove its security screen from the island, which is held by the Chinese Nationalist Government of Chiang Kai-shek, and does not intend to compromise on its determination to "liberate" Taiwan and assert its complete sovereignty.

The Chinese reject and shun any discussion of the possibility of a plebiscite to determine the preferences of the 12 million indigenous people of Taiwan. In a dinner conversation with this writer, Premier Chou for the first time gave a hint of what Peking's attitude toward the Taiwanese and two million mainlanders on Taiwan would be if the Communists took it over.

He said that there would be no reprisals against the Taiwanese if they yielded to Peking's sovereignty and that their economic conditions would improve. He said that unemployed mainlanders would be permitted to return to their home provinces without being subject to discrimination.

Foreign observers speculate that Peking might work out some bilateral deal directly with the authorities on Taiwan once President Chiang passes from the scene. The island with its prosperous, well-developed economy and different social system, might be too difficult for Peking to administer directly without conceding a measure of autonomy.

Peking seems content to wait for an evolution of the political situation in the United States and on Taiwan itself rather than launch an armed invasion to bring the island under its rule. However, observers feel that what danger exists of a war between the United States and China now lies not in Southeast Asia but in the Taiwan Strait.

Chinese officials dwell on the Taiwan issue but rarely refer to the Indochina war, presumably taking it for granted that the United States is withdrawing from the region. There is an ambiguity in Chinese attitudes about the postwar presence of the United States in the Pacific. One senses that they might prefer an American presence to a resurgence of Japanese militarism, which Peking obviously dreads.

Present evolution of Chinese policy suggests that Peking will not attempt any military expansion into Southeast Asia or seek military bases abroad. Rather than trying to exercise the type of control that Moscow exerts over Eastern Europe, the Chinese are bent on forging links with Communist governments in the region based on ideological attraction, economic and technical assistance, and supply of military equipment.

Competition between Moscow and Peking for influence in Southeast Asia is sharpening, giving Communist governments there an opportunity to balance one off against the other and thus retain greater independence.

Premier Chou intends to continue to expand people-to-people contacts with the United States by admitting more newsmen, scholars and a range of other interested individuals. Chinese officials have become convinced that the program is helpful in mobilizing American public opinion to bring about changes in Washington's China policy.

Peking, delighted by the lengthening parade of nations marching to recognize the People's Republic, expects its admission to the United Nations and the expulsion of the Taipei Government at the fall session of the General Assembly or, at the latest, 1972. It is expected that Peru, Tunisia, Iran, Turkey and Libya will soon follow on the heels of Austria in setting up diplomatic ties.

The Chinese Communists have apparently dropped two former preconditions for accepting a seat in the United Nations. These were basic organizational changes in its charter and repudiation of the 1951 resolution condemning Peking's entry into the Korean war.

Once in the United Nations, the Chinese Communists have indicated, they intend to press their "united front" tactics and seek organizational changes that would curb the power of the United States and the Soviet Union.

Judging by their military precautions, the Chinese now believe there is more likelihood of war with the Soviet Union than with the United States.

Trade relations with the Russians have improved and some tensions eased since border clashes in 1969 when Moscow mobilized more than a million troops on China's borders and hinted at the possibility of nuclear strikes. Nevertheless, the Soviet Union is reportedly continuing its military build-up in Outer Mongolia for a possible confrontation with China.

Outer Mongolia is heavily dependent on Moscow's economic and technical aid and has become a tremendous base area for Soviet tank divisions, air forces and rocket installations. The Russians have been observed recently improving airfields in Mongolia, building permanent barracks for troops rushed there during the 1969 crisis.

Political analysts believe Soviet forces in Mongolia constitute essentially a strike force rather than a purely defensive grouping. There has been no attempt by the Russians to conceal their activities from passengers on the railroad between Ulan Bator and Peking. Open military activity serves as a warning to the Chinese Communists, who are continuing their bitter ideological attacks on the Soviet Union and taking a stiff line in boundary negotiations.

The Chinese-Soviet border talks, which have been in progress in Peking since October, 1969, appear stalemated. The Chinese have offered to accept present boundaries, with minor adjustments, if the Russians will concede publicly that 19th-century treaties that transferred great slices of Chinese territory to Czarist Russia were unequal. Moscow, fearful of future difficulties, has rejected this.

Although the Russians have overwhelming nuclear superiority over the embryo Chinese nuclear force, Peking is making military preparations that indicate it has no intention of backing down in any confrontation with Moscow or of being as vulnerable again as the country was in 1969.

The Chinese are completing an enormous air-raid shelter program throughout the country. Population shelters are to be seen in every city and village. In Shenyang, or Mukden, a big industrial city in the northeast, the writer observed construction work at a machine-tool plant for a large bunker to house an emergency workshop.

Decentralization of the economy and vast stocks of reserve grain believed to have been built up in every region has been aimed at giving the country the capacity to absorb heavy military blows and to carry on.

At Changsha air force base and at other airfields, this writer saw in operation Chinese-built versions of Soviet MIG-19 jet fighters, which are not highly sophisticated but serviceable. The intense training activity indicated that China has overcome its former shortage of jet fuel.

The Russians cut off military and other aid to the Chinese in 1960 when their ideological dispute exploded into the open.

In talks with Rumanian and Yugoslav leaders in Peking recently, Premier Chou has offered to stand with them and other Communist governments against further extension by Moscow of the Brezhnev Doctrine. Leonid I. Brezhnev, the Soviet party chief, in justifying the Soviet-led invasion of Czechoslovakia in 1968, enunciated the doctrine of the right of the Soviet Union to intervene when the party system of a Communist state is threatened.

The Chinese leader put the label of "imperialist" on the Soviet Union, an epithet previously reserved for the United States.

The Yugoslavs and Rumanians, like other nations to which Premier Chou has appealed for a "united front," have welcomed cooperation with Peking. But virtually all have expressed reservations about unnecessarily antagonizing the United States and the Soviet Union.

Many governments are looking for aid from Peking or trying to get to the head of the line for trade. Peking made new aid commitments last year totaling nearly $1-billion despite its own pressing domestic needs. Such countries as Rumania, Tanzania and Pakistan have received substantial aid while North Vietnam and Albania have been beneficiaries of continuing military and economic assistance programs.

Within the last weeks, in the ornate, colonnaded reception rooms of the Great Hall of the People, Premier Chou has told West Europeans that he favors expansion of the Common Market to include Britain and others so that the continent will be shored up against United States influence.

The slightly flabbergasted trade delegation of the Peruvian military junta was assured that China stands beside South American nations in insisting on a 200-mile limit for territorial waters.

Two sisters of the Shah of Iran were charmed when they were congratulated on their brother's successful fight to get British and American oil companies to increase oil royalties.

When a government appears wedded to the Taipei Government, Peking does not hesitate to invite leaders of opposition parties to visit the Chinese capital.

An Australian delegation, members of the opposition Labor party, will arrive here soon. The Australians will be reminded that this year Peking is importing 2.5 million tons of wheat from Canada, which recently recognized the Chinese Communist Government. The Labor party will be able in the next general elections to speak out against the government whose policies led to the loss of contracts for export to China of millions of tons of surplus wheat annually, although Australian grain is cheaper than the Canadian variety.

Chinese Communist ideologists see no contradiction between a policy of "peaceful coexistence" with non-Communist states and their commitment to world revolution and support of "liberation movements."

Ideologically, Peking believes it is not possible to "export" revolution, which must develop its own indigenous roots and energy. Once a revolutionary movement of this kind generates, however, the Chinese feel obligated to support it with propaganda, economic and technical assistance and with military equipment when the situation allows.

There is a twilight or tactical zone in which Peking maneuvers when it sees an advantage to continue dealing with a government while giving limited encouragement to a revolutionary movement.

In recent weeks, Peking has received warmly a trade delegation from Malaysia although Communist guerrillas have operated in border areas of that country since 1948. Similarly, relations with Burma have improved although Communist splinter groups in northern Burma get some Chinese help. Peking is reported to have made discreet contacts through third parties with the Burmese Government while giving relatively strong support to guerrillas operating in the Northeast.

Chinese Communist diplomats who are renewing their worldwide activity will be no less committed to eventual world revolution than they were in 1965, when a policy of more overt intervention resulted in some disastrous setbacks, especially in Indonesia and Africa.

Since the Cultural Revolution, the Foreign Ministry has been purged and reorganized under a "Revolutionary Committee," including army and party delegates. Virtually all diplomats, including Huang Hua, the new Ambassador to Canada who is one of Premier Chou's most trusted aides, have been through ideological re-education schools or undergone similar reindoctrination in peasant villages.

Foreign governments are likely to find Peking's diplomats more ideologically committed than ever before. Their world outlook is drawn from the party program adopted in April, 1969, which declares:

"Mao Tse-tung thought is Marxism-Leninism of the era in which imperialism is heading for total collapse and socialism is advancing to worldwide victory."

Implying that the center of world communism has shifted from Moscow to Peking, the program says: "Comrade Mao Tse-tung has integrated the universal truth of Marxism-Leninism with the concrete practice of revolution, inherited, defended and developed Marxism-Leninism and brought it to a higher and completely new stage."

There is an echo in this doctrine of the old imperial attitude that led Mandarins to describe China as being at the center of the civilized world. This cannot be forgotten as the United States and other Western nations look at Maoist China and engage with Premier Chou's new pragmatic foreign policy.

Chinese Court
U.S. Public Opinion

by Seymour Topping

HONG KONG, June 26—The Chinese Communists guards at the bridge leading from this British Crown Colony to mainland China are pretty nonchalant these days about the passage of Americans into the once forbidden country. Nine young American graduate students and four of their wives trooped across the narrow railway bridge last week, and in Peking Premier Chou En-lai said such visits would become reciprocal in due time.

The question that persists is: Why is Peking pressing ahead with its people-to-people approach after so many years of self-imposed isolation from Americans? During a five-week stay in China, this correspondent was provided with some hints as to the reasons for the new hospitality.

The decision to adopt the current policy was apparently taken in 1970, when President Nixon began to signal his desire for an improvement in relations. It was a year in which Premier Chou, the shrewd pragmatist of Chinese Communist leadership, assumed a stronger role in day to day management of the Government.

Prior to 1966, the Premier had been subordinate to the Chief of State, Liu Shao-chi, who had been locked in a power struggle with the party chief, Mao Tse-tung. Mr. Liu was deposed in the Cultural Revolution unleashed by Mr. Mao, and Premier Chou's own future became uncertain during 1967–68, when leftist extremists became dominant in the Cultural Revolution Group.

By 1969, Mr. Mao was back in full control. Then, largely

51

because of concern over the border conflicts with the Soviet Union that year, the party leadership assigned greater license to Premier Chou to set the nation's domestic and foreign policies in order.

The Premier was aware by then that the American people, disillusioned by the experience of the Vietnam war, were wavering in their attitudes toward Asia. Today there is an obvious belief in Peking that American public opinion can be made a potent ally in the realization of Chinese foreign policy aims.

At a dinner in Peking last Tuesday with this correspondent, William Attwood of Newsday and Robert Keatley of The Wall Street Journal, Premier Chou said he felt that American visitors could help to mobilize their fellow countrymen to bring about the withdrawal of American forces from Taiwan and Indochina.

The 73-year-old leader remarked that it would be "glorious" if United States forces were withdrawn from the island and the Taiwan Strait, thus removing the key obstacle to the establishment of diplomatic relations with Washington.

The Premier's aides are now culling the deluge of visa applications from American politicians, scholars, businessmen, writers and others, in search of those who are most influential or sympathetic. Proud of material improvements in their country, the Chinese Communists are ready to show them off. They also are convinced they have persuasive arguments in support of their foreign policy.

The experience of this writer in China during the last five weeks suggests that however the Chinese Communists may try to use American visitors, the people-to-people exchanges will prove worthwhile on balance for the United States. Most independent observers will emerge from a tour of China with at least three salient conclusions:

• Access to China is essential if the country is to be understood and intelligent policy toward its Government formulated.

• China is on the way to becoming a first-rate power.

• The Chinese Communist society is disciplined, militant and committed by its leaders to the ultimate goal of world Communism, with Peking as its ideological center.

Many illusions about China dissipate before these realities.

What American visitors tell their hosts may be more important to the future of Sino-American relations than what they hear.

The Chinese Communist leadership forms its impressions of the United States on a meager ration of information and through the spectrum of its ideology. Chairman Mao believes, if one is to judge by his writings, that American society is headed for collapse and revolution. In support of this analysis, Peking points to anti-Vietnam war agitation, racial disorders and economic dislocations.

Peking leaders draw some of their impressions about what is going on in the United States from a daily compendium of Western news agency reports monitored by Hsinhua, the Chinese Communist press agency. Chinese diplomatic reporting from abroad was disrupted by the recall of ambassadors during the disruptions of the Cultural Revolution. Only now are the embassies being fully restaffed. Few of the Chinese Communist leaders have traveled abroad in the last decade, most not at all.

Premier Chou, the most worldly of the top leaders in China, has not been in a Western country since 1954, when he attended the Geneva conference on Korea and Indochina. Hungry for information about the West, particularly the United States, the Premier often bombards visitors with more questions than they can address to him.

There is a tiny coterie of men around the Premier who have had first-hand experience in dealing with Americans. One of the top two, Chiao Kuan-hua, a Vice Minister of Foreign Affairs, is ill. The other, Huang Hua, Ambassador-designate to Canada, will be setting up in Ottawa Peking's most important post for monitoring developments in the United States.

The people-to-people program could provide Peking with a direct channel for an exchange of information and ideas with

Americans. These exchanges might help make the next Government-to-Government talks more meaningful than the discontinued sterile dialogue at Warsaw.

Peking Is Pleased Over Nixon Visit

by James Reston

PEKING, July 16—Chinese officials expressed pleasure today over the planned visit of President Nixon, but offered no information about the talks between Henry A. Kissinger and Premier Chou En-lai that arranged it.

The head of the Foreign Office information department, Chen Chu, said the mission involving Mr. Kissinger, the chief White House adviser on national security, was arranged and carried out in the greatest secrecy and that he did not know personally what had been discussed. The Peking radio broadcast the text of the joint announcement without comment.

In the three days that this correspondent has been in Peking, however, officials have been showing great interest in the Nixon Administration's forthcoming decision about China's seat in the United Nations, and Secretary of Defense Melvin R. Laird's visit to Japan. On both they have been taking a very hard line.

The official theme here is that the seat on the United Nations Security Council properly belongs to the People's Republic of China, that Nationalist China should be ousted from the world organization, that the United States Seventh Fleet should be removed from the Taiwan Strait and that the United States security treaty with Chiang Kai-shek is illegal.

While this stern line is clearly in opposition even to the Nixon Administration's new efforts at accommodation with Peking, it is assumed in diplomatic quarters here that the United States Government did not arrange the Kissinger mission and the President's visit here while it was planning to lead the fight against the admission of the People's Republic into the world organization. On the contrary, this latest move toward normalization of Chinese-American relations is expected by diplomats here to encourage other nations to support Peking's entrance into the world organization.

Officials here seem to be taking a more critical attitude toward United States efforts to encourage the defense efforts of Japan than on the United Nations seat or anything else. A Foreign Ministry official said today that the Nixon Administration's efforts to arrange what he called the remilitarization of Japan were regarded as a threat to China.

He said Peking's information was that Japan now had an armed force of over 300,000 men, two-thirds of them officers, and that such an army could be rapidly expanded. He said that Japan was doing her best to infiltrate Taiwan and to arrange for Taiwan to remain in the United Nations under Chiang Kai-shek or an independent Taiwan Government.

These points, however, tend to distort the generally friendly atmosphere toward Americans here. Officials are insisting that they have no ambitions in Southeast Asia and merely want peace restored there.

Press Is Silent
On President's Trip

★

by James Reston

PEKING, July 17—The Chinese Government seems to be making less fuss over President Nixon's forthcoming trip to Peking
than most other governments in the world.

The Peking daily Jenmin Jih Pao, which comes out any time
of the day that there is news, gave the story seven lines in the
corner of its front page yesterday. It did not mention the matter
today and ignored the comments of President Nixon and Henry
A. Kissinger on it.

The Peking radio merely read the official communiqué yesterday and then dropped the subject today in favor of a long denunciation of "American imperialism" and "Japanese militarism."

Foreign Ministry officials passed on to Premier Chou En-lai
requests for information about the Kissinger mission, but these
were ignored.

People in the streets and even at Peking University seem
wary about discussing what for them is a surprising development. For years they have been urged from billboards and propaganda racks to "unite and defeat the United States aggressors
and all their running dogs," so the switch leaves them cautious
if not speechless.

Not so the members of the Western diplomatic corps, who
have had a hard time here for years. They were outspokenly,
almost joyfully, complimentary to Mr. Nixon for what they regarded as a bold mission that might finally lead to normalization
of relations between Washington and Peking.

President Nixon, they noted, must have known that so dramatic an American diplomatic initiative, coming on top of his public statement that China's cooperation was essential to the building of any durable world order, would encourage many wavering nations to support the mounting drive to expel Nationalist China from the United Nations and give its seat to the Peking Government.

It is hard to imagine, diplomats here observed, that the President would time Mr. Kissinger's trip to Peking before the September meeting of the United Nations General Assembly and his own visit to Peking after the Assembly if he intended to lead the fight against Peking's entry into the world organization this autumn.

Aside from this awkward dilemma over who should represent China in the United Nations, and what seems to be a rising campaign here against "United States-Japanese militarism," the timing of the President's move seems ideal. The general tone of official talk here is moderate and even friendly. Chinese Foreign Ministry officials go out of their way to say that China is a big but poor country, not a superpower and with no ambitions to be one. They say the Chinese want what is theirs—meaning Taiwan—but that Peking can wait. They say Peking does not want war and could not impose its social and political system on Southeast Asia if it wanted to.

Unless one gets to the top of the Chinese Government, however, it is hard to get dependable information. Even the Foreign Ministry was not told about the mission by Mr. Kissinger, President Nixon's adviser on national security, and apparently it has yet to be filled in on his talks with Premier Chou. The diplomatic corps was given no advance information about the joint communiqué.

It is probably significant that the Chinese Government is not saying much about the affair. Officials here are well aware that Mr. Nixon's initiative will help Peking get into the United Nations, but there is not a whisper of this even in their private conversation.

On the whole they seem rather pleased with all the attention of a Nixon visit, especially since it was arranged before any official Presidential visit to Moscow, but they are not raising any hopes about it.

Tactics Change, ★ But Principles Don't

by James Reston

PEKING, July 31—China's attitudes and tactics toward the United States are obviously changing, but her strategy and principles remain the same. This is the main impression of a reporter here.

Eleven years ago, Chou En-lai told Edgar Snow, the American journalist: "We believe that a solution to Sino-U.S. relations will ultimately be found, it is only a question of time. But there is one point: If the United States does not give up its policy of aggression and the threat of war against China, no solution is possible. We do not believe that the people of the United States will allow their Government indefinitely to pursue such a policy. There is no conflict of basic interest between the peoples of China and the United States, and friendship will eventually prevail."

Now, while Chairman Mao Tse-tung is making a philosophy

of history, it is Chou En-lai who is making history itself, and what he told Snow in 1960 is very similar to what the Western diplomats here believe he told Henry Kissinger here the other day.

Agreement on principle between Washington and Peking must be reached first before concrete issues can be settled, and these principles, as China sees them, are as follows:

First, there are not "two Chinas," but one Chinese Government over both the mainland and Taiwan, here in Peking.

Second, all disputes between China and the United States, including the dispute over Taiwan, must be settled through peaceful negotiations, without the threat or use of force.

Third, accordingly, Washington must agree to withdraw its armed forces from Taiwan and the Taiwan Strait. As to when and how these forces are to be withdrawn, these are matters to be settled by subsequent negotiation.

It is assumed in the Western diplomatic community in Peking that Mr. Kissinger was authorized to give assurances to Chou En-lai that President Nixon accepted these principles, and further assure him that it was the policy of the U.S. Government to withdraw all its armed forces from Vietnam.

Otherwise, diplomats here say, Chou En-lai would not have been authorized to invite President Nixon to come to Peking in opposition to strong feelings within the high command of the Chinese Army that no negotiations should take place with Washington so long as American forces remained on Taiwan.

Convincing Chou En-lai on the seriousness of Washington's desire to normalize relations with Peking has not been an easy exercise. Early in the Nixon Administration, the French Ambassador in Peking, Etienne Manoel Manac'h, was instructed by President de Gaulle to tell Chou En-lai that Mr. Nixon had told de Gaulle that he intended to withdraw from Vietnam and re-establish diplomatic relations with China, but the Chinese Premier was not at that time convinced.

Since then, however, President Nixon has been faithful to the policy he outlined to de Gaulle. He cancelled most of Washington's restrictions against trade, travel, and cultural exchanges with China. He resumed diplomatic talks with Peking's representatives in Warsaw in 1970, and after Mao Tse-tung indicated to Snow that he would welcome personal talks with the President, Mr. Nixon has kept pressing for a summit conference, finally through the Kissinger mission.

For this, Mr. Nixon has been generously praised in the Western diplomatic community in Peking, but now that his visit here has been arranged, even the diplomats who are most enthusiastic about his initiative are asking: Is he really prepared to pay the price?

Does he know that China will make absolutely no concessions on Taiwan to get into the United Nations, make no compromises for a peace settlement in Vietnam, and oppose violently Mr. Nixon's policy of increasing Japan's military role in the defense of the Pacific?

In short, the question being asked by Western diplomats here is what Mr. Nixon hopes to get out of all this except a relaxation of tension as an argument for re-election.

For the judgment of well-informed men in Peking is that China is changing its attitudes and tactics here, not because it needs Washington's support in its quarrels with Moscow, but because it wants Taiwan and Taiwan's seat in the United Nations.

Officials here are still cautious and even skeptical about what Mr. Nixon will do in the debate in New York about bringing Peking into the United Nations. They are hoping for private talks with Washington about their basic principles on Taiwan, Vietnam and Japan before President Nixon gets here. For they still cannot quite believe Mr. Nixon is ready to meet their terms for China's representation in the U.N., and the "normalization of relations." And they insist that Washington must get out of Vietnam and out of Taiwan before there can be any normal diplomatic relations between the two countries.

U.S. Is Told
To Get Out of Asia

by James Reston

PEKING, Aug. 1—Despite President Nixon's recent efforts to establish normal relations with China, powerful officials of the People's Liberation Army are mounting a campaign for total withdrawal of United States troops not only from Taiwan and Vietnam but also from Korea, Japan, the Philippines and Thailand.

During celebrations this weekend of the 44th anniversary of the founding of the Communist armed forces, the army for the first time opened a military exhibit in Peking to the foreign press and stressed the political functions of the armed services.

On the whole, the exhibit emphasized that the army was not only a fighting force but a work force and a production force as well. But the presentation ended with a statement that the army was "determined to liberate the sacred soil of Taiwan."

The climax of Army Day was a reception for the Central Committee of the Chinese party and the Peking diplomatic corps. During the reception—and in the presence of Premier Chou En-lai and Chiang Ching, Chairman Mao Tse-tung's wife—the chief of the general staff of the army called for the withdrawal of all American troops from this part of the world.

"United States imperialism," said Huang Yung-sheng, "must completely withdraw its aggressor troops from Indochina, the southern part of Korea, Japan, the Philippines and all other countries and regions which it has occupied and stop its interference in the internal affairs of the peoples of the Middle East and the Arab people as well as the peoples of Asia, Africa and Latin America."

To the applause of the audience of more than a thousand people, the chief of the general staff added: "We are determined to liberate Taiwan. The United States must withdraw all its military personnel and military installations from Taiwan Province and the Taiwan Strait area.

"We firmly oppose any schemes of creating 'two Chinas, one China, one Taiwan, or an independent Taiwan.' The liberation of Taiwan is China's internal affair, which absolutely brooks no foreign interference."

In his speech, the only one of the evening, Huang Yung-sheng said that China would not attack any other nation unless it was attacked. He said China stood for "the normalization of relations between states on the basis of the principles of peaceful coexistence."

He added that Peking supported the peoples of Vietnam, Cambodia and Laos and specifically backed the seven-point peace proposal put forward in Paris by the "provisional revolutionary government of South Vietnam."

In short, there is no evidence here that the Chinese Government is preparing the Chinese people for any compromise with President Nixon on the Taiwan issue or anything else.

Mr. Huang's speech contained a denunciation of "Japanese militarism," which he said was being organized by "United States and Japanese reactionaries."

There has still been not a single word of official commentary or analysis here about President Nixon's forthcoming visit to Peking or about the mission by the President's assistant for national security affairs, Henry A. Kissinger, who arranged the Presidential visit, and radios continue their propaganda against the Nixon Administration's policies regarding Taiwan, Southeast Asia and Japan and condemn the Nixon doctrine of encouraging Asian allies to defend themselves as a device to militarize Japan and "let Asians fight Asians."

The guests at the head table during Huang Yung-sheng's speech indicated the importance of the occasion. In addition to Premier Chou and Chairman Mao's wife, those in attendance included Prince Norodom Sihanouk, the ousted Cambodian chief of state, and the following members of the Central Committee of the Chinese Communist party: Chang Chun-chiao, Chi Teng-kuei, Chiu Hui-tso, Chu Teh, Kuo Mo-jo, Li Hsien-nien, Li Teh-sheng, Li Tso-peng, Wu Fa-hsien, and Yeh Chien-ying.

U.S. 'Two China' Stand Irritates Peking

by James Reston

PEKING, Friday, Aug. 6—China is taking a hard line against the Nixon Administration for trying to have both the Peking Government and the Chinese Nationalists in the United Nations, but this has not changed its decision to welcome President Nixon here some time before next May.

It can be said on the highest authority that officials here are not only irritated by Secretary of State William P. Rogers's announcement that Washington will vote for the seating of Peking in the United Nations and oppose the expulsion of Taipei, but furious because they think this formula was reached as a result of pressure from both Japan and Chiang Kai-shek, the Chinese Nationalist leader. The Government here is still counting on private negotiations and President Nixon's visit to straighten things out.

Peking has four ways of making its official views known here. In order of importance, they are Government or Communist party official statements, pronouncements in the official press by "Commentator," a signature usually denoting a member of the Central Committee of the Communist party, editorials in the official newspaper, Jenmin Jih Pao, and articles in the official press agency, Hsinhua. The sharp attack on Mr. Rogers's "two China" statement came in the form of a Hsinhua commentary.

The Government here hesitated for a day before its attack on Mr. Rogers's statement. Finally, they characterized the "two China" formula as "absurd," a "preposterous" proposition that proved that the Nixon Administration was "lying" in its determination to support the "Chiang Kai-shek gang" and demonstrate that it was "the enemy of the Chinese people."

There was also a suggestion in the official comment that Peking was not only disappointed but felt that it had been deceived, for it talked about the Nixon Administration's saying one thing and doing another. Did this mean that Henry A. Kissinger, Mr. Nixon's foreign-policy adviser, had led Premier Chou En-lai in their talks last month to believe President Nixon would take a more pro-Peking position? Or that a Peking Government that accused an American Government of being an "enemy of the Chinese people" was about to cancel the Nixon visit?

Again, on the highest authority, despite disappointment in the Rogers formula, it can be said that no responsible official here is asserting that Peking was misled or deceived. Mr. Kissinger, they agree, made no promises. There were no "deals."

The two things that seem to trouble the highest officials here are not Washington's intentions but the danger that, as the United States withdraws from Asia, Japan will become militarist and expansionist, and the Taiwanese will develop a powerful independence movement.

Oddly, less talk is heard in Peking about American ambitions in this part of the world than about Japanese ambitions, and less concern about Chiang Kai-shek or the American security treaty with Taiwan than about a Taiwanese independence movement.

Peking is in a peculiar spot. It talks endlessly about "American imperialism" and Chiang Kai-shek's "feudalism" but at the nub of the problem here, if one hears these top officials clearly, Japanese economic power and military potential, and the Taiwanese independence movement—independent of both Chiang Kai-shek and Mao Tse-tung—are this capital's nightmares.

Officials here seem to concede that Mr. Nixon is withdrawing from Vietnam and that President Chiang is not immortal, but as they see it, Japan is expanding, and the Taiwanese independence movement is more of a menace than Generalissimo Chiang or his son, Chiang Ching-kuo, who is his political heir apparent.

The Chinese are watching all this very carefully. They have heard the cries of dismay from North Vietnam and North Korea after the Kissinger visit to Peking, and for the moment they are reassuring their Communist allies by condemning Secretary Rogers and President Nixon, but, visibly concerned by the million Russians on their northern borders, they are closing no doors to a better understanding with Washington.

China clearly wants to be in the United Nations and it wants Taiwan. Only after that does it want a place as one of the five great powers. But curiously its ambitions seem less important here than its anxieties over Japan. Probably the most important paragraph in the Hsinhua statement Wednesday is not the vilification of Mr. Rogers but the reference to Japan. "The Japanese reactionaries," it said, "have offered advice and worked energetically openly and behind the scenes for the 'two China' plot dished up by Rogers. Before Rogers issued his statement, the reactionary Sato Government of Japan had played up 'two Chinas' singing one and the same tune as Rogers."

The most surprising thing to a visitor here is this pervasive anxiety about Japan. Actually Hsinhua's statement condemning Mr. Rogers for his "two China" policy, despite its vivid language, is almost amiable compared with what the controlled press here has said about Secretary of Defense Melvin R. Laird's recent visit to Japan. Mr. Laird got much more than a mere Hsinhua rebuke, for the Chinese thought he was directly concerned in raising the military power of Japan, and in Peking, that seems to be more of a menace than anything else.

A View of Nixon
From Peking

by James Reston

PEKING, Aug 7—President Nixon is handling his relations with this sensitive and suspicious capital about as well as anybody could do under the circumstances. He is tip-toeing through a mine field, which extends from here through Tokyo, Moscow, Taipei, Saigon and Hanoi, and could easily be blown up at any point, but so far, as seen from here, he has been remarkably effective.

Mr. Nixon has made the bold and historic move to establish communications with China. He has not been the prisoner of his own past politics, prejudices and propaganda. He has taken risks with Japan—very serious risks—and with the Soviet Union, to change the questions and the players on the world board, and he has not been thrown off balance by the mutterings of protest in Tokyo or Moscow or by the savage public reaction of the official Chinese news agency here to his proposal that both Taiwan and Peking remain in the United Nations.

Fortunately, Mr. Nixon is dealing here in Peking with a wise and experienced professional, who understands the ambiguity of life. Premier Chou En-lai hasn't survived the revolution of China and the turmoil of the world in the last fifty years by being rigid or silly.

Chou En-lai is angry about the Nixon Administration's "two Chinas" policy in the United Nations. He is particularly angry about Secretary of State Rogers' use of the word "Government" in reference to Taiwan, as if Washington still thought Chiang Kai-shek was, at this late date, the head of a potential "Govern-

67

ment" of China. But he doesn't lose his temper on the point, or let the Rogers statement get in the way of the Nixon visit to Peking.

In short, Chou En-lai draws a distinction between propaganda and policy. Let Washington say what it likes, he says, and Peking will disagree, even in violent terms, but after both sides sound off, let's keep to the main point and have Nixon come here for serious conversations. That, at least, is what I believe Chou En-lai is saying in private conversation.

President Nixon has been equally careful. He has kept to the main point of opening up serious talks with Chou En-lai and not letting propaganda interfere with policy. He quickly and as seen from here wisely did not allow himself to be provoked by the Chinese news agency's savage attack on the Rogers "two Chinas" policy in the United Nations, and emphasized the importance of ending China's diplomatic isolation, even if this did not promise to produce any spectacular agreements, which it obviously won't.

Chou En-lai has watched all this very carefully. I have had a long five-hour conversation with him, and am not yet free to report what he said, but it is clear that he understands the President's problems, at home and in Tokyo, Moscow and Taipei, and accepts Mr. Nixon's sincerity in wanting to come here and talk out the problems of common concern about the future of the post-Vietnam world.

It is clear that Chou En-lai regards this as a very important and maybe even decisive moment in history. He is 73. He is very conscious of the passage of time, of the age of the leaders of China, of the transformation of philosophy and politics and power in America, Europe, the Middle East and Asia—particularly of the gathering power of Japan—and wants to talk about the future with President Nixon before it is too late. Henry Kissinger must have sensed this during his visit here, and President Nixon seems to be acting cautiously and prudently on the human and political facts. Chou En-lai is clearly ready for change, and intrigued by Mr. Nixon's dramatic move toward talks, but he is still skeptical, still wondering whether Mr. Nixon is reaching for a genuine settlement in Asia or merely conniving with Tokyo and Taiwan and striving for the appearance of accommodation and the hope of re-election.

In the short range, Peking wants Taiwan; it is more worried about a Taiwanese independence movement than about Chiang Kai-shek or America's troops on that island. It wants to replace Taiwan in the United Nations, for this is the last symbol of its humiliation by the West, and its isolation as a great power.

Also, Peking seems to be more concerned about the threat of the Soviet Union on its northern border and about the threat of Japan's growing economic and military power, than it is about America's future role in the Pacific. So whatever the official press here says about Secretary of State Rogers and America as "the enemy of the Chinese people," Chou En-lai obviously wants to talk to President Nixon, and Mr. Nixon has been just delicate enough in dealing with all this to make serious talks possible.

Chou Looks To Broad Talks With Nixon

★

by James Reston

PEKING, Aug. 9—Premier Chou En-lai is prepared for a very broad discussion of world problems when President Nixon comes here some time before May.

In a recorded interview that the 73-year-old Chinese leader reviewed and approved for publication, he stressed that he was not solely preoccupied with the short-term problems of ending the Vietnam war and the controversy over Taiwan and China's seat in the United Nations, but also wanted to talk about the changing roles of the United States, Japan and the Soviet Union in Asia and the Pacific.

Mr. Chou expressed some concern over what he insisted was the rise of Japanese militarism and ambitions in Taiwan and Korea and over the mobilization of massive Soviet power on China's northern frontier.

The interview took place in the Fukien Room of the Great Hall of the People in the center of the capital. Present were members of the Foreign Ministry staff and my wife.

It somehow seemed that Mr. Chou, who wore a plain gray Mao Tse-tung jacket, has shrunken physically as his power has expanded. Courteous and grave, he seemed eager to get on with the experiment in diplomatic exploration with Mr. Nixon while there was still time.

Critical as he was of past United States policy in China, Taiwan, Indochina and Japan, he said nothing that could be regarded as critical of the President personally and was obviously eager for any information he could get about his psychology.

He praised the boldness of Mr. Nixon's initiative in seeking the meeting with China. He showed detailed knowledge of Mr. Nixon's speech in Kansas City July 6 on world economic rivalry and said he was waiting for a transcript of the President's news conference last week.

While Mr. Chou conceded that there was a lot of formal underbrush to be cleared away before the President arrived and that perhaps some of it could be done by technicians, he insisted that "if these questions are to be solved, they can only be solved when the President himself comes."

He also made a point of stressing that no private deals had been made during the recent visit here by Henry A. Kissinger, the President's adviser on national security affairs, and he went out of his way to recall the friendly relations between the American and Chinese peoples in the past.

At no time, however, did the Premier concede the slightest point on the Indochina, Taiwan or United Nations controversies.

As to China's seat in the world organization, it was all the way in or all the way out. Mr. Chou was less vehement than the official commentaries here on Secretary of State William P. Rogers's "two Chinas" formula. It was "not a step forward," he said mildly.

China will not mediate between the parties in the Indochina war, he insisted, but is backing the forces opposing the United States and will continue to do so until the United States withdraws.

Discussing questions of nuclear armament, Premier Chou referred calmly to the possibility of a Soviet attack on China. "We Chinese are not afraid of atom bombs," he said. "We are prepared against their attack, against their launching a pre-emptive attack on us. That is why we are digging underground tunnels."

"You probably heard about this," he added almost casually.

His visitors had noted great mounds of gravel and odd excavations all over the capital; I said I understood that there was a network of civil-defense bunkers in Peking.

"Not only Peking," Mr. Chou replied. "The great majority of our big and medium cities now have networks of underground tunnels."

That rather ominous note at the end of a long evening does not typify the mood of the conversation. Mr. Chou was often critical of the United States, the Soviet Union and especially Japan, but never belligerent, emotional or bitter about the past.

"China," he said, fanning himself slowly and talking very softly, "is a country which was blockaded by the United States for more than 20 years. Now since there is a desire to come and look at China, it's all right. And since there is a desire to talk, we are also ready to talk."

"Of course, it goes without saying that the positions of our two sides are different," he continued. "To achieve relaxation, there must be a common desire for it, so various questions must be studied, and all these questions may be placed on the table for discussion."

"We do not expect a settlement of all questions at one stroke. That is not possible. That would not be practicable. But by contacting each other, we may be able to find out from where we should start in solving these questions."

That was nearer to his general approach and tone. There was, he thought, the problem that had to be sorted out between President Nixon's doctrine of encouraging other nations to assume more of the military burden in the Pacific and the President's desire for normalizing relations with China.

As the Premier sees it, the Nixon doctrine only encourages the militarists in Japan—a growing problem anyway, in his view —to follow the country's economic expansion with military expansion. Indeed, Mr. Chou almost stated it as a rule of life that military power follows economic power.

He was quite generous about the Japanese people in general. "A diligent and brave people and a great nation," he called them, but he said, the United States is promoting their economic and military power, and if Washington does not handle the Taiwan and Korean questions carefully, Japan will move in as the United States pulls back. The militaristic movement has to be nipped soon, he added.

If Mr. Chou was worried about the Japanese getting out of hand, he was asked, why was he so eager to get rid of the United States-Japanese security treaty, which has been a restraining force on Japan, particularly in the nuclear field.

The Premier rejected that as "a forced argument." Despite the treaty, he maintained, "Japan with her present industrial capabilities is fully able to produce all the means of delivery."

"She is able," he said, "to manufacture ground-to-air missiles, ground-to-ground missiles and sea-to-ground missiles. As for bombers, she is all the more capable of manufacturing them. The only thing lacking is the nuclear warhead."

"Japan's output of nuclear power is increasing daily," he added. "The United States supply of enriched uranium to Japan is not enough for her requirement, so she is now importing enriched uranium from other countries. And so her nuclear weapons can be produced readily."

If Japan gives up her ambitions in Taiwan and Korea, Mr. Chou said, it might be possible to negotiate a Chinese-Japanese mutual nonaggression pact, but she wants to control Taiwan and is conniving with "American reactionaries" to keep Peking out of the United Nations and establish "an independent Taiwan."

In remarks about the role of the United States in Asia, Mr. Chou said that it had committed offenses in this part of the world and that it was for "the doer to undo the knot."

On the whole, however, Premier Chou sounded like a man who had made up his mind that a major reappraisal was now in progress among the major nations and that China wanted in on the talks this time. To him Taiwan is a symbol of Western domination over China's territory and he is determined to resolve the question, and, in particular, to keep Japan out of it.

Despite his alarmist talk about the Soviet Union and the danger of a Soviet attack on China, he reserved by far his most critical comments for Japan.

"When you oppose a danger," he said "you should oppose it when it is budding. Only then can you arouse public attention."

For the rest he was at least much milder than Peking's revolutionary propaganda. He saw no conflict between the United Nations principle of the peaceful settlement of disputes and Peking's doctrine of supporting wars of national liberation. He even denied that New China, as he called it, was a nuclear power, saying it was only an experimental one, out of necessity.

In short, he made it clear that he was very much for new and serious talks with the President—not very hopeful about them, but at least eager to discuss the changing world and see what happens.

An Evening With
The Premier of China

by James Reston

PEKING, Aug. 9—The Premier of China is an austere man with thick John L. Lewis eyebrows, cool and inquisitive dark brown eyes and very white, expressive hands.

Premier Chou En-lai greets his visitors in the vast Fukien Room of the Great Hall of the People on Tienanmen Square, across from the main gate to the Forbidden City.

In the formal part of our conversation, when he was discussing China's relations with the United States, the Soviet Union, Japan and Taiwan, he talked very slowly, as if he were tired and perhaps a little suspicious, but when we moved to dinner in another part of the room shortly after 10 o'clock, he brightened and talked on a wide range of subjects.

The Foreign Ministry stipulated before the interview that I could use a tape recorder but not for broadcast purposes, and that it was not to be used during dinner. However, my wife was permitted to take notes at the table.

The Premier, asked whether he was an optimist or a pessimist, replied with a smile that he was an optimist because he was a Communist. He then talked about the United States and showed some interest in its race problem and in the American experts on China who were so severely criticized during the McCarthy era.

Mr. Chou said a friend of his just back from the United States had told him that the American blacks were making progress and he seemed pleased about it. He asked whether many of them worked in the Government, and when he was told that 64

75

per cent of the population of the District of Columbia was Negro, and that many worked in the Government, he observed
that this was a good thing because you get used to them.

He said he had no old friends in the United States except the
journalist Edgar Snow, but he inquired about John Stewart
Service and John Carter Vincent, formerly of the State Department, and the Orientalists Prof. John K. Fairbank of Harvard
and Owen Lattimore, formerly of Johns Hopkins.

When I said that it would be good if they were able to come
back and see the country they had devoted their lives to studying, he replied that it was a worthwhile idea. "Take good wishes
to them," he added. "If they want to visit China we will welcome
them."

Premier Chou expressed some admiration for the late Gen.
Joseph W. Stilwell, United States commander in China during
World War II, mainly because he quarreled with Generalissimo
Chiang Kai-shek. But he was rather grudging in his praise for
Gen. George C. Marshall, who tried unsuccessfully to mediate
between the Chinese Communists and Nationalists, though he
expressed a preference for him over Gen. Albert C. Wedemeyer
and Patrick J. Hurley, who also served the United States here
during the postwar period.

At one point Mr. Chou's mind jumped from General Marshall to the Marshall Plan for the reconstruction of Europe, and
he was particularly interested in what the plan had cost the
United States and whether it got any of the money back.

The United States has apparently not learned in Vietnam the
lessons of its failures in China, he said, and is trying a Vietnami-
zation program of arming and supporting reactionary forces that
do not have the backing of the people. That, he observed, was
precisely what the United States tried in China—America had a
"Chinaization" program of supporting President Chiang, who
had five million men and plenty of American arms.

That was where the Communists got their arms, he said, by
destroying General Chiang's millions and taking their arms.

There was a very interesting photograph, he recalled, showing Mao Tse-tung entering Peking in an American jeep and reviewing whole rows of American guns and tanks.

The Premier had taken time to read what I wrote from China before the meeting and brought up, without offense, an observation I had made that China was an old civilization that seemed vigorous and young but was run by "old men."

The reason for this, he said, is that China's revolution has gone on for 22 years and actually for 28 years before that, from the founding of the Communist party. Accordingly, the leaders grew old in the struggle and did not come to power until they were in their fifties.

The American Revolution was quite different, he observed, lasting only a few years, and the early Presidents were young.

The Americans numbered only three million at the time of the revolution yet were able to resist a colonial power of 30 million, so they depended on guerrilla warfare, he said. It was Americans who started guerrilla warfare, he added; "George Washington started it."

China is thinking about the problem of succession and younger men, Mr. Chou said. It operates on the three-in-one combination, he added, explaining that all instruments of government are now run by a combination of the old, the middle-aged and the young.

While Premier Chou talked an elaborate dinner was served. Also at the table were Chang Wen-chin, director of the Foreign Ministry's Department of Australian, European and American Affairs; Chen Chu, director of the Foreign Ministry's Information Department; Chi Chao-chu, the Premier's principal interpreter, who did all the translating, and three other interpreters, including Chin Kuei-hua, who has squired us around since we arrived July 8.

It would be misleading to say that the meal was served in courses. It was a never-ending stream. First hors d'oeuvre of prawns, green beans, cold duck and chicken, and delicious morsels of fish. Then the first of three soup courses, this one oyster broth with tiny oysters the size of a quarter and floating slices of cucumber, followed by a dish of shrimp balls, quails, eggs, cabbage and sea slugs.

There were small glasses of sweet red wine and a strong liquor called mao tai, which Mr. Chou used to propose a toast, without swallowing a drop.

At about this point he began talking about the Chinese revolution and Stalin.

I observed that parents owed their children a record of the years before a child has its own memory and asked whether the leaders of the Chinese revolution felt the same obligation. Had they kept personal records in the form of diaries or journals of their long political struggle?

"No," Mr. Chou replied, "none of us have kept a diary—not Mao or Lin Piao or I, and none of us want to write our memoirs." Maybe, though, he continued, a history of China from the Opium War on should be prepared, and perhaps it would be a good idea to try to get the record down on tape, but, he added, "we are not quite accustomed to the tape recorder in China yet."

Premier Chou, who, in the formal part of the conversation, had criticized the Soviet Union, nevertheless expressed his admiration for Stalin. Looked at from certain points of view, he said, Stalin no doubt had his shortcomings, and even from a Chinese point of view he was not good for China at the Yalta Conference with Roosevelt and Churchill, but from a world point of view there was much to be said for him.

"We consider him to be a great Marxist-Leninist," Mr. Chou said. "Also, you must admit he made great contributions to the world war."

Unfortunately, Mr. Chou added, Lenin died early, and after his death "no one but Stalin could have held the Soviet Union together—no one." Without the 15 years of Soviet construction before the outbreak of World War II, he added, it would have been impossible to defeat the Germans.

Though the dinner had run through almost two hours and

many courses, Mr. Chou never let the conversation loiter. His mind seemed to jump from one topic to another, and as it was getting on toward midnight, he suddenly began talking about America again.

"America has its merits," he said. "It was composed of peoples of all nations and this gave it an advantage of the gradual accumulation of the wisdom of different countries. You are also a big country. We both have about the same amount of land and room for development."

"Of course," he continued, "you plead that your economic and political system is good, but let's not argue about that. You will not oppose progress, and if you are going to make progress, of course you must expect change."

"You will undoubtedly develop faster because of your industrialization," he added.

That turned his mind to the question of language, which seemed to have a special fascination for him. He said, English was now the second language in China though the Chinese attach considerable importance to French. There is a tendency in China now, he added, that he did not quite approve of: too little attention to Russian. A lot of people speak Russian and there is a lot of knowledge to be gained through it, he commented.

Commenting on General Chiang at another point, Mr. Chou noted that he was well acquainted with the Nationalist leader and that account must be taken that he is a man who can stand up to American pressure, unlike President Nguyen Van Thieu in Saigon. General Chiang has a sense of national respect, Mr. Chou added, but that is not the case with all the people around him, as the Central Intelligence Agency will know.

In a discussion of population problems, the Premier said it was not good for China to expand the population, now estimated at 750 million to 800 million. Living standards cannot be raised with rapid population growth, he explained, and it is not good for mothers. He added that progress was being made on the problem, but not everywhere in the country.

By this time, naturally, more fuel was needed, and in some

mysterious way it was bountifully replenished without anyone's noticing. Suddenly the quail eggs and sea slugs were gone and there were some minidumplings with meat and, of all things the first time in our experience here—beautiful white expanses of bread and butter, which the Premier consumed with delicate satisfaction.

Then a separate helping of ground pork, served in lotus leaves —"Please don't eat the lotus leaves," Mr. Chou said after I had started—followed by not one but two soup courses, first corn and bean soup and, finally, a sweet soup, then tangerine tarts, bananas and small triangular slices of watermelon.

In short, it was not exactly a TV dinner, and not a typical American interview either. A few minutes after midnight Premier Chou gave the signal to disperse, but first he sat us down to make a forgotten point about Korea and then took us to the door which could not have been more than a quarter of a mile away.

It was, as we say back home, quite a night.

Transcript of Reston Interview With Chou

PEKING, Aug. 9—Following is a transcript of a recorded interview with Premier Chou En-lai of China conducted Thursday night by James Reston, vice president and columnist of The New York Times. The conversation took place in Mr. Chou's reception hall here, and the translator was Chi Chao-chu, a former Harvard student who is on the Premier's staff. Mr. Chou authorized the official transcript on the condition that both questions and answers be printed verbatim.

MR. CHOU—Have you recovered your health completely?

MR. RESTON—I am a kind of an old dog, you know. And I've never been sick in my life, and I was rather surprised to be struck away from home.

MR. CHOU—Perhaps you had this trouble before but because of your good health you didn't quite feel it.

MR. RESTON—There are specific things, particularly in the last few days, I wanted to be sure that we understood the clarity of your thought. The first thing in my mind was whether you were surprised by Secretary Rogers's statement. In the Chinese news agency—sorry, it was said that the United States Government was saying one thing and doing another, and therefore I wondered whether you were not only surprised but perhaps felt deceived, whether you have been led to believe something by Dr. Kissinger other than what was in the Rogers statement.

MR. CHOU—I do not plan now to make a comparison for you on this. The position of the Chinese Government has all

81

along been clear. That has been the case throughout the 16 years of the Sino-U.S. ambassadorial talks, first in Geneva and then in Warsaw. And that has also been the case with the whole series of statements we have recently made.

This statement issued by the U.S. Secretary of State was a self-contradictory formula worked out under the pressure of the talks between the Japanese Government and the Chiang Kai-shek representative in Tokyo. This, of course, must be pointed out by our press.

As for the position of our Government, it has never changed. It is possible that you already heard about this from the French friends because I had a talk with the French parliamentary delegation, and I also had a talk with some American friends from the Committee of Concerned Asian Scholars. And do you want me to reiterate our position?

MR. RESTON—The central question that is in my mind is whether you felt that the statement by Rogers in any way interfered with the movement which I believe was taking place toward a normalization of relations between the United States and China?

MR. CHOU—At least it is not a step forward. And what is more, a confused debate is bound to take place in the United Nations and in the international arena, in which case we are compelled to speak out.

MR. RESTON—I thought that there was a misjudgment here, frankly, in what it was that Rogers and President Nixon were doing. I thought that the President, by seeking a conference with you before the U.N., was saying to members of the U.N. who had wavered in past years or followed our line in past years: We have now changed, we want to see the People's Republic seated in New York. And by that process he had started a procedure which inevitably would lead to the seating of your Government in the U.N., particularly on his third point, which clearly implied that he would not use the veto in the Security Council, yet as I interpreted the news agency's remark, this was not taken into account at all.

MR. CHOU—The central point of that statement is to retain the Chiang representative in the United Nations, and that means that it would be impossible for us to go in.

MR. RESTON—Perhaps this is not a subject that lends itself to useful conversation at this time. Maybe it's too delicate. And if it is, I hope you will tell me so and we'll go on to other things.

MR. CHOU—You are not planning to make clear our position in an all-round way?

MR. RESTON—I want to do that. I mean——

MR. CHOU—As I have seen from your talk with our friends, your proposition is that since the United States is to recognize the People's Republic of China, then it should give up the Taiwan representative.

MR. RESTON—I believe very frankly that we've come to an unusual moment in the history of the world that neither in your life nor in mine will we see again. In my own country there are great changes taking place, philosophical and political. In Europe we are seeing a transformation, with the British coming into the Common Market. In the Middle East we see more evidence, I think, that force does not prevail for anybody. The only place where force seems to have prevailed is for Russia in Czechoslovakia. And therefore what I've come here to do is to find out, during this long period when China had not been actively participating in these affairs of the U.N. and elsewhere, how you see the world of this great transformation? Do you really believe that the United States is ready for change, as I do, or do you feel that we are engaged again in maneuvers and manipulations for imperialist purposes, as you seem to be saying in your press?

MR. CHOU—We admit we also are seeing some changes. As you said to our friends, you are also seeing changes taking place in China. But there is one question and that is we will not barter away principles. And so once this question is raised, there is bound to be a dispute.

As for Taiwan, who occupied Taiwan? And so if you want to have a change, then you should act according to a Chinese saying, that is, it is for the doer to undo the knot.

The latest discussions between Japan and Taiwan were obviously designed to create an obstacle so that it would not be possible for us to get into the U.N. After Rogers's statement, the Japanese Acting Foreign Minister, Kimura, and the Secretary General of the ruling Japanese Liberal-Democratic party, Hori Shigeru, made similar statements.

Both Kimura and Hori Shigeru said that this basic policy of the United States was determined after many consultations between the United States and Japan. And Japan's demand was put forward after two secret talks held between the Chiang representative and Sato in the later part of July and on Aug. 1.

And so the statement made by the so-called Foreign Ministry of Chiang Kai-shek did not touch on Rogers's statement at all but concentrated on attacking the Albanian resolution.

Japan has ambitious designs with regard to Taiwan. Japan wants to control Taiwan in her hands. So it's not a simple matter that Japan is supporting Taiwan in the United Nations.

In fact, we can even go on further from there. That is, not only will there be a question of two Chinas or one China, one Taiwan—it's even conceivable that they are trying to separate Taiwan from China and, under the direction of Japan and also possibly with support from some quarters in the United States, to bring about a so-called independent Taiwan.

And because of this, we cannot but make our attitude very clear. We have stated very clearly that should a state of two Chinas or one China, one Taiwan appear in the U.N., or a similar absurd state of affairs take place in the U.N. designed to separate Taiwan from China to create a so-called independent Taiwan, we will firmly oppose it and under those circumstances we will absolutely not go into the U.N.

It is indeed true that the world is undergoing changes. But these changes must not cause further damage to the Chinese people. Over the past 20 years and more, it's not we who have caused harm to others, but the U.S. Government who have been causing harm to other countries and other peoples. We have waited already for more than 20 years and we can wait for another year. That doesn't matter. But there must be a just solution.

MR. RESTON—May I ask whether, in the event that your present position proves to be too pessimistic and the General Assembly and the Security Council without any veto by the United States decide to seat China, will you at this meeting of the Security Council go to New York yourself and represent China at this meeting of the General Assembly?

MR. CHOU—Will Chiang Kai-shek still be there or not?

MR. RESTON—No, on the assumption that he is not.

MR. CHOU—He has left?

MR. RESTON—Yes.

MR. CHOU—Only if he has really left can I express an attitude, and Taiwan must be a part of China. But if in the U.N. resolution there is anything to the effect that the status of Taiwan remains to be determined, then we will not go in.

MR. RESTON—I understand that. But I am assuming by my question that the Albanian resolution will have been put up and voted to your satisfaction in the General Assembly, and that you will go on and be voted into the Security Council, at which time Taiwan will be expelled, and my question is: Would you at that time personally go to New York?

MR. CHOU—But I was asking the question that would they still consider the status of Taiwan undetermined and the status of Taiwan an outstanding question? You cannot answer that question now, nor can I.

MR. RESTON—I don't see that that question would be a question for the U.N. at all. At that time it's a question between you and the Taiwanese. As early as 1955 I believe that you said that this was an internal question and it should be settled between the Government of the People's Republic and the local authorities, I believe you called them at that time, on Taiwan. Is it still your view, that it should be settled in that way? And second, is there anything to Edgar Snow's remark that he believes there already has been contact between the People's Republic and officials on Taiwan?

MR. CHOU—I've said on many occasions that the liberation of Taiwan is China's internal affair which brooks no foreign interference. That is still our position now. At the same time, I've said that the United States has committed aggression against and occupied China's Taiwan Province and the Taiwan Strait, so we are willing to sit down and enter into negotiations with the U.S. Government for a settlement of this question.

This has been going on for 16 years, first in Geneva and then in Warsaw. And what is more, I've said that the Chinese people are friendly to the American people, the two peoples have been friendly with each other in the past, and in the future they should all the more live together in friendship, because the Chinese people have now stood up.

That was said far back in 1955 at the Bandung conference. Afterwards, we tried to accept the visit of some American correspondents to China, but John Foster Dulles's State Department did not approve of that. And so, since the way was blocked by the U.S. Government, then we on our side would no longer want any such contacts. We have thus been cut off for more than 20 years, but it doesn't matter.

But now since there are some changes in the world, then we should see to it no damage is done to anyone, that concern should be shown to the wronged party and the wronged party should not continue to be wronged. Therefore, the question of Taiwan is not merely an internal question. If it were merely an internal matter, then we will be able to settle it ourselves. The solution of this internal problem has been obstructed now for already 21 years, and so changes are taking place. And in this process some country has started to harbor ambitions. That is quite evident.

MR. RESTON—You mean by that Japan?

MR. CHOU—Yes.

MR. RESTON—May I ask you to state the principles again.

You have been very clear about this in the past, you have told Snow, in '60 I believe. Principle one was nothing between us on Taiwan shall be settled by force or the threat of force. Principle two, there is only one China. Now are these the two and only two principles to be settled? What about withdrawal of forces, what about the question of the treaty between Washington and Taipei?

MR. CHOU—When you say us, you mean China and the United States?

MR. RESTON—Yes, the United States and China.

MR. CHOU—If Taiwan is to be returned to the motherland, the U.S. forces must withdraw, because otherwise how can it be returned to the motherland? And since the United States is to withdraw all their troops and military installations from Taiwan and the Taiwan Strait area, then as a matter of course the so-called U.S.-Chiang mutual defense treaty, which we had all along considered to be illegal, would become invalid.

MR. RESTON—I understand. It is clear, I think, since the differences over Rogers's statement, that there is a lot of underbrush to be cleared away before you and the President are to meet. I wondered what ideas you have about whether preliminary technical talks at a lower level should take place and where, between now and the President's arrival?

MR. CHOU—It is possible. But if these questions are to be solved, they can only be solved when the President himself comes. He expressed a desire to come and we have invited him to come.

MR. RESTON—Could I ask one final question about the U.N. and China? In your mind, is there a conflict between the basic principle of the U.N., namely, that all disputes between nations shall be resolved without the use of force or the threat of force, and the principle of revolution and support for national liberation movements in the world as espoused by your Government in the past? Is there a conflict between these two things?

MR. CHOU—No. Who has committed aggression against

other countries? China hasn't. Over the 22 years of the history of our People's Republic, we only went abroad to assist Korea, but that was under certain conditions. We made it very clear to the so-called U.N. Command, composed of 16 countries led by the U.S. We said to them that if they press toward the Yalu River, then we will not sit idly by, although at that time our Taiwan and Taiwan Strait area had already been occupied by the U.S. Seventh Fleet and the U.S. Air Force. It was the U.S. which first committed aggression against China, and not vice versa. It was only after the U.S. forces had reached the Yalu River that we sent our C.P.V. [Chinese People's Volunteers] to resist American aggression and aid Korea.

As for our help to other countries of the world, that is in the case when they are subjected to aggression. And in the view of the U.N. itself, aggression is wrong and should be stopped. So we are merely helping them to resist aggression. And in the view of the U.N. itself, they should be given support. And a striking instance is Vietnam.

As for Vietnam, we will continue to give them assistance to the end, until the complete withdrawal of the U.S. forces. At present the most urgent question is still Vietnam. You wondered very much why I said to the Committee of Concerned Asian Scholars that it was our position that first of all the question of Vietnam and Indochina should be solved, and not the question of Taiwan or other questions.

Because the status quo of Taiwan has remained for 21 years. There is no war there. That is because of restraint on our part. But this is not the case with Vietnam. Not only did the U.S. send troops to commit aggression there, but the U.S. is expanding the war there. When President Nixon took office, he started withdrawing troops from Vietnam, that is anyhow changing the former situation. But in March last year, the peaceful rule of Samdech Norodom Sihanouk in Cambodia was subverted, and then the U.S. troops went in. Even your New York Times criticized that action.

MR. RESTON—Especially The New York Times.

MR. CHOU—And then this year there was the attack on Route 9. Isn't that an expansion of the war?

MR. RESTON—Yes, I think so.

MR. CHOU—And so that has brought even greater harm to the Vietnamese people and the Indochinese people as a whole. Such a small place as Indochina, with a small population. Yet such a huge sum has been spent. The American Government itself admitted that in 10 years' time it spent $120-billion and suffered such heavy casualties. And the American people are unhappy about the American casualties. We on our side feel they are needless casualties. But the Vietnamese people have suffered even greater casualties.

MR. RESTON—I agree.

MR. CHOU—Just take a look there and you can see that. Shouldn't we sympathize with them?

MR. RESTON—Absolutely. It's a tragedy.

MR. CHOU—So why shouldn't the United States stop its aggression?

MR. RESTON—Yes. Now what do you think we should do to stop it? I went straight there from Panmunjom in 1953, and I have been fighting against our involvement in that war ever since. As a matter of fact, when I went to Saigon in 1953 I saw the British brigadier who was the observer there at that time and I asked, was there any way in which the West can possibly deal with the Vietminh, as they were then called. And he said, yes, there may be one way: If you would give foreign aid, military program to the Vietminh, especially tanks, then you might be able to find them. That will be the only way, said he, the West will ever win a war in this part of the world.

MR. CHOU—You did some work, your New York Times, by making public some of the secret Pentagon papers.

MR. RESTON—Yes.

MR. CHOU—Indeed, back in the time of Truman, the U.S. Government started helping the French in their aggression and colonial war in Indochina. And after Dulles took over from Acheson, this further developed.

MR. RESTON—Are there some Peking papers on that period on the war that have not been published. If there are, then The New York Times would like to accommodate you and publish them.

MR. CHOU—We have no secret papers like that. But we did send some weapons to the Vietnamese people to help them in their resistance. The French Government is aware of that. Within less than half a year after the founding of our People's Republic, we recognized the DRVN [Democratic Republic of Vietnam] headed by President Ho Chi Minh. Actually the French Government was prepared to recognize the P.R.C. [People's Republic of China], but because of that matter, France put off the recognition until the time of General deGaulle. So if you are interested in secret documents, this is a document but not a secret one.

MR. RESTON—Yes. Your commentator the other day made it quite clear that your Government is opposed to the Geneva conference for a settlement of the Indochina war. Now, do you see the Laotian and the Cambodian questions being settled separately from the Vietnam question?

MR. CHOU—This is a matter within the sovereignty of the Government of the DRVN, of the provisional revolutionary government of the Republic of SVN [South Vietnam], of the royal government of national union of Cambodia and of the Laotian Patriotic Front. It is within their sovereignty to decide whether the Indochina question is to be settled together or separately.

Judging from the present situation, negotiations are going on now only on Vietnam. And so maybe the Vietnam question will be first solved. As for Cambodia, the U.S. refuses to recognize Prince Sihanouk's Government, and Prince Sihanouk has clearly stated his just position in his message No. 24 to his compatriots. I haven't heard anyone say anything more on that score. As for

Laos, they are planning to discuss among themselves. And there is correspondence between Souvanna Phouma and Prince Souphanouvong, and the Laotian Patriotic Front has put forward a five-point proposal, one of which is cease-fire throughout Laos.

We support this five-point proposal of the Laotian Patriotic Front. As for the summit conference of the Indochinese peoples, the four sides of the three countries issued a joint statement in April last year and they put forward a common proposition. They demand all troops from countries outside of Indochina to completely withdraw and let the three peoples of Indochina solve their question by themselves. And we support this principle.

MR. RESTON—You are not interested in mediating this struggle between the U.S. and the North Vietnamese and Liberation Front?

MR. CHOU—We don't want to be a mediator in any way. And we were very badly taken in during the first Geneva conference. If you are interested, I can go into it now. If not, we can discuss it at the dinner table.

MR. RESTON—Yes, but I want to hear all about your confrontation with John Foster Dulles at dinner. You know, nothing has surprised me quite so much since coming here as the vehemence of your feeling about Japan.

MR. CHOU—You too were victims of Japanese militarism. But you said the Americans are more forgetful. But I know you still recall the Pearl Harbor incident.

MR. RESTON—Yes, but this is one of—in my view—the endearing qualities of the American people: They have no memory. They have every reason to be aggrieved, if not full of hatred, about Japan and about Germany. There is no hatred in our country toward Japan or Germany. And if there is one thing that has troubled me a bit since I have come here, it is a sense that, while you are, in your domestic policy, looking forward toward the 21st century, in your foreign policy I think you are looking backward to the old disputes. And that saddens me. Now am I being unfair to you? Because I don't want to be.

MR. CHOU—It is unfair. Because you didn't have any direct talk with us about our foreign policy, you just heard about some of our slogans.

Why is there such sentiment among the Americans? Because the U.S. benefitted from both World Wars, and the U.S. losses were rather small. Why is it that the American people have a rather deep impression about the present U.S. war of aggression against Vietnam? Because they have really suffered. And so the American people demand the withdrawal of the American troops. It is not that the American people don't summarize their experience.

So I don't quite agree with your estimate that the American people are easily forgetful. Any nation is bound to summarize its own historical experience. Just yesterday I met a friend who had come from the U.S. some time ago, and he said that among the Americans there are now some changes toward the black people and that is a good thing. And it shows that many white people in the U.S. are becoming awakened to the fact that it is not right to continue the exploitation and oppression of the black left over from history. So isn't that a summary of historical experience? And it is very good.

MR. RESTON—Yes.

MR. CHOU—We oppose the Japanese reactionaries. It is not that we have any hatred for the Japanese people. After the end of the Pacific war, we have not stopped our contacts with the Japanese people. New China has never imposed a blockade against them. The Japanese people have kept on visiting China, and we are also willing to go there.

The Japanese people are a diligent and brave people and a great nation. And it was the U.S. Government which after the war strengthened the Japanese reactionaries. And when they have developed to the present stage they are bound to develop militarism.

Just look at the economic development of Japan. According to your President, the steel output of Japan is about to catch up to that of the U.S., as he said in Kansas City on July 6. Why is it that Japan has developed so quickly? I've heard that you also admit that the reason was that not only was no indemnity exacted from Japan, but Japan was protected and provided with raw materials, markets, investments and technology.

And then there is another thing. That is, the U.S. has promoted the development of Japan toward militarism by the indefinite prolongation of the Japan-U.S. security treaty. The Japanese people are opposed to this treaty. And according to the report of the American Congressmen who went to Japan to study the matter, Japan does not need such a huge defense budget for its fourth defense plan for the purpose of self-defense.

The budget for the fourth defense plan reached the amount of more than $16-billion. And Defense Secretary Laird himself admits that according to Japan's present economic strength and industrial and technical ability, she will not need five years (1972–1976) to complete that plan, and two to two and a half years will be sufficient.

In Japan, in South Korea and when he returned to Washington, Laird said that there were three pillars to the Nixon doctrine. The first is to arm your partners, and of these partners, the principle one will be Japan. The second is nuclear protection, and only thirdly is negotiation. And what is more, he made it clear that these negotiations have to proceed from a position of strength. And without the previous two pillars, there would not be the third.

MR. RESTON—Could I ask you, sir, what you want us to do about Japan? Because it seems to me there is a dilemma here. If we stay allied to Japan, with some control over her, particularly in the nuclear field, that is one thing. If we end the security pact with Japan, is it in your view that it is more likely then that Japan will become more militaristic or less militaristic?

It seems to me that, confronted by two nuclear powers in the

Pacific, both China and the Soviet Union, and freed from us and our pact, she would almost certainly have to go nuclear, would she not? Therefore I find myself puzzled by your desire to see this pact with the United States broken.

MR. CHOU—That argument is quite a forced argument. Despite this treaty, Japan with her present industrial capabilities is fully able to produce all the means of delivery, she is able to manufacture ground-to-air, ground-to-ground missiles and sea-to-ground missiles. As for bombers, she is all the more capable of manufacturing them. The only thing lacking is the nuclear warhead.

Japan's output of nuclear power is increasing daily. The United States supply of enriched uranium to Japan is not enough for her requirement, and she is now importing enriched uranium from other countries. And so her nuclear weapons can be produced readily. She cannot be prevented from doing so merely by the treaty. You have helped her develop her economy to such a level. And she is bound to demand outward expansion.

Economic expansion is bound to bring about military expansion. And that cannot be restrained by a treaty. Look at all your nuclear bases in Japan. Even if you are to withdraw your nuclear weapons, the nuclear bases are still there, and they can make use of them.

When you said that there is no militarism, well, I'll argue with you on that score. This is not only borne out by the film which we have shown you and by the activities of Mishima, who had committed suicide.

Just when you were ill in Peking, you probably heard of the incident of a Japanese fighter colliding with a Boeing civil airliner, causing heavy casualties. Why? Because the air corridor in Japan is very narrow.

You have been to Japan. You know that the Japanese air corridors are divided into several levels, the higher for Boeings, the lower for the propeller-driven aircraft. And with the Japanese Air Force being equipped with more and more planes, they

just fly everywhere with them at will for training. And the pilot
of that fighter parachuted to safety but let his fighter collide
with the Boeing. And when asked why they did that, the trainer
just said there was no place for training. What could they do?

That of course gave rise to public indignation. And among
those voicing indignation were the opposition within the ruling
Liberal-Democratic party itself, who said this is one of the harms
of militarism. It is not something said by the Chinese alone; they
themselves are saying that.

MR. RESTON—You are really worried about Japan, aren't
you?

MR. CHOU—Because you know we suffered a long time, for
50 years. Such calamities can be prevented by opposition from
us and from the Japanese people together.

Of the four opposition parties in Japan, only the Japanese
Communist party has differing views with China; that party sup-
ports Sato on this question.

The Japanese Socialist party admits to revival of Japanese
militarism. The Komeito party admits that Japanese militarism
is being revived, the Democratic Socialist party does not deny
this fact, and the opposition wing of the Liberal-Democratic
party also admits this fact.

When you oppose a danger, you should oppose it when it is
only budding. Only then can you arouse public attention. Otherwise, if you are to wait until it has already developed into a
power, it will be too strenuous. If the Far East situation is really
to move towards relaxation, and if Japan gives up its ambitions
of aggression against Korea and China's Taiwan, then it will be
possible for China and Japan to conclude a mutual nonaggression treaty on the basis of the five principles of peaceful coexistence.

MR. RESTON—Could I ask you at that point whether you
can foresee an expansion of such a pact to include the United
States and the Soviet Union?

MR. CHOU—That must go through a whole series of steps

and I cannot at the present time give an immediate answer. Because at the present time the two superpowers, the U.S. and the Soviet Union, are involving themselves in affairs throughout the world. And it is not an easy thing to bring about a solution of world problems, so we would rather like to have a discussion with your President.

MR. RESTON—On this subject——

MR. CHOU—Various questions can be discussed. This question, too, may be discussed.

MR. RESTON—This is too serious a question to be dismissed lightly. Could you define as you have done so often in the past and so helpfully in the past, what are the principles that must precede such a far-sighted move as such a four-power non-aggression pact.

MR. CHOU—This question can be thought about only after we come to it because international questions are too complicated. It is easy to say the five principles of peaceful coexistence which we advocate. But to go into an examination to see whether or not these principles are observed, then many problems will arise.

For instance, it was with India that we had first reached an agreement on the five principles of peaceful coexistence. Because both China and India are two big countries, and in history there was no aggression by either against the other, with the sole exception of Genghis Khan's descendants, who went to the subcontinent but then stayed here and intermarried with the local inhabitants.

As for the two peoples, we had lived together in friendship for generations. As for the boundary question, it was something left over by British imperialism. But precisely over this boundary question, they fell out with us.

On this question, it was India which occupied Chinese territory. They even crossed the so-called McMahon Line. As for us, we did not press forward and were ready to solve the question by negotiations. As for Aksai Chin, in the western sector, that had all along been Chinese territory, there was never a boundary dispute over that territory before, but suddenly they raised the question about the western sector.

I went to India to negotiate this boundary question with the Indians on three occasions, and no solution was reached. What is more, they want to further occupy our territory north of the so-called McMahon Line. You didn't know much about this. Now you should know about it. A very good proof of the facts about this situation was a book written by a British author, Mr. Maxwell.

MR. RESTON—Yes.

MR. CHOU—That book is similar to the Pentagon papers which you published. They did not make use of a single Chinese document. All are from Indian sources.

MR. RESTON—May I ask you, sir, how you view the control of nuclear arms? You are now one of the nuclear powers.

MR. CHOU—No, we are not a nuclear power. We are only in the experimental stage. And what is more, that has been the case throughout the period from 1964 to the present, seven years already. We will not test when there is no need. We know it is quite expensive and a waste. And it is not beneficial to the improvement of the livelihood of the people.

It is quite clear, we can see, that the two big powers, the United States and the Soviet Union, have embarked on the mass production of nuclear weapons—cannot get down from the horse, so to speak. But can they thereby monopolize nuclear weapons? No, they cannot.

We produced nuclear weapons by ourselves. We manufacture nuclear weapons because we are forced to do so in order to break the nuclear monopoly. And our aim is the complete prohibition and thorough destruction of nuclear weapons. And so every time we make a test, we declare that we will never be the first to use nuclear weapons. You will see what we Chinese say counts.

MR. RESTON—Do you want to see a world conference on

this question? How can this ghastly problem be solved when the world is now spending about $220-billion a year on arms. It is a disgrace to the intelligence of the human family. What are we to do about this question, and what can China do to help?

MR. CHOU—We do not agree with the Soviet proposal for a conference of the five nuclear powers. They want to lasso us by that means. We have expressed our disapproval, Britain said that she would not take part in the conference, and France too now says that she would not take part either.

We are calling for the convening of a conference of all countries of the world, big or small—because all the countries of the world, regardless of their size, should be equal—for the purpose of reaching an agreement on the complete prohibition and thorough destruction of nuclear weapons, and as a first step, on the nonuse of nuclear weapons. Once everyone agrees on the nonuse of nuclear weapons then what will be the need for the production of nuclear weapons?

MR. RESTON—Why do you use the word "lasso"?

MR. CHOU—When I said "lasso," it means if they want to drags us into such an affair. They will, first of all, demand that we sign on the partial nuclear test ban treaty, on the nonproliferation treaty and so on. How can we sign them?

But we undertake not to be the first to use nuclear weapons. The people of the world have indeed noted the fact that these two big powers are using so much money on nuclear weapons. Your Defense Secretary, Laird, himself admits that with so many nuclear weapons it is not possible for the United States and the Soviet Union to fight a nuclear war. The two peoples will oppose such a war.

MR. RESTON—True.

MR. CHOU—Since you do not want to have a nuclear war, then the United States and the Soviet Union should first undertake forthrightly that neither of them will be the first to use nuclear weapons, and then to go on to the next business. Because by reaching such an agreement, people will feel at ease.

Secretary Laird said, now the U.S. should be prepared for conventional warfare. So Laird is telling Japan to strengthen the modernization of conventional weapons in Japan.

MR. RESTON—Is there a conflict between the so-called Nixon doctrine or Guam doctrine and our efforts to reach an accommodation with China? The thought I have in mind is this: I am afraid there is a puzzling and troubling point here that as we try to reduce our commitments in the Pacific, we encourage Japan and other countries to assume a larger military role, and that, in turn, leads to a greater dismay and anxiety on the part of China. Is there a conflict here? Is this one of the things to talk about with President Nixon when he comes to Peking?

MR. CHOU—You put it well. It is indeed a contradiction. I also discovered this contradiction because this is to encourage the militarization of Japan. There should be an effort at relaxation by all parties concerned. Indeed, there are a lot of questions. And as you know, your President spoke to the correspondents on the fourth after Rogers made his statement. We have not yet seen the full text of his interview, we have read only a partial text. Have you seen it?

MR. RESTON—You mean the Rogers?

MR. CHOU—No, Nixon's.

MR. RESTON—No, I have not seen it.

MR. CHOU—I have only received very fragmentary reports, and probably I might get the full text tonight. President Nixon said that there were no preconditions for the forthcoming talks with China. Neither side has made any commitments. That is, there was no tacit understanding previously reached between the two sides.

MR. RESTON—I think it is useful to clarify this point because I think your allies and ours have both been a bit suspicious on this point.

MR. CHOU—China is a country which was blockaded by the United States for more than 20 years. Now since there is a desire to come and look at China, it's all right. And since there is a desire to talk, we are also ready to talk. Of course, it goes without saying that the positions of our two sides are different. And there are a lot of differences between our points of view. To achieve relaxation, there must be a common desire for it, so various questions must be studied, and all these questions may be placed on the table for discussion. We do not expect a settlement of all questions at one stroke. That is not possible. That would not be practicable. But by contacting each other, we may be able to find out from where we should start in solving these questions.

MR. RESTON—We are a very impatient people, you know, Mr. Prime Minister. In the old grocery stores up in our countryside there used to be little signs which said the improbable we do today, the impossible tomorrow. How long do you anticipate that it will take for reasonable men to resolve these problems of Taiwan, Vietnam and get the principles solved and get down to diplomatic relations between these two countries.

MR. CHOU—We hope that the Indochina question will be solved first, because the war is still going on there. I have read some of your articles, and you said in one of your articles that you felt that your President lacked courage. But of course, in deciding to come to China this time, it is something which even the opposition party say others dare not do. So on this point he has some courage. Mr. Mansfield himself said that.

MR. RESTON—Courage or lack of courage, those are fighting words. What I was trying to say is that I do not think that he is a bold-minded man in the sense that de Gaulle was when de Gaulle said, "I was wrong about Algeria, therefore, I stop it, and I move to change it now."

I think the trend of the President's thought is bold and even right on both Vietnam and China. His timing and his politics are rather ambiguous. That was what I meant, not a lack of courage—it is not a lack of courage, it's a lack of clarity and definition and boldness to cut and end the killing and end the stupidity of isolation of China.

You asked me before about what did I mean by favoring China and the end of the Taiwan relationship. It's very simple. We cannot resolve the problems in the world without China. It's just that simple. We can resolve the problems of the world without Taiwan. It's not a question of sentiment, it's a question of reality and power.

That is why I want to see this resolved, and resolved at a moment when the country is ready for it. That is why I am worried about the China news agency and their story of the other night. If we leave it to journalists, the world will be in a mess. It has to get down to quiet diplomacy.

MR. CHOU—Well, some things can be dealt with quietly, but when some things have been openly declared by the other party for several times, then it must be openly answered in the press.

I agree to your estimate of the character of President Nixon, and of course there is also the question of the position he is now in. The then position of General de Gaulle in France was a bit different. But as there are going to be conversations between us, I hope he will clearly see the future, as you said, to look forward.

For instance, a complete withdrawal from Vietnam will be quite an honorable thing. What is there dishonorable about their withdrawal from Vietnam? I think that is most honorable. When General de Gaulle withdrew from Algeria, the whole world expressed their approval, and the Algerian people expressed approval, too. The relations between France and Algeria improved in de Gaulle's time.

MR. RESTON—I should say one thing to you privately about this. I think it is very important that you say you should look forward. I think the President does look forward. I think there are two things about him that are particularly interesting.

One, he is a Californian and he looks to the Pacific in the way that we who live on the other side of the continent do not. Second, he has an ambition. His ambition is to preside over the

200th anniversary of the Declaration of Independence in 1976. There is one small barrier in the way of that, which is he must get re-elected in 1972. And beyond that, I think he is a romantic, and I think he is dead serious about China.

I think he sees an historic opportunity here to repair the damage that has been done and even the injustice that has been done to China, and also perhaps, in his own sense, a certain rebuke to his own past and a feeling that the role he has played in the cold war is something that might be altered by a great and generous move to unify the peoples of the Pacific before he ends his term.

MR. CHOU—Thank you for providing me with this information. And you are motivated by your concern about the over-all world situation.

MR. RESTON—Yes, one doesn't come abroad to criticize one's own President, and I don't do that. It is true and it is still part of the mythology of America—I believe it's true—that the White House—you know, Woodrow Wilson once said that in the White House a man either grows or he swells, but most men are ennobled by it, and I think President Nixon is focusing on China, where he sees a historic role. This I think is terribly important psychologically.

MR. CHOU—We've noted this.

MR. RESTON—May I, because I don't want to impose on or weary you. There is one thing I want to have you clarify for me if you will. You see we can talk philosophy, and that is interesting. But when we get down to it and listen to all the specific conditions to which I've heard since I have come to Peking, I get rather depressed. The condition on Vietnam I understand, and I can see that it can be met. The conditions and the principles of Chou En-lai on Taiwan, I think, can be met. But when I hear General Huang say that we must withdraw from the Philippines, we must withdraw from Japan, we must withdraw from Thailand, I think this is asking us, in a way, to withdraw from the Pacific, and I get depressed at that point because this doesn't seem to me to be a realistic basis which any President could accept.

MR. CHOU—If one really wants to achieve a relaxation throughout the world and not the aggravation of tension, then the troops of all foreign countries, not only the U.S. troops, should be withdrawn from the territories of the countries they have occupied and let the peoples of various countries solve their own problems by themselves.

This is a question of principle. But as to when and where these withdrawals are to take place first, and how to discuss and reach agreement with the governments concerned, they are concrete matters.

When the principle has been put forward, and if one really goes in this direction, there are many specific details which have to be discussed for the implementation of this principle.

MR. RESTON—I have a feeling that perhaps we'd better end on this point. There are two great movements in the world today. There is a movement of withdrawal by the U.S. in Vietnam and a retrenchment of its commitment overseas, and, on the other hand, the most visible movement, it seems to me, is the enlargement and the expansion of Soviet power across the Middle East and along the southern shore of the Mediterranean, and once the Suez is opened, into the Indian Ocean and the Pacific. Is one justified in being troubled by this Soviet movement in your view? Are you bothered by it?

MR. CHOU—Of course, for us it is an even more urgent matter. The assistant managing editor of your paper, Mr. Salisbury, had been to Mongolia. He testified to the fact that there are massive troops concentrated on our borders in the north. So, in general, we stand for withdrawal of all foreign troops back to their own countries so that the people of various countries may settle their own questions by themselves.

This is a matter of principle. But to put that into concrete form, of course, requires a process. In a word, in the past 25 years, first the U.S. tried to manage affairs of the whole globe, and then after Khrushchev took office it was a matter of striving for hegemony between the two superpowers.

The so-called disarmament conference is in fact a conference for arms expansion. Although there has been no world war, yet small wars have never ceased. We are not for demanding only the U.S. withdrawal and not the Soviet withdrawal, because that would be unfair. We say so in general terms, and specific matters will be dealt with concretely.

So if you say one should relax the situation, it is indeed not an easy matter. The reason is they have a few more atom bombs. But we Chinese are not afraid of atom bombs. We are prepared against their attack, against their launching a pre-emptive attack on us. That is why we are digging underground tunnels. You probably heard about this.

MR. RESTON—Yes, I did. As a matter of fact, you have a great network of tunnels under Peking.

MR. CHOU—Not only Peking. The great majority of our big and medium cities now have a network of underground tunnels.

[*At this point the formal interview broke for dinner, but after dinner, though it was then past midnight, Mr. Chou asked that the formal discussion be resumed. The official transcript was renewed.*]

MR. CHOU—There is one thing I've forgotten to mention. We have just discussed the question of Japan without discussing the question of Korea. As you know, there is still only an armistice agreement in Korea, and there has been no peace treaty. In this connection, we have to revert to John Foster Dulles.

In the Geneva conference, the first stage was devoted to the Korean question. As for the armistice in Korea, on your side it was a result of the decision taken by President Eisenhower. One of your generals admitted that the Korean war was a wrong war fought at a wrong time at a wrong place.

MR. RESTON—Gen. Omar Bradley.

MR. CHOU—At the 1954 Geneva conference there should

have been a result on the Korean question, at least a decision should have been made to continue the conference in the future. But even that was disrupted by Dulles. And so even now there is a demilitarized zone, a Military Armistice Commission which meets once every one or two weeks in Panmunjom.

On your side there is an American representative and a representative from what we call the puppet Government in South Korea. And on the northern side is a representative of the Democratic People's Republic of Korea and a representative of the Chinese People's Volunteers. So the state of war has not ended. And you may recall the two incidents caused by your side, one of the Pueblo spy ship and the other a spy plane which was downed.

MR. RESTON—Yes.

MR. CHOU—And so the situation remains tense. And this is a matter which should be discussed.

MR. RESTON—Yes. If you could give me your views about that, I would be very happy to report them.

MR. CHOU—Our people's volunteers were withdrawn back in 1958. And the troops of other countries under the so-called U.N.C. have also been withdrawn. Only American troops remain there. And of the 60,000 troops or more in Korea at that time, 20,000 troops have been withdrawn and 40,000 and more still remain. And the American troops should all be withdrawn.

To solve the Korean question, a way should be found to bring about a rapprochement between the two sides in Korea and to move toward a peaceful unification of Korea. That of course requires time. But this demand is reasonable.

Now in the U.N. there is still a so-called commission for the unification and rehabilitation of Korea which is completely unilateral, composed of those countries of the so-called U.N.C. participating in the Korean war, and not a commision of both sides.

That presents a problem too. And so the Korean question is also linked up with the problem of Japanese militarism. If things do not go well, Japan may use the treaty it has concluded with South Korea, i.e., the Japan-R.O.K. treaty, to get into South Korea immediately upon the withdrawal of the U.S. forces.

MR. RESTON—It is extremely useful to have this view because, for one thing, we have not been able to do is to define those questions, of which I presume this is one, that really should be on the agenda when the President comes here.

MR. CHOU—The Korean question also involves a question of preventing the rise of Japanese militarism. If Japanese militarism is to expand outward, it will first aim at these two wings, Taiwan and this wing. I only dealt with Taiwan. This is just what I would like to add.

MR. RESTON—Prime Minister, thank you very much for your kindness. I would like to ask the Prime Minister while I am here, would it be presumptuous for me to ask whether it is at all possible to see the Chairman?

MR. CHOU—Not very possible this time, because the Chairman is preoccupied with other matters. But of course you can come with your President next time.

MR. RESTON—No, I don't think I'll do that. I'll worry about him from now till then, and let you worry about him after he gets here.

China's Goals: National Unity And Security

★

by James Reston

PEKING, Aug. 10—China is now obviously reappraising if not yet changing its foreign policy but its list of demands is longer and clearer than anything else on the coming agenda.

It has agreed to receive the leader of its arch-imperialist, the United States, and talk to President Nixon about anything he wants to discuss, but so far that is the extent of its proposals.

China's objectives are more tangible: it wants to complete its national unity by the restoration of Taiwan; it wants to improve its national security by getting rid of American forces in Southeast Asia and South Korea; it wants the withdrawal of the Soviet Union's massive forces on its northern border; it wants assurances against the rise of Japanese economic and military power in the Pacific basin, and it wants its sole place as the most populous nation on earth on the Security Council of the United Nations. Peking has not been able to achieve these goals, which it has had for a generation, through a policy of diplomatic isolation, open hostility toward both Moscow and Washington and mass revolutionary propaganda at home and abroad.

It has made great progress toward evangelizing its people and mobilizing their energies, consolidating the national territories except Taiwan, increasing agricultural and industrial production, establishing its independence from Moscow and producing some experimental nuclear weapons.

But its influence and power in the world are clearly nowhere close to its size and potential, and despite its economic and military efforts, it still feels under military threat from the north and southeast and under economic threat from the spectacular industrial and commercial miracle of Japan.

In this situation, China had to decide whether to go along in isolation with its ideological zeal and its offer of revolutionary leadership to the hungry, yearning nations of the world, or try for a limited accommodation with Moscow or a limited truce with the United States or, more complicated and less likely, some kind of partial easing of tensions with both Washington and Moscow.

President Nixon's series of gestures toward Peking, together with his movement toward ending the Vietnam war and finally his dramatic proposal to come here himself, probably persuaded Chou En-lai, if not the more militant revolutionaries here, on Peking's procedures, if not on its policies.

After all, in the short run, Washington can do more for Peking's shopping list than any other capital. Officials here are not so worried about an American-backed Chiang Kai-shek running Taiwan as they are about an independent Taiwan attracted, if not dominated, by Japanese economic power. Chiang is not immortal, as officials here see it, and oddly, they seem more concerned about an expansionist Japan than an expansionist United States.

Besides all that, it is America and not Russia that has troops on Taiwan and in Southeast Asia, Washington and not Moscow that has influence over Japan, and President Nixon rather than anybody else who—by praising China as one of the great powers and offering to come here—could help produce votes for the entrance of Peking and the expulsion of Taiwan at the United Nations.

Maybe Chou En-lai and the others here are ready for more ambitious talks with Mr. Nixon on a new world order, but a visitor can find little evidence that China thinks it has to change its strategy. The theme here, even in the Premier's more moderate and appealing language, is that Washington has been wrong, and if this has now become apparent to Mr. Nixon, Peking will be glad to listen and talk.

But so far the People's Republic has had little to give. Officials here are very conscious of the possibility that they might just by accident give the President the means of re-election, but important as this is, the asking price in Japan—and if we are to take the chief of staff of the army here, Huang Yung-sheng, at his word, also in Thailand and the Philippines—is very high indeed. In fact, it is an invitation to the United States almost to withdraw from the Pacific.

This is not to say that President Nixon's opening toward China is not a good thing and that Chou En-lai's attitude is anything but receptive to the talks, but beyond that, with the best will in the world, it is hard to go.

We know what China wants from the world but not what it is prepared to contribute to a general settlement, and this recalls the advice of a wise Oriental specialist in the Britsh Foreign Office many years ago: "Do not waste your time," he said, "trying to imagine in advance of negotiations what is in the Oriental mind. Just be sure you are very clear about what is in your own mind."

In China, Dollar
Crisis Is No Crisis

by James Reston

SHANGHAI, Aug. 19—The "dollar crisis" was no crisis in China. Even here in this commercial capital of the People's Republic there was no public evidence that anybody was paying the slightest attention to Washington's "new economic policy."

Two days after President Nixon devalued the old greenback and sent a hiccup through all the banks and stock exchanges of Europe, I cashed $500 worth of American travelers checks at the old exchange rate in Peking. No problem. No questions asked. And even a day later, the banks here in Shanghai were still paying out on cabled dollars from New York as if nothing had happened.

It isn't that the news of Mr. Nixon's latest troubles hadn't got through to this part of the world. All the details were on the B.B.C., and The Voice of America even gave us Secretary of the Treasury John Connally's mystifying clarifications. More than that, the official Japanese radio has been stuttering into China with amazement all week, but the Chinese have almost ignored it all publicly, and even privately their officials have treated it as the normal aberration of the "war-oriented capitalist system."

Later on, the Chinese Central Bank here will undoubtedly adjust to the new realities of the international monetary exchange, but for the moment the devaluation of the dollar is primarily a political question which raises some awkward problems in the relations between Washington and Peking, and particularly between Washington and Tokyo.

Peking is not primarily interested in the play of the international markets or exchanges. China's economy is mainly internal. It is not particularly worried about world trade because it doesn't have much. It buys and sells very little from and to the United States, but its political stake in this dollar crisis is another matter. For Washington is now clearly preoccupied, not with "normalizing diplomatic relations with China" but with stabilizing its domestic economy and avoiding a trade war with the major trading nations of the world, including Japan.

At the beginning of July, despite his mounting economic problems, President Nixon was concentrating on establishing a new and friendly relationship with China. For this purpose, he sent his White House Assistant on Security Affairs, Henry Kissinger, on a secret mission to Peking, without telling the Japanese Government about it until the last minute; but now the preoccupation in Washington is obviously on economic questions, and in this field, Japan is clearly a more important consideration for the time being than China.

Officials here are very conscious of Japan's economic power. They see Tokyo's gross national product increasing by about 13 per cent a year and her steel production about to outreach America's.

More important, Peking is visibly alarmed about Japan's economic influence in Taiwan and what it regards as Japan's ambitions to create an independent Taiwan under Tokyo's economic and political influence. All this seemed to be going very well from Peking's point of view so long as Washington was concentrating on establishing a new and friendly relationship with China, even at the risk of irritating the Sato Government in Tokyo; but with the sudden switch of interest in Washington to economic questions, the emphasis has obviously changed.

You couldn't tell it, however, from talking to officials here. They made very little publicly of the Kissinger visit or their agreement to receive President Nixon in Peking before next May. They are not saying a word publicly about the dollar problem, but privately they are saying they will wait and see. They will not be surprised if the United States puts commercial interests ahead of everything else; it has happened many times before. But meanwhile they will "await developments."

China is under no pressure on any of this. It doesn't even bother to pick up a little extra foreign exchange by noticing the devaluation of the dollar. It won't even send its newspaper reporters to the United Nations to send back dispatches on the fight there betwen Taiwan and Peking on China's seat, so long as Chiang Kai-shek has representatives at U.N. headquarters in New York.

The attitude here is that China has waited for over twenty years and can wait for another year or more and couldn't care less about the economic problems of the United States or Japan.

The unfortunate thing about the economic crisis in the United States, as seen from here, is that it seems to support Peking's propaganda line about Washington, namely that, even when President Nixon makes dramatic moves to establish "normal diplomatic relations with Peking," everything can be changed within a few days by internal American economic or political considerations.

Even so, officials here are acting as if the Washington economic crisis, with all its repercussions in the other capitals of the world, has nothing to do with Peking. They are not acknowledging any "crisis." They are paying out on the dollar as if it were gold. They are not even trying to lobby for votes to get a seat in the United Nations, or so they say. They are merely waiting, they insist, in the belief that, despite temporary arguments over economics or the claims of Taiwan or Japan, China's place as one of the major nations in the world will finally be recognized and accepted.

China's First Order of Priorities

by James Reston

SHANGHAI, Aug. 24—After wandering around China for six weeks, this reporter has the impression that the "sleeping giant" is awake all right, but is not really very interested in "shaking the world."

It is true that the propaganda billboards from Canton in the South to Manchuria in the North summon the Chinese people to unite against "the American imperialists and all their running dogs," but if this running dog heard the Chinese officials clearly they are less interested in leading a worldwide revolution than in three more practical projects nearer home.

First, they are not only trying to feed and educate 750 million people—give or take a hundred million—but attempting at the same time to modernize, revolutionize and even reform the character of a quarter of the human race. This in itself makes Franklin Roosevelt's revolution in America seem like a minor adjustment.

Second, they say they have a million hostile Soviet troops on their northern border and an expanding and militaristic Japan coveting Taiwan and Korea on their flanks, and while they sound almost paranoiac on the subject, they cannot forget the past.

And third, they are relying for the defense and moral reformation of China to a very large degree on the legendary figure of Mao Tse-tung, who is 77, and on Premier Chou En-lai, who is 73, and must anticipate the problem not usually easy in Communist societies of passing power to the next generation.

All this leaves very little time for plotting the downfall of capitalist scoundrels in Bolivia or organizing the hungry millions of Africa, Asia and Latin America against the Soviet revisionists and the American imperialists.

Besides the Chinese attitudes and approach to life make one wonder why Washington was so worried about an aggressive and expansionist China. They are the most careful and meticulous people I have ever met, and despite their world propaganda, more inward-looking than any major nation on earth.

Mao Tse-tung has given them a phrase about making the past serve the future and the outside world serve China, but they are at great pains to explain that they are going their own way, not copying the West like Japan, not revising the true socialist doctrine or seeking spheres of influence like the Soviet Union or the United States, and certainly not sending soldiers or navies abroad like the two "superpowers." They draw a distinction between giving moral and even material support to other peoples fighting for independence and liberation on the one hand and actually sending men abroad for this purpose. No foreign aggressions for them, they insist, and no Monroe Doctrines or Brezhnev Doctrines either.

One has the impression that long before the United States tried to "contain" China, they were self-contained, quite satisfied that they had enough land, resources and people, and not at all sure that they wanted any more outsiders in their ancient "middle kingdom."

Officials here seemed quite proud of the fact that their self-containment immunized them to the monetary fever now sweeping the Western world, and it was explained to us at a fishing factory at Dairen in northeast China that Chinese fishing boats never go out to sea because they had all the fish they needed in their own territorial waters.

Similarly, at almost every factory we visited it was emphasized with pride not only that all the machinery was made in China but also that most of it was actually produced by the men in this particular factory. They didn't actually say that producing goods for export was a bad thing, but somehow they managed to convey the feeling that it was at best an unfortunate necessity.

The defense of China, however, is another matter. They are quite determined and even militant about that and for a people so obviously unemotional they seem excessively concerned about the danger of a preventive war by the U.S.S.R. and the militarism of Japan.

There is not the slightest whisper of a suggestion here that China's recent limited moves toward cooperation with the United States is in any way connected with her anxieties over Moscow and Tokyo, but one has the impression that Peking was beginning to feel that fussing with Washington, Moscow, Tokyo and the United Nations all at once was maybe not the best way to defend China's vital interests.

In any event officials here are moving on the world diplomatic stage but primarily for nationalistic reasons, or so it seems here. They want first to complete the geographical unity of their country, which means getting control of the island of Taiwan. They want the withdrawal of American troops from this part of the world, but, interestingly, not on any irrational helter-skelter basis that would encourage Japan to replace American influence in Taiwan and Korea.

They want to take China's place in the United Nations at least partly because denial of that seat, like the presence of American troops on Taiwan, is a symbol of China's past humiliations by the West.

In short, the conclusion of this blind man's guide to China is as Confucius did not say: Keep shirt on. Officials here, or at least Chou En-lai, seem to be persuaded that maybe the trend of American military policy in Asia is toward disengagement and that they will have to worry about the Soviet Union and Japan long after all American troops are withdrawn from the mainland of Asia and Taiwan.

Meanwhile, far from being impressed by President Nixon's suggestion that both China and Taiwan take seats in the United

Nations, they are furious, for again the unity and security of China are their primary concerns and any suggestion of an independent Taiwan is a more serious threat to that unity than the temporary existence of Chiang Kai-shek.

For Mao Tse-tung and Chou En-lai, who are also mortal, this is undoubtedly an important question. For they would like to unify the country, deepen its revolution, and establish China as one of the five permanent members of the UN Security Council before they leave the scene. This, rather than all the ceaseless talk about world revolution, seems to be their first order of priorities.

Hong Kong and China, a Contrast

by James Reston

HONG KONG, Aug. 28—Coming out of China into the reck-lessly beautiful city of Hong Kong is almost more of a shock than going the other way. Suddenly everything is different, everything is speeded up, as if somebody had flicked a switch on a gigantic movie camera and all the sights and sounds of life began to race and scream.

Hong Kong is San Francisco squeezed into a narrower dimension. The Victoria Peak of Hong Kong is Nob Hill only twice as high, and the inner harbor between Victoria and Kowloon is much tighter than the wide expanse of water between the San Francisco docks and Oakland and the gentle hills of Berkeley beyond.

You don't look *at* Hong Kong. If you are at the ferry dock on the water's edge you look up because Hong Kong itself is a kind of natural skyscraper, with soaring man-made apartments standing up like trees on its bony face. Or if you wind your way up its cement streets—not straight up like the cable car avenues in San Francisco—you look almost straight down on the water, which is a parking lot for ships and the commercial traffic of the world.

Across the narrow bridge that separates the "new territories" of Hong Kong from China at the railroad junction of Lowu, the sights and sounds are quite different. The land suddenly flattens out, and the noise changes.

Very few cars or trucks on the China side. No commercial advertisements. No tipping to get your baggage across the border and a different kind of noise. Not the quick beat of jazz or the

117

sad, yearning regrets of unrequited love of Western music but the incessant sound of modern Chinese martial music and the glorification of Mao Tse-tung.

Even time is different on both sides of the border, and not only that Hong Kong is an hour ahead of Canton. China thinks in generations and even in centuries. Hong Kong lives on borrowed time. The British have to give it up to China by treaty, down to the water line across from the Victoria Peak by the end of the century, but the British keep on digging and building, as if they were going to be here forever.

The Chinese watch and listen to all this development of Hong Kong without any official comment. They talk about the wonderful new life for the young in the new China and how the educated growing generation of China loves to go to the countryside, but every month more young Chinese risk their lives to swim in the dark to Hong Kong.

They come across "Deep Bay," so named because it is shallow, and across Mirs Bay, swimming about half a mile despite Chinese and British patrols, and between 400 and 500 of them are picked up by the British every month.

In July, the British Hong Kong patrols intercepted and arrested and permitted to live here 397 young men between ages 17 and 24, and 83 young women, all of whom had made their way through the Chinese border and water patrols, and the flight of the young from China seems to increase every month.

So, while there is no massive defiance of the Communist Government in China, there is obviously some defection by the young in the border areas, and the reason for their defection is interesting.

The British interrogate the young Chinese defectors very carefully. They estimate that while they intercept between 400 and 500 every month, two or three times that many make their way to Hong Kong. But even when they land here, the young defectors are not saying that they are political refugees but mainly that they are economic refugees, looking primarily for a better chance for education in Hong Kong.

So these two totally different worlds coexist within a few swimming miles of each other. Peking seldom mentions Hong Kong. Hong Kong has its Chinese Communist political head-quarters. The Chinese travel bureau operates here with efficiency and elaborate courtesy and guides confused Americans from Kowloon to the Chinese border. The press covers the activities and disputes of Communist and anti-Communist parties as if this were a local and not an international concern.

In short, Hong Kong is a remarkable, spectacular and in many ways a hopeful symbol. For it is a link between the con-tending worlds. Logically, it should give up the struggle between the Communist and capitalist giants, but it keeps going, keeps building and somehow keeps betting and investing millions in the belief that somehow common sense will in the end prevail.

CHAPTER TWO
The Transformation of China

Elimination Of 'Four Olds' Transforms China

★

by Tillman Durdin

HONG KONG, May 18—One of the early objectives of the Cultural Revolution in China, which began in 1966 and goes on today, was to wipe out the "four olds"—old ideas, old culture, old customs and old habits.

The "four olds" had already suffered setbacks in the years of Communist rule preceding the Cultural Revolution, but the Maoist leadership tried to use the new revolutionary upsurge launched in 1966 to eliminate them completely.

In the turbulent years from 1966 to 1968, what remained of old religious practices, old superstitions, old festivals, old social practices such as traditional weddings and funerals, and old ways of dress were violently attacked and suppressed. Visual evidences of old things were destroyed, and there was an orgy of burning of old books and smashing of old art objects.

Young Red Guards invaded homes and shattered family altars that denoted continued Confucian reverence for generations of forebears. The few temples, mosques and churches still used for religious purposes were closed and put to secular use. Even those that had been left open for sightseeing purposes, such as the great Buddhist, Lama and Taoist temples of Peking, were barred and their statues, altars and other furnishings were removed.

The Forbidden City—the walled enclosure in Peking of palaces, ceremonial halls, pavilions and residential quarters from which Chinese imperial rule was exercised until 1911—was shut.

The evidence, mainly visual, during three weeks of travel by this correspondent in the east coast areas of China, indicates that the drive against the "four olds" has had sweeping effect.

In not a single home seen by the writer was there any family altar, any tablets to ancestors or any representation of the old gods formerly worshipped by the Chinese masses. In as Westernized a city as Hong Kong, still under British rule, such things are still commonplace in Chinese homes.

No religious practices were discoverable during the trip in China, and guides said there were none. Religious edifices have been turned to use as schools, warehouses or recreational centers.

The Forbidden City, with its evidences of great traditional art and architecture, remains closed to the general public, and the showplace temples and mosques of Peking and elsewhere are still barred except for a few that are reportedly kept open to be shown to visiting Buddhist and Moslem delegations.

Collections of traditional Chinese art objects of second-class quality—porcelains, jades, paintings, lacquerware and jewelry—are for sale in special shops in Peking, Tientsin, Shanghai and Canton, but only for foreign visitors. The Chinese never get a sight of these examples of a great artistic past.

Before the Cultural Revolution it was not uncommon to see women wearing traditional sheath dresses and using cosmetics. Now the old styles in women's garments are gone, and today women wear the same frumpy blue or gray trousers and jackets as men. The writer saw no use of lipstick or rouge. Dressed like men, women work alongside them in manual as well as office jobs at the same pay.

The traditional big Chinese family apparently is gone, too. Cramped living quarters and social conditions today dictate a small family composed of husband, wife and one to three children.

The only old festival observed now is at the time of the old Chinese New Year, based on the lunar cycle, and it is not called

a New Year festival any longer but a spring festival. Celebrations are not the colorful traditional kind. There are holidays,
but the activities then are of a political nature—political dramatic performances or politically oriented mass meetings and
sports events.

No old literature, either Chinese or Western, is on sale. Instead, the bookshops are stacked with the works of Mao Tse-
tung, and the few periodicals on politics, literature, medicine
and other matters that are being produced these days.

In a library inspected at Tsinghua University in Peking, the
section devoted to old Chinese literature was still intact, but a
look into the classic novel "Water Margin" showed that it was
last taken out for reading in January, 1967.

No traditional operas, no traditional music and no traditional
plays are performed these days. There are only the 10 new
standard dramatic works developed during the Cultural Revolution and performed everywhere now in full or in excerpts.

Even the manners and attitudes of the people seem changed.
Weddings and funerals are plain and simple without public display of any sort.

People seem more direct and less polite. They appear to be
more motivated than before by considerations of time and of
cause and effect, as in Western societies.

The exotic, the traditionally pictured and the traditionally
colorful things are gone from Chinese life, at least in the areas
that were visited. In the Chinese People's Republic there is no
"mysterious East" any more, just workaday people following
workaday routines that seem essentially familiar and ordinary
to the Westerner, even though they operate within a Marxist
totalitarian framework.

Old folk sayings are occasionally heard, but these have largely
been replaced by the maxims of Chairman Mao. The first of
January is celebrated as the real New Year's Day, and the other
fixed holidays, besides the spring festival, are May Day and the
Oct. 1 National Day.

A new generation has appeared, and though much of the old China is too indelible to erase as yet, a new China with ways quite different from the old is in existence.

Dirt Is Now A Dirty Word

by Audrey Topping

CANTON, China, April 27—The most visible change in China since the Communist take-over in 1949 is cleanliness. The People's Republic of China is faultlessly clean. Dirt is a dirty word.

In walking from the Hong Kong side across the railway bridge extending from British customs in the village of Lowu to Chinese customs in Shumchun, the contrast is startling. On the Hong Kong side, the railway tracks are littered with garbage and paper, while the Chinese side not only is tidy, but an antiseptic smell rises from the scrubbed building to replace the earthy odors of the British side.

After a gourmet Chinese lunch served with cold White Cloud beer, we boarded an air-conditioned train to Canton. Posters of Chairman Mao Tse-tung surrounded by smiling faces hung on both ends of our railway car, and hot jasmine tea was served by young girls with long braids and dark blue suits with Mao buttons on them.

The train floor was polished to a high shine, and an attendant kept walking around with a cloth to flick off any traces of dirt. At one point, a great commotion was caused by a fly that had managed to slip into the train and land on a window sill. It was soon dispatched by two girls flailing away with fly swatters.

The improvement in China's attitude toward cleanliness seemed incredible to my father, Chester A. Ronning, who was born in China in 1896 and who served as a Canadian diplomat here from 1945 to 1951. He remembered the days when sanitary conditions were unspeakable and when train passengers were often packed in like cattle.

The Chinese stared incredulously at this gray-haired giant who spoke flawless Chinese. Before long, the captain of the train and most of the attendants were gathered around listening to and laughing at his Chinese stories and riddles.

There is nothing like laughter to break the ice in China. Even the most solemn passengers who at first turned their backs on my camera were soon laughing and smiling for photos.

From the train window one still sees the eternal China that has been attracting and enchanting travelers for centuries.

Terraced emerald-green rice fields stretch to the horizon, and the peasants, wading knee-deep in water, plow their fields behind brown water buffaloes. Arched willow and bamboo trees edge the winding path that seems to lead to a distant pagoda. Children in large straw hats drive flocks of fat white ducks and shrieking black pigs.

People still carry their burdens on poles across their shoulders and squatting women beat their clothes clean on rocks by a stream. In the distance, groups of peasants spoon out fertilizer from wooden buckets. Their stone houses with tile roofs are close together and surrounded by artistically shaped haystacks.

But now the scenes are set in an immaculate background. The crops look richer and more abundant. The pigs and chickens are no longer in the family house but in a place of their own and there are no stray dogs. Many of the houses have slogans and quotations of Mao written across the walls in large red characters: "Down with U.S. imperialism!" "Long Live Chairman Mao!"

The peasants have added red stars to their hats and wear neat blue suits. There are concrete walls, large gates hung with red stars signifying district party headquarters.

The trees and buildings of Canton are as clean as the countryside. Each person is responsible for keeping the front of his own shop or home clean.

Since my last visit to Canton—in June of 1966 at the beginning of the Cultural Revolution—the only discernible change in the city's appearance is the increase in the statues and paintings of Chairman Mao that appear in and on the public buildings and in the squares. Quotations from Chairman Mao's red book in gold lettering on large red billboards can be seen everywhere. Many are in English for the benefit of visitors and businessmen attending the Canton trade fair. Others are in the Chairman's own neatly executed calligraphy and to the foreign eye look more like abstract paintings.

An In-Depth Look at Shanghai

by Tillman Durdin

SHANGHAI, April 19—A small group of foreign newsmen, including this correspondent, two Japanese, one Swiss, three Britons, and four Canadians, today started a four-day program that promised to give them the most extensive look at affairs in Shanghai, China's largest city, that any journalistic group has had in recent years.

After spending yesterday afternoon in quick tour of the city and attendance at an evening performance of the ballet "White-Haired Girl," the newsmen entered the more serious activities of the Shanghai visit this afternoon.

Our visit here still has a link with international table tennis, Peking's justification in the first place for letting us come into the country.

Traveling with us is a British table tennis team scheduled for a series of matches with Chinese players in Shanghai. But while officials arranged journalistic appointments so as to allow for attendance, they gave no indication that attention to the matches was an obligation. When all but the Reuters correspondent chose not to attend tonight's matches on the plea that news dispatches had to be written, there were no official demurrers.

Our journalistic group was told this morning that it would spend the morning seeing an exhibition of Shanghai industrial products and hearing about the city's industrial development and this afternoon inspecting and studying the political and social patterns of the big Shanghai machine-tool plant. We were informed that tomorrow we would be taken on a trip into the

129

countryside to visit a commune and would spend the afternoon at a factory that makes table tennis balls.

Wednesday morning is to be occupied by a visit to a hospital and talks with the staff and the afternoon by a visit to a workers' settlement. Thursday morning the group will depart at 11 o'clock for two days in Tientsin, a major port on the Yellow Sea 70 miles southeast of Peking.

So far the Chinese have fixed the group's itinerary and daily program on a rather arbitrary basis, and the newsmen have accepted the arrangements as offering good opportunities for initial insights into the situation in China. It remains to be seen whether any differences will develop over a "this is the way it will be" program after the party leaves Shanghai.

This writer's own one-month visa is valid through May 1, after which, he has been told, an extension will be considered.

So far we are being shown places and institutions that have been on the list for many visiting individuals and groups before us. There has been no opportunity for any extended roving about unaccompanied, but this may be possible later.

A request has been made for a meeting with the chairman of the Shanghai Revolutionary Committee, Chang Chun-chiao, the equivalent of the mayor of the city, and the response so far is that the matter is being considered.

Questioning by members of the group has been intensive and the responses immediate and candid during encounters so far. Dispatches are being sent out without censorship and the conducting officers, a Peking Foreign Ministry representative and official interpreters, are proving courteous and cooperative.

This morning's visit to the products exhibition, housed in a huge columned structure with a Stalin-type tower and spire rising above the main hall, which was flanked by two wings, revealed an impressive sample of Shanghai manufactures from both light and heavy industry. No information was available, however, on the scope or costs of production of most articles and a number of the more advanced machines were frankly described as experimental models that were still under development.

One thing emphasized by Chou Wen-yu, head of the exhibition's revolutionary committee and guide for the tour of the display, was that the items were thoroughly Chinese and not copies of foreign products and that workers had participated extensively in designing and fabricating the articles in accordance with the present Chinese Communist policy of self-reliance and self-sufficiency.

A featured item was a huge 125,000-kilowatt turbogenerator with inner water-cooled stator and rotor that foreign engineers have pronounced quite an achievement. It was described as still under development and not in service yet.

The display of motor vehicles included two examples of a sedan called the Shanghai, a neat-looking medium-sized car bearing a considerable resemblance to a Checker cab. No figures could be given on output.

Also exhibited was a 32-ton-capacity dump truck, a full range of other trucks running from small to standard-size carriers, an attractive range of buses with windows providing all-around vision from inside, and a rice transplanter said to be another test version of a long line of machines already in use but not entirely satisfactory.

Several of the complicated machines, including the generator, were said to be run by computers. But upon questioning, it turned out that this was merely automated control apparatus.

A section devoted to the making of the basic materials for sophisticated electronics equipment such as radar, radio and guidance apparatus made evident that progress enough has been made to account for Peking's firing of missiles, launching of space satellites and explosion of hydrogen test devices.

The section on consumer electronic items such as transistor radios, tape recorders and television sets, showed items below world standards in styling and higher than world levels in prices at retail.

Mr. Chou explained that the exhibit was not just for visitors and the general public but mainly a demonstration center for workers. From 8,000 to 9,000 a day come through to study the machines and make suggestions on how they can be improved, he said.

The Shanghai machine tool plant, with a work force of 6,000, is the largest of its kind in the country and obviously a major link in the Chinese industrial system. It has been built up from a small plant that was a joint Chinese-American venture before the Communist take-over in 1949 and still contains some machinery made in the United States.

The plant now specializes in making grinding machines and doing precision grinding, and a member of its revolutionary committee asserted that many of the latest machines and automated processes it has developed with intensive worker participation were unsurpassed in the world.

"We produce mainly for China's needs," said Yu Chi-ching, the plant spokesman and member of its revolutionary committee, "but some of our output is exported and has gone to 30 countries. Under the impetus of the Cultural Revolution we have greatly increased output and turned out 2,600 sets of machines in 1970 as compared with 1,600 in 1966."

The blue-clad workers, with many women among them, receive pay ranging from $20 to $55 a month and looked cheerful and efficient. When it is considered that they get housing at nominal cost in a big state housing complex adjacent to the sprawling factory building and that they have job security, cheap food, clothing and medical services, and education for their children at little cost, their pay package is not as low as it might seem.

That all is not pure happiness in the plant, however, was indicated by Mr. Yu himself, who said there were still problems of "revisionism"—the deviation attributed to the purged chief of state, Liu Shao-chi, and his partisans—within the factory ranks. Another revolutionary committee member, Chen Hsieh-kuei, declared that "struggle-criticism-transformation" sessions were still being held and individuals were from time to time called to account by the workers.

With some embarrassment, he related how he himself had been subjected to a criticism session recently.

The plant is famous for its workers' college, established to give higher technological education to selected workers in accordance with the new nationwide system of sending laborers to universities for higher studies. The factory has 52 men and women who have almost completed a two-and-a-half-year course, the standard for the new higher education.

The workers' college lays heavy emphasis on political indoctrination. After graduation the students will return to work in the factory.

The head of the Revolutionary Committee that runs the factory is an army political commissar and simultaneously head of the factory's Communist party committee.

In one room where the newsmen were asked not to take pictures, precision threading was in progress that could have been for defense-related equipment.

Shanghai's Bright Lights Give Way to Smog

★

by Tillman Durdin

SHANGHAI, April 18—A view from one of the city's tall buildings makes it easy to accept the official statement that Shanghai is the premier industrial city of China.

In every direction as far as one can see factory chimneys pour out smoke that hangs in a murky smog reminiscent of that of New York or any other major American city.

On the streets everyone seems a worker. In frumpy blue-clad millions, they overflow the sidewalks and almost choke the roadways. It is fortunate that there is little motor traffic, only the plying of motor and electric trolley buses, for there would not be space for both pedestrians and even a moderate number of private cars.

What private transportation there is comes in the form of the ubiquitous bicycle, which is not yet motorized as it is in many other developing Asian nations. The bicycles vie in formidable battalions with the press of pedestrians.

Officials here giving a cursory briefing today to visiting Western newspapermen put the population of the city proper at six million. The suburbs and the areas beyond that are administered as part of the city encompass 2,223 square miles—four times the size of the inner city—and have a population of four million.

Thus Shanghai has a total population of 10 million, which makes it by far China's largest city. It easily outstrips Peking, which has a population of seven million.

Before the Communist take-over of China, Shanghai already had many light industries and the beginnings of heavy industry.

134

Officials today noted that the light industries have been expanded and heavy industries established on a scale that makes Shanghai a major industrial center. Heavy industry was said now to represent more than 50 per cent of the total.

Shanghai makes electronic equipment, machine tools, turbines, textiles, chemicals, machinery, pharmaceuticals, steel, cars and trucks, plastics and a wide range of general consumer goods. The total of industrial workers is 1.2 million.

Shipbuilding was already a sizable industry here before the war with Japan but has been greatly expanded. Officials today said that vessels built last year included six of 10,000 tons.

The port is the country's largest and today it was obviously in full use. In one short stretch of the Whangpoo River more than a dozen ships could be seen unloading.

The city's steel production was today given as "more than 5,000 tons a day." Officials saved the newsmen some arithmetic by saying that this represented "more than 1,825,000 tons a year."

The city's rural areas go a long way toward supporting its populace in basic foods such as rice, vegetables and cooking oil.

The changes seem drastic to someone returning after an absence that began before the Communist take-over.

The solid edifices within the old inner city, standing in a semicircle along the Whangpoo River waterfront, are still the same. The massive Hong Kong and Shanghai Bank building, however, is now municipal headquarters, the Cathay Hotel is now the Peace Hotel, and the great stone offices of the British trading firm of Jardine, Matheson & Co. are now a Communist financial institution. And the human component is radically different.

In its heyday in the nineteen-thirties Shanghai was a cosmopolitan metropolis of rushing traffic, of bright lights, of innumerable places of pleasure, of rampant vice and high intellectualism, of an enormously wealthy, high-living élite, of an emerging middle class and of millions of people toiling in poverty.

One downtown street, Nanking Road, scintillated with smart shops, high-rise department stores and worldly people. The city's 100,000-odd Europeans mingled with its Asians without any thought on either side of their being strangers to each other.

Today Shanghai is a proletarian city, obviously full of energy and drive but with little of the ebullience and sparkle of old. Bright lights are few on Nanking Road, the shops dowdy, the goods seemingly plentiful but utilitarian.

The atmosphere is provincial where before it was sophisticated and international. The foreigner walking down Nanking Road today is stared at and if he pauses he is surrounded by a curious crowd of such density that further progress is difficult.

A whole new generation has come into being without even the remembrance of the gaudy, greedy Shanghai of old.

Shanghai Suburbs: ★
Dynamic and Cheerful

by Tillman Durdin

SHANGHAI, April 22—The Chinese Communist Government has clearly concentrated attention on the suburbs, factories and rural areas attached to Shanghai rather than to the old inner core left from the era of foreign rule.

Only an occasional new building is to be seen in the former International Settlement and the former French Concession. The old structures, shabby and begrimed, still serve as offices, dormitories, workers' clubs, stores full of utilitarian goods, warehouses and schools. Not a bourgeois touch remains.

Central Shanghai may look run down, but the outer areas present a newer, cleaner, more dynamic aspect. New factories ring the city, many spewing coal smoke that is causing a smog problem, and many new workers' apartment buildings and spruced up old single-family dwellings stand amid trees and parks.

Farther out each of five satellite communities of apartment buildings in garden settings houses some 20,000 people and provides manpower for nearby industrial plants.

New paved highways lead beyond into fields lush with flowering rapeseed—for the city's cooking oil—wheat, barley, clover, beans, cabbage and melons, and on into the area of the collective farms, where peasant communities that are part of the Shanghai complex produce what the city eats.

The suburbs and the rural areas, like the central city, swarm with people, all dressed roughly alike, all working or playing at the same mass, group-activity level. But in the suburbs and rural areas life seems more cheerful, more open, more relaxed.

Everywhere, downtown and out of town, youth is on the move. About the most common sight is marching columns of youngsters and teen-agers, packs on their backs, heading off somewhere for physical and military training.

Visiting newsmen were never quite able to learn just what the marching columns did at their destinations. Work in the fields? Pitch camp? The reply was always "They are just training" or "They are just marching."

The marchers added to the congestion of millions of pedestrians and cyclists in this swarming city, which has a metropolitan population of about 10 million, the largest in China.

A system of staggered days off for workers insures that there are always crowds in public places, and night work requires that some shops and public transportation function.

Brightening the teeming but otherwise dull spectacle were great portraits of Mr. Mao that hang everywhere, huge posters heralding performances of ballet and new-style opera and placards portraying husky uniformed soldiers on guard at frontiers as well as Maoist quotations in man-high lettering on almost every wall.

The massive Bank of China's Bund headquarters, built when T. V. Soong and his brother-in-law, H. H. Kung, dominated the finances of the Kuomintang regime in the nineteen-thirties, is still the Bank of China, but Mr. Soong would never recognize the bizarre mingling of banking with politics. Scores of placards bearing the thoughts of Chairman Mao Tse-tung dangle from twine strung between pillars and walls, a great portrait of the chairman beams from the back of the main hall, and posters and bulletin boards proclaim the themes of the "struggle-criticism-transformation" campaign going on among the bank staff.

Still the liveliest corner of the downtown area is the department store complex at the upper end of Nanking Road, which, as in the old days, draws teeming masses to its four multistoried emporiums. The biggest, formerly Wing On and now Shanghai No. 1 Department Store, retains an aspect of glitter, but its stocks of luxury goods from all over the world have given way to utilitarian items entirely of domestic manufacture.

The international group of journalists that has been visiting China, ostensibly in connection with tours by foreign table tennis teams, has in fact been permitted to function separately, and most of its members have paid little attention to the games.

They have looked into conditions in a rural collective, in factories, among workers and their dependents, and in a hospital and have been able to talk with individuals in many walks of life, but they did not succeed in seeing the officials who run the city administration.

A request for a meeting with Chang Chun-chiao or some other member of the Revolutionary Committee that governs Shanghai drew the response that they were too busy.

The visitors had no contacts with people except through interpreters on conducted tours to places regularly shown to foreigners.

Canton: A Society Transformed

by Seymour Topping

CANTON, China, May 20—In 1949, a few months before the Communists seized Canton, two Americans clambered out of rickshas at the entrance to a hotel on Shameen Island, the old foreign quarter.

In a boisterous mood, one American flung a handful of nearly worthless Chinese Nationalist currency into the air in payment for the ricksha fares. The other watched the sweating, panting ricksha men scramble in the dust for the bills and reflected on this humiliation brought on by war, government corruption and inflation.

On returning to this teeming southern metropolis after two decades, one finds the face of society transformed. A new Canton man has emerged. His old verve and individuality seem to have yielded to passivity, but he also obviously lives better and carries himself with restored dignity.

Old brawling Canton with its raucous downtown neon lights is gone. Also gone are the emaciated beggars who stood outside restaurants with outstretched palms and looked in at banquet tables where most of refulgent dishes were left half-consumed by the rich. Forgotten are the brothels where round-faced girls with flashing eyes and chattering birdlike voices insisted to rough foreign seamen on the civility of sipping tea ceremoniously before sex was dispensed.

Strolling down narrow sidestreets planked by two- and three-story white plastered buildings one does not hear the clack-clack of mah-jongg tiles.

140

On broad clean streets traffic moves in a disciplined procession. There are few cars or trucks and none of them are driven by swearing, argumentative drivers who once abused each other and hapless traffic policemen. Today unarmed policemen dressed in green military tunics over blue trousers effortlessly direct streams of bicyclists and pedicabs.

The people, dressed in white or blue shirts over unpressed trousers, look well-fed and content but strangely silent and ordered.

On larger thoroughfares such as Liberation Boulevard, people crowd grimly but politely into efficient-looking buses powered either by overhead electric lines or conventional gasoline motors.

Big shops and department stores remain open until 9 P.M. Still later into the night tiny shack-like booths stay open selling hot steaming food, cigarettes and basic commodities. Some of these cubicles are privately operated, but the owners are forbidden to hire employes and they must adhere to uniform government price levels.

In the years before the Communist take-over on Oct. 14, 1949, shops were crammed with luxury foreign goods. Foreign businessmen still come to Canton, the international trading center of China, by the thousands during the official one-month fall and spring fairs. But they no longer peddle silk stockings, French wines and automobiles. The 3,000 businessmen, half of them Japanese, who went home this week after the spring fair came to sell essential industrial machinery and buy raw materials.

In the dining room of the Tung Fang Hotel, foreign businessmen patiently waited to be served by waiters whom they addressed as "tung chih," or "comrade," not crying "Boy!" as in the old days.

In the poorly lighted three-story Nanfang Department Store, the largest in Canton, crowds surged about counters buying such household necessities as thermal jugs, soap, preserves and bolts of plain cloth.

The average worker in Canton is said to earn 60 to 70 yuan ($25 to $30) a month. At Nanfang, a customer was paying 7 yuan for a large aluminum cooking pot, 227 yuan for a table electric fan, 21 yuan for a medium-sized plastic suitcase and 51 yuan for a cheap-looking portable transistor radio.

A woman's cotton blouse was selling for 4.85 yuan, with matching slacks for 4.25 yuan.

While store prices are high, Cantonese can afford some such purchases because of their low rents. An unmarried worker can bunk in a factory dormitory for less than a yuan a month. His food costs 15 yuan more. A family can get living quarters, including a bedroom and kitchen facilities, for 3 or 4 yuan.

Adjoining the Nanfang Department Store is a Friendship Shop for foreigners, where officials of Polish and North Vietnamese consulates in Canton as well as seamen and visiting businessmen shop. Here there is a better selection of goods, including a sewing machine made in Canton, fine bicycles and brocade cloth. Payment is in yuan purchased with foreign currency.

Housing developments seem limited, but driving down the Embankment of the Pearl River, which divides Canton, some new construction can be seen, notably the 27-story Canton Hotel, the largest building in the city, which towers over the trade fair complex. On the south side of the river, new housing has been constructed for fishermen and their families who once lived in sampans by the quayside.

Adjacent to Shameen Island, which is linked by a bridge to the north bank, there is a new handsome stone bridge across the Pearl River. It was constructed in 1967 at the height of the Cultural Revolution. The only other bridge across the river is Haichu, which was repaired in 1952, three years after the Nationalists blew it up in their retreat.

Foreigners have been moved off Shameen Island. The great consulates and the mansions of the rich and diplomats have been converted into Government offices or shabby and crowded living quarters.

Schoolboys in blue shorts play volleyball on old tennis courts. On lovely stone walks beside the gardens where English and French governesses once parked their prams under banyan trees, Chinese youngsters rough and tumble. They have no memory of foreigners on Shameen Island.

Peking: A Tense City for Foreigners

by Tillman Durdin

PEKING, May 1—For foreigners Peking is still a tense and touchy place to live, though large areas of the capital long closed to them are in bounds again.

Among those still barred, perhaps the most notable is the southern part of the city beyond the Temple of Heaven. And foreigners are not able to go more than a few miles outside the city without a permit. Innocent transgressions of the regulations, even by half a car's length, can bring overnight jailing or hours of detention and lectures in a police station.

Arrest in Peking is usually a procedure called "surveillance by the masses," which means that vigilant civilians, usually young people, who think a foreigner has done something wrong hem him in while he is harangued by some neighborhood activist until regular security personnel come to deal with the case.

As for associations, foreigners meet Chinese by official arrangement only. There is no such thing as having a casual chat on the street or making a call without official approval. After any contact of that kind the Chinese in question is likely to be interrogated by policemen and made to repeat and explain the conversation.

In a building for foreign residents, the aged elevator operator whose perfect English seems to point to education in a Western university has not gone beyond formal good mornings and good evenings in talking with the tenants after years in his job. They assume he has been consigned to a lifetime of monotonous labor because of some objectionable bourgeois background and does not dare have any but the most limited contact with foreigners.

The Chinese gate to the one-time compound of the United States Legation in Peking—it was a consulate general in its later days—appears to have recently received a bright coat of paint, but it is hardly likely that the area is being readied for return to its former occupants. The paint is probably a part of the normal process of maintenance by the Foreign Ministry, which controls the compound.

The Chinese-Soviet border talks are reportedly being held in one of the compound buildings, which are on a thoroughfare now called Anti-Imperialism Street instead of Legation Street.

All the buildings on Anti-Imperialism Street that were the property of foreign missions are in Chinese control except those occupied by the Rumanian Embassy. The Rumanians are in an area just across from the former American compound, and there are no indications that the Chinese will require them to move, as they have all other foreign missions in the process of dismantling a little enclave that represented foreign powers' grip of special privilege for more than a century. Foreign missions are mainly in a new area in the eastern part of the city.

The Chinese have compensated countries owning the old buildings either by payment or in new quarters elsewhere.

Whether the United States would get such treatment if relations are established is the subject of lively speculation.

Three weeks ago the Forbidden City, which had been closed since the Cultural Revolution began in 1966, was opened to a group of foreign table tennis players and accompanying journalists. Since then the magnificent collection of yellow-roofed halls, pavilions, gardens and palatial residential quarters has been seen almost daily by visiting groups and members of the Peking diplomatic corps.

The walled imperial sector, built in the main by the first Ming Emperor, Yung Lo, in the 15th century, was barred to protect it from rampaging Red Guards in pursuit of the directive to destroy the four olds—old habits, old culture, old customs and old ideas. To make doubly sure, truckloads of art treasures were hauled away to guarded warehouses.

There are indications that the prearranged tours through the imperial quarter mean that it will be reopened to the general public soon on a permanent basis.

Peking Is Handsome ★
But Other Cities
Are Grim

by Tillman Durdin

HONG KONG, May 10—"Peking gets the best of everything" is a common saying among foreigners who have spent some time in China.

That is certainly reflected, a visitor finds, in the general appearance of the ancient capital. There has been wide-scale reconstruction and the addition of hundreds of large buildings. Much of the brooding medieval beauty and massiveness has been eliminated, particularly by the removal of the city walls and towering gates, but a modern metropolis of wide boulevards and imposing structures has grown up.

The same cannot be said of the other big eastern cities. Tientsin, third largest after Peking and Shanghai with a population of five million for urban area and satellite countryside, is the grimmest in appearance. In the downtown area, where little new building has been done, many structures are grimy and dilapidated, debris clogs many side streets and factory chimneys belch uncontrolled coal smoke.

Canton, a little smaller than Tientsin, is only a little less depressing in appearance though it is cleaner and is brightened by the buildings of the great semi-annual foreign trade fair. Shanghai also looks grimy and run down, particularly in downtown areas where old foreign-built structures are used but not maintained and show dirt-encrusted windows, sagging doors and trash under staircases.

All cities are teeming, with people in their monotone uniforms surging through the streets afoot or on bicycles, purpose-

146

fully and with splashes of animation. Municipal transport everywhere is good—solid, clean, Chinese-built, wide-windowed electric trolleys and gasoline buses.

Apart from parks and a scattering of theaters, the cities have few bright spots. Restaurants are simple, proletarian and poorly lit. At night there is little illumination to relieve the gloom.

Officials frankly acknowledge that the old inner cores of the cities have been neglected. "We have given higher priority to investing in factories and suburban communities," a Foreign Ministry spokesman said.

The suburbs are brighter, newer and livelier, streets have been broadened, trees planted and apartment buildings and shopping centers erected.

Everyone seems employed, men, women and teen-agers, but the impression is given that the pace of work is generally moderate. This fits the pattern of the Soviet Union and other Communist societies, where job security and universal employment inspire temperate exertion. "The Chinese work hard but not too hard," reported a foreign resident of Peking who has long observed them under Communism.

Overemployment seems to rule in many factories, which experts say often have many more hands than they need.

The satellite rural areas, with their neat villages, scattered factories and rich, green, well-tended fields, look more attractive than the cities. With communal living and home-made entertainment they may well be.

A young doctor at a commune 15 miles outside the city, asked how often she went to Peking, said: "Not very often. There is nothing to take me to Peking."

Fancheng Sees First Foreigners In 20 Years ★

by Audrey Topping

FANCHENG, China, May 19—Five gray cars with horns rasping drove right onto the platform of the railroad station here early today to pick up the first foreigners to visit this area deep in the Chinese interior in more than 20 years.

A group of district and municipal dignitaries headed by two vice chairmen of the regional Revolutionary Committee were gathered at the station along with masses of intensely curious people.

It was 7:30 A.M., but we—my father, Chester A. Ronning, my sister Sylvia and I—had been up since sunrise looking out through the train windows.

We had traveled by plane the 550 miles south-southwestward from Peking to Wuhan and all night by train the 175 miles northwestward from there. The hilly green, plush countryside here in Hupeh Province was a welcome contrast to the flat fields in the Peking area.

Chester Ronning, who was born here in 1894, spent his first 13 years in this area and later taught in the school his father had founded. He was welcomed home as a native, a "lump of mud," as people here often modestly call themselves.

He spent the years from 1945 to 1951 as chargé d'affaires of the Canadian Embassy in Chungking and Nanking, but this was his first visit to his birthplace since 1927. He was amazed by the changes.

"In those days," he said, "the villages were clusters of mud huts surrounded by high mud walls. Every village had a watch-

148

tower and guards on constant surveillance against bands of robbers and soldiers who would loot and rob the villages."

Now the watchtowers are gone and most of the houses are of brick.

Our cavalcade of honking cars drove over a bridge across the River Han to Fancheng's twin city of Siangyang.

We had expected to rough it in the interior of China, so we were amazed to arrive at a very good guest house. It had been built in 1966 and the interior was freshly whitewashed. It is also used for meetings of the revolutionary committee.

The rooms were comfortably furnished with bamboo furniture and double beds with embroidered satin quilts and pillow cases.

Four smiling girls in white jackets were assigned to bring us all the hot water we could use. They did their job so well that every time we came in we were ushered to the bathtub.

After breakfast, we went sightseeing—first a walk on the city wall.

With a thousand eyes watching us we climbed to the drum-and-bell-tower on top of an old pavilion where, as Father explained to our Chinese guides in fluent Chinese, scholars used to retire for study.

When the guide said the broken bronze bell on top had been used to tell the time, Father interrupted him, to the amusement of our Chinese friends.

"The bell was not used for telling time," he said, "but for ceremonial purposes. The time was given by a man called a ta-ken-ti who would walk through the streets sounding a gong and singing out the time."

The ta-ken-ti also beat a night song to warn of thieves, he explained.

The Chinese soon gave up trying to show us around and urged Father to take over.

We visited the north gate at Siangyang and looked across the river to Fancheng. From there we could see the house in the old Lutheran mission compound where Father had lived. His parents, Halvor and Hannah Ronning, were among the first Lutheran missionaries to come to China. She died here in 1907.

Father recalled how the people in Fancheng and Siangyang lived in terror of the fierce Han River. During flood periods both cities were often submerged. In 1938 more than 3,000 people were drowned in a flood. Even as late as 1960 and 1964, the area suffered from flooding.

In 1964, however, the people turned out to widen and strengthen the dikes. Now with 26 miles of sturdy embankments along both sides, the river is contained. The water can rise five or six feet above the former danger level without flooding.

In the afternoon, we paid a visit to a rural commune, and in the evening we were invited to a banquet given by the chairman of the revolutionary committee. It was a multicourse dinner, including wild chicken, rabbit, fish eggs and a delicious monkey-head mushroom soup.

Ho Fung-wu, a vice chairman of the Revolutionary Committee, explained that the population, which was 40,000 "before the liberation," had risen to 189,000. This is mostly a result of new industry.

"Before the liberation," he said, "there was no modern industry in this area. We had a machine repair shop with 21 workers, four handicraft shops, a cigarette rolling shop and over 100 blacksmiths. Now we have transformed a consumer city into a productive one."

He said that 106 of the 200 large and small factories now here had been built during the campaign of the late nineteen-fifties for rapid industrialization that was known as the Great Leap Forward.

In a discussion of education and culture, it was pointed out that my grandfather founded the first modern school here in 1893 and when Father returned as a lecturer in 1922 there were only three middle—or junior high—schools with a total of

1,500 students. Now there are 38 middle schools with 13,000 students.

When asked about the average income, Mr. Ho said it was comparatively low as a result of an influx of new workers into the area.

He said that there was no unemployment and that there was still a need of more manpower.

"Mr. Ronning knows better than I do what it was like here 44 years ago," Mr. Ho said. "He can also see our shortcomings. He knows, for instance, that we must raise our standard of mechanization of agriculture and raise our potential to fight against natural catastrophes. Last year our cotton yield dropped and there are still many unpaved roads and highways.

"The work on our buildings is not fast enough. We have a long way to go."

Father replied: "When I was a child here, many of the people did not even have a roof over their heads. Only the merchants, officials and landlords had adequate housing.

"Today, on our trip, I saw many new houses. They are not so big or elaborate, but they are adequate and clean."

"The changes in Hupeh Province," he remarked, "are beyond my expectations. If there were no Chinese on the landscape, I would almost think it was a foreign country."

Rural China: Change and Continuity

★

by Seymour Topping

PEKING, May 27—At the gate to the village compound of Shih Ke Chuang, peasants in blue tunics wearing Mao Tse-tung buttons came out with undisguised curiosity and broad smiles to welcome the first American they had seen in more than 20 years.

For this equally curious American, it was the beginning of a day-long glimpse into the life of a people's commune, a microcosm of the transformed rural society of Communist China. The one visited, the Chinese-Vietnamese Friendship People's Commune, north of Peking, is a fairly advanced unit, having been set up in 1958. But it is said to be typical of many thousands of communes across China in its political, social and economic organization as well as in its techniques of operation.

"Know the anatomy of a single sparrow and you know all sparrows," said my Chinese guide as we began to explore the nearly self-contained world of 38,000 people living on about 38 square miles of flat, green, fertile land.

There were Mao portraits everywhere and red letter propaganda slogans blazoned on the sides of buildings. Army propaganda units operate in commune villages, but this writer found more than he had expected of the traditional China he had last seen in 1949, the year of the Communist take-over.

There is the same gentle civility of people, although they seem to speak with more self-conscious dignity and pride. Family ties remain strong, it appears, and the individual household continues to be the basic social unit. Members of the Revolutionary

152

Committee that governs Shih Ke Chuang chuckled and dismissed as "inventions" stories that peasants in communes had been regimented in dormitories.

The Communist party now shares with parents the old profound loyalty of children. Ancestral grave mounds have been cleared from the countryside so that more land can be tilled, and old family shrines have been replaced in homes by portraits of Chairman Mao. But parents still are obviously revered, and small children, as always, are left in the care of grandparents who live with the family.

In the commune there are three well tended "respect-for-aged" homes, where about 100 of the elderly who have no family or are disabled are cared for.

While there is a high degree of centralized political and ideological control, the villages of the commune have considerable economic independence and enjoy communal democracy in management of their local affairs.

The Chinese-Vietnamese Friendship People's Commune embraces 35 original villages organized into six production brigades, which are in turn subdivided into 95 production teams. The production team is the basic operating economic unit of the commune. The village of Shih Ke Chuang, with 628 inhabitants, makes up one of these production teams.

The commune was created in 1958 out of six cooperatives to permit the concentration of a large labor force capable of physically reshaping the land. In 1960, 5,000 of the commune's total force of 19,000 workers labored for seven months to dam the Sha River to create a reservoir.

Two hundred miles of irrigation ditches were dug and pumping stations were built to give the region its first flood control system and continuing water supply in time of drought.

Today the commune has rich, leveled farmland, with extensive fields of rice, wheat, soybeans, corn and orchards divided by tree-lined roads.

Ma Ching-chang, vice chairman of the Revolutionary Committee, said that the grain output of the commune area had quadrupled since its founding in 1958.

Fine, red brick buildings have been built to house the dairies, the pigs, cattle and horse-breeding stations and the duck-breeding yards, where fowl are force-fed and sold for slaughter 60 days after they are hatched in incubators.

There is a farm-tool factory in the commune, but mechanization is proceeding slowly. There are only 45 tractors and 17 trucks.

In contrast to the new animal husbandry and central administration buildings, the villages themselves have not been rebuilt.

In Shih Ke Chuang there are still old tile-roofed, small houses behind white walls made of lime-painted bricks and mud. The narrow streets are paved with stones, as are the small courtyards and floors of houses.

Villages are cleaner and more orderly than they were in the China of 20 or more years ago. People wear worn but adequate clothing, and they look healthier and are better educated. Looking into faces of peasants one no longer sees eyes swollen with trachoma and open skin sores. Beggars and opium smokers are gone.

Mrs. Li Yang-shih, 54 years old, lives in a typical small two-room house, whose walls are decorated with the portrait of Chairman Mao and posters depicting scenes from revolutionary plays of Peking Opera. She shares her house with three children. Her husband works in Peking in a carpet factory, and he bicycles home 14 miles every Sunday rather than pay bus fare.

The Li family sleeps on the traditional kang bed, which is made of brick with an oven for heating below. It is covered with straw mats and bedding. Water hauled from an outside well stands in a tall jar in a corner, and the main room is illuminated by a single electric bulb, which is the only utility Mrs. Li pays for. The house is owned by the family.

In a tiny courtyard outside there are a few chickens and a black pig. The state supplies fodder on the condition that the pig be sold to the Goverment slaughter house. The money is used to buy processed pork in a shop. Nearby is a private family plot to raise vegetables.

Mrs. Li shops for cloth and other necessities in the village store, where prices are the same as those in Peking.

"I am happy now," she says. "Before liberation I worked hard for a landlord."

For entertainment she likes to go to performances of an amateur troupe in the village and to see films shown by a touring projection unit. A loudspeaker brings her wired music and political commentaries.

Mr. Li earns 60 yuan a month, about $25, at his factory job. Mrs. Li, from her job in a nursery, and an unmarried daughter, who works in the field, earn an additional 60 yuan. On that income the family eats well daily, with dishes of rice, meat and vegetables.

The production team pays each peasant in terms of work points. Generally each worker is classified in one of four grades, according to skills, physical ability and cultural and ideological development. Each grade, on a graduated basis, receives from seven to 10 points for each day's labor. There are some non-grade peasants who receive less than seven points.

At the end of the year, the grade rating is multiplied by the number of days worked to arrive at total credit. Earnings of the production team from sales to the state are then distributed proportionately according to individual labor credits. But first, the state is paid a fee for use of the land and a local committee decides how much should be retained for reinvestment.

Last year the Shih Ke Chuang team, which is one of the most productive in the commune, harvested 7.5 tons of rice and paid each worker 1.5 yuan a day. This compared to the rate of pay of one yuan in other, less productive, communes. Some 10,000 yuan was withheld for investment and used to purchase small tractors.

During the year, peasants draw advances against their annual payment to meet food and other living costs.

Each person in the commune is charged 1 yuan a year for

medical care. This includes everything except the services of the commune dentist and purchase of eyeglasses, which cost about 10 yuan.

In Shih Ke Chuang, medical treatment begins at the village dispensary, two small rooms with white lime walls and stone floor where Chinese herb medicine and Western medication is provided by Miss Lo Hui-ying, a pert 24-year-old graduate of a six-month medical course.

Miss Lo is one of 120 "barefoot doctors," in the commune who work directly with peasants as part-time medical practitioners. Her fellow "barefoot doctor" in the dispensary is on leave in Peking, where he is supplementing his two-and-a-half year medical education.

Miss Lo treats peasants mainly for minor ailments and finds them generally in good health. She also gives them advice on sanitation and urges them to brush their teeth every morning, which they probably do judging by white teeth one sees among the younger Chinese.

When her patients have more serious ailments they go to one of the commune's six medical centers served by 50 doctors or to a Peking hospital, where treatment is also free.

Adult education classes are available in commune villages and there is universal education for children through the three years of secondary school. About 6,000 students are attending 35 primary schools and 2,000 are in six secondary schools.

At the Hei Lung Kuan secondary school, class was in session for 400 students under the supervision of 30 teachers meeting in simple one-story classrooms with some 40 students assigned to each teacher.

Hung Yu-lo, a teacher and chairman of the Revolutionary Committee of the school, said that it had been under supervision of a board of education made up of poor and lower middle peasants since the Cultural Revolution of 1966–68.

However, he said examinations were prepared by teaching

staffs and given periodically during the two semesters of the year.

On the wall of Mr. Hung's office was posted the class schedule for that day for the second-year students. It called for seven 45-minute periods. The initial period was given over to study of Chairman Mao's works. This was followed by Chinese language and literature, mathematics, agricultural biology, musical instruments and singing Peking Opera, politics and ideology, and, finally, a marching and sports period on the red clay outdoor fields where there are a basketball court and gymnastic parallel bars.

When students leave school, they must put in two years of manual labor. Then they can be selected for university training by peasants of their village.

"Academic grades are not the only criteria," said Mr. Hung. "They are judged in all-around way, taking into account their political and cultural development."

Miss Sun Fu-chi, a 30-year-old graduate of the Peking Teachers Training University, who was wearing braids and a gray tunic over a white blouse, was teaching agricultural biology to her second-year class. The ages of her 47 students varied because the school had been closed during the upheaval of the Cultural Revolution.

The students sat two-by-two at wooden desks writing with fountain pens in copy books. They had just studied some plants under microscopes.

Miss Sun used a paperback textbook that had been revised since the Cultural Revolution to include more pratical applications. It was marked "provisional and experimental."

On a wall, a slogan in large characters declared: "Heighten our vigilance and defend our motherland."

In another classroom, politics was being taught. Miss Han Lu-chu had written on a blackboard a denunciation of "revisionist traitor Liu Shao-chi," the former chief of state who was purged during the Cultural Revolution.

Leaving school and returning to the commune center Mr. Ma, vice chairman of the commune, confessed that he too had for a time been led astray ideologically by the ideas of Liu Shao-chi and Peng Chen, purged Mayor of Peking. Mr. Ma said he had been "unable to distinguish between the proper road to socialism and capitalism" and had been removed from his post as vice director of the commune and subjected to mass criticism by the people.

Later, after studying Chairman Mao's works, he became ideologically rehabilitated. When the Revolutionary Committee of the commune was formed in March, 1968, Mr. Ma, a tall obviously highly intelligent man of 42, was elected vice chairman.

The 35-member Revolutionary Committee, which controls the commune, is headed by Kuo Shao-hung, formerly a Communist party functionary. All 11 standing members, three women and eight men of the revolutionary committee are members of the Communist party.

As this writer drove out of the commune, he waved goodby to Mr. Ma and the vice chairman waved his little red book of Mao quotations in reply.

For Most ★
Of the Peasants
Things Are Better

by Tillman Durdin

CANTON—With their patchwork of well-groomed fields and their little villages of tile-roofed, bamboo-tufted houses, the farmlands of China in the springtime were always among the charms of the country's peasant-based society. Today, the beauty of China's rural landscape is, if anything, more pronounced than ever.

The little villages are still there, but a greater variety of crops on somewhat larger collectivized fields, together with newly grown trees along roads and embankments, add new tones to the color patterns. Collectivization has also evened out peasant income levels, eliminating the poor, unkempt farm and bringing an attractive neatness and uniformity to the whole countryside. New rural factories with their smoking chimneys are an occasional blemish, but not yet seriously disfiguring.

What does this more-pleasing visual aspect imply for the material life of the 600 million peasants who are still the backbone of Chinese life and economy?

As of 1971, after nine years of good harvests and a stabilization of the Communist system for rural areas, the answer must be that things are better for a large proportion of the peasantry than they have been in decades.

Last year's harvests were probably the best in Chinese history. Premier Chou En-lai has claimed that grain production reached 240 million tons. Although foreign observers might not completely accept this figure, their estimates would put the output at well above the 200 million mark.

This writer recently visited communes near Peking, Shanghai and Canton, and the individual members of the farm collectives all reported better incomes in 1970 than in many years previously. Sewing machines, radio sets, recently acquired bicycles and other items in homes attested to their purchasing power. Annual cash earnings per working individual were still exceedingly low—in the $40 to $60 range—but this represents money left to spend after food, housing and medical needs are taken care of. A family with three or four workers ends the year with a sizable packet of ready cash.

The farmer on a rural collective in the People's Republic of China has no rent to pay—he owns his own home—and receives medical services, rudimentary though they often are, at nominal cost and free schooling for his children. His work is often grueling, but he still finds enough time to cultivate a small private plot that usually provides a family with most of their vegetables and with enough grain to raise several pigs and a flock of chickens.

The ration of low-priced cotton cloth is just about enough for one suit of clothing a year, but other kinds of cloth are unrationed. Peasants look ragged and clothing appears a problem, but good clothes seem to have a low priority—even when the peasants can afford them.

The peasants' standard of living varies widely, depending on whether the farms are on the infertile hills of Kweichow or on the high-yield flatlands of the Yangtze Valley, but the basic assurance of home and livelihood exists for all. This is something that the poorer farmers of pre-Communist times never had, particularly the tens of millions of tenants subject to eviction by landlords.

The collectivized farm system, with its controls and constant round of political pressures and exhortations, is irksome to peasants because it provides income based on both the amount of work done and on political attitude. This provokes resentments. The system is one that gives the hard-working farmer an income that is not much better—or sometimes not at all better —than that of the poor and easygoing farmer.

Today's system has certainly raised the level of all peasants above that of the poor peasants of pre-Communist times. It may well have raised the level of all above that of the middle peasant. However, the well-to-do peasant of former times who had some land of his own, and could hire seasonal workers, would not be as well off today as of old.

Thus the masses benefit, and that is the way Mao Tse-tung planned it.

Since 1966, ★
A Kaleidoscope
Of Changes

by Audrey Topping

NANKING, China, June 1—Today's visitor to China—to commune, department store, factory or school—invariably hears officials describe their achievements by comparing 1971 with 1966.

That was the year that saw the start of the Cultural Revolution, in which Mao Tse-tung purged Chinese society of what he called "revisionist tendencies" and demanded a new upsurge of production.

In the past, the comparisons had been with the way things were before the Communist take-over in 1949.

For the visitor who toured China both in June, 1966, at the onset of the Cultural Revolution, and in recent weeks—and lived here in Nanking from 1946 to 1948, when it was Chiang Kai-shek's capital—the changes were registered in a kaleidoscope of impressions.

In Shanghai, new bells ring out the time every half hour.

Before the Cultural Revolution, the Shanghai clock tower sounded like London's Big Ben. Now it chimes out the strains of the song of praise to Chairman Mao, "The East Is Red."

The Bund, Shanghai's famous waterfront, is lined with propaganda posters and loyalty testimonials written by workers and intellectuals. In 1966, I saw such confessional letters concerning ideological experiences tacked on bulletin boards inside factories.

Now there are larger ones, and they have been put on public display. They are on the entrance to every factory and commune and on walls and billboards throughout the main cities.

Canton has more propaganda posters than any other city that I visited on this tour, which I made in the company of my father, Chester A. Ronning, a retired Canadian diplomat, and my sister Sylvia. But in the twin cities of Fancheng and Siangyang in the interior, I saw only one, and that was still being painted.

The biggest visual change in Shanghai since the Cultural Revolution is in the harbor, to which foreign ships have returned.

On a boat tour of the harbor we saw two of the six 10,000-ton ocean-going ships that the Chinese said they had built since 1966.

We sailed through the merging yellow waters of the Yangtze and Whangpoo rivers and then down the Whangpoo through the main harbor area. We passed hundreds of sampans and cargo junks with their colorfully patched, bamboo-ribbed sails, contrasting with the modern Chinese ships and vessels from France, Britain, Canada, Greece, Italy and the Soviet Union. The river banks were bustling with drydock shipbuilding activities.

"Before the Cultural Revolution," a vice chairman of the Shanghai Revolutionary Committee told us, "we only repaired ships. Now we build them."

He told us they also make 32-ton trucks, "in spite of the fact that the Soviet Union tried to impose an economic blockade on us."

Everywhere there is more open criticism of the Soviet Union than in 1966. We have heard it voiced by workers, leading members of revolutionary committees, People's Liberation Army men as well as at dinner with Premier Chou En-lai.

In the outskirts of Hangchow I was welcomed once again by Mrs. Cheng Wu-yen to the Tea Brigade of the West Lake People's Commune.

We stepped into the same teak-panelled reception room in the home of the former landlord of the area. A portrait of Chairman Mao still hung over the Ming Dynasty psaltery table made of rare rosewood. Elaborately carved, marble-backed chairs still felt deliciously cool as we leaned back to sip our green tea and talk.

Two thing about Mrs. Cheng had changed.

One was the size of her Mao button. Like most others in China it had increased from the size of a dime to the size of a silver dollar.

The other was her title. In 1966 she was brigade commissar, now she is a vice chairman of the Revolutionary Committee.

The Revolutionary Committees were organized during the Cultural Revolution and their chairmen and vice chairmen, we were told, head virtually all establishments in China.

Here in Nanking, the most striking change is the completion of a four-mile-long, two-level bridge that spans the Yangtze River. It was begun in 1960 and finished in 1968. Now the giant ferryboat that carried my train across the Yangtze in 1966 is being used as a freighter, and trains, often two at a time, are travelling across the bridge, along with the cars, trucks, ox carts, donkey and horse carts and people that make up Nanking's traffic. Along one side of the bridge are 10 giant Chinese characters reading "Long live our great leader Chairman Mao Tsetung." Each character is said to weigh five tons.

We drove over the bridge to see the four red-flagged bridge towers, which rise 70 feet, and four massive stone sculptures depicting heroic groups of workers, peasants and soldiers.

Another not so obvious change since 1966 is the removal of a mosaic of the Chinese Nationalist flag from the ceiling of the Sun Yat-sen Mausoleum in Nanking's outskirts.

In 1966, I wanted to visit the University of Nanking, where I had studied in 1948. However, the rector of the university had been purged the previous day, and I was unable to go because of the revolutionary activities at the university. Instead they took me to visit a political prison.

This time I requested to revisit the prison but instead they took me to the university. The old buildings remained, but new ones were being added and hundreds of trees were being planted.

We also visited the old Canadian Embassy compound and the prefabricated houses where we had lived when my father was Canadian chargé d'affaires.

In 1966 the three buildings were being used as dormitories for Ginling College, but now they stood empty and in need of paint and repair.

In Peking the big change since 1966 is the disappearance of the city wall. The massive gray-stoned, century-old structure, which separated the Manchu emperors from the Chinese city, has been torn down. Only a few gates remain. The new subway with its palatial underground stations now runs beneath the old foundation, and the Peking Eastern District Cadre School for official functionaries has been built from some of the old bricks of the old wall.

The Revolutionary Museum and the Museum of Chinese Art are now closed, presumably for updating after the changes of the Cultural Revolution. But others have been opened.

The 2,500-year-old Great Wall and the Ming tombs near Peking are now main tourist attractions. They were closed during 1969 and 1970. The only change is a huge portrait of Chairman Mao hanging over the main portal of the wall and the addition of scores of flag poles on the parapets. Walking on the wall in 1966 I saw few Chinese. Now it attracts hundreds. They come by bus and truck to see the historic structure that stretches like the backbone of a dragon some 3,400 miles over the western hills.

The Door Is Still Only Open a Crack

by Tillman Durdin

HONG KONG, May 15—Chinese Communist leaders in Peking, from Premier Chou En-lai on down, are on record as saying a regular flow of visitors from the United States and other countries will be admitted into Communist China from now on. Last week there were more signs that at least a trickle had begun.

A Peking broadcast reported that two American biologists, Dr. Arthur W. Galston of Yale University and Dr. Ethan Signer of the Massachusetts Institute of Technology, had arrived in Peking from Hanoi. It was reported also that an American geophysicist, Dr. Robert Coe, had received word that he could enter the Chinese mainland.

The Peking Government has not yet shown its hand regarding criteria, timing and numbers in connection with admissions. So it is not possible to say whether giving visas to the three scientists reflects criteria or whether the trickle marks the beginning of a new inflow.

The three visitors admitted last week could be special cases. Dr. Galston and Dr. Signer are Vietnam war opponents whose views and visit to Hanoi, where they were given their China visas, may have put them in a special category as far as Peking is concerned. Dr. Coe is the son of Frank Coe, an American who has been working for the Chinese Communists in Peking for many years.

Even before Peking's recent opening of frontiers to foreign table tennis teams and journalists, the Chinese Communists had admitted Americans for visits with relatives. A fairly recent example was the granting of a visa to a grandnephew of the late Anna Louise Strong last year to dispose of her belongings in Peking.

Nor can the admission of American newsmen in connection with last month's tours in China by American and other foreign Ping-Pong teams provide much of a guide to future policy on admissions. Preference appears to have been given to correspondents who had served in China before the Communists took over and who were personally known to the Chinese Communist leadership.

American newsmen who have been in China were questioned by officials in Peking about Americans who had applied to enter. They were also asked about the policies of newspapers and magazines toward the Communist Government.

Foreign officials said they had basketfuls of visa applications from Americans—so many they were overwhelmed by the problem of handling them—and their questioning embraced politicians, scholars and newsmen. Businessmen were not mentioned.

The Peking Government has a distinct preference for group travelers rather than individuals. Groups are easier to handle than individuals and they require fewer interpreters—which are in relatively short supply. China's foreign language schools were closed for more than two years during the Cultural Revolution.

A factor that may delay the entry of Americans in any numbers is the large total of visitors in China now—trade delegations, goodwill missions from friendly countries and technical study groups—and with more to come. Not only are hotel accommodations being taxed but guide and interpreter facilities as well.

Whoever gets in will go only to places approved by his hosts and see and talk with Chinese under the surveillance or with the knowledge of officials. At present in China there is no such thing as a foreigner striking out on his own, entering offices or knocking on residential front doors and talking privately with anyone that he would not be dealing with—such as personnel of public service organizations and taxi drivers—as a necessary part of his travels.

Signs on all main roads in the suburbs of cities say, "Foreigners not permitted beyond this point." No foreigner can go anywhere without permission outside cities. This means if he wanted to fly from Peking to Shanghai, or make a rail journey from Canton to Wuhan, he would have to get permission. There is no censorship of what he might write from the country, but he would, under present procedures, be asked to leave if he wrote repeatedly in ways obnoxious to the regime.

Aside from the dozen or more correspondents of Communist countries, there are just five resident Western newsmen, all stationed in Peking. They represent the German press agency, The Toronto Globe and Mail, and the French news agency. They operate under severe restrictions. For months they sit confined to Peking without even permission to visit a factory or a school.

In addition to the Western and some Japanese newsmen and foreign diplomatic personnel, the remaining foreign residents number in the thousands if one includes all the Africans, Latin Americans, Vietnamese, Cambodians, Arabs, Indonesians and others who are in Communist China for technical or political training. There are a few dozen Europeans and Americans working for the regime and a few British nationals of mixed Chinese-European parentage who live and work as ordinary Chinese but have kept their British passports.

The reasons for restrictions on foreigners are the same as those that bring similar restrictions in Russia and other countries of the Communist East European bloc—only more so. The Peoples Republic's highly suspicious attitude toward the outside world is reinforced by a traditional xenophobia evident in China long before the world had heard of Communism. At this stage, opening the door a little to some foreigners and treating them cordially does not mean Peking has suddenly decided to expose a regimented people freely to disconcerting contacts and influences from outside.

Restrictions of Foreign Newsmen Eased

by Seymour Topping

CANTON, China, June 24—The Government eased some of its restrictions on the activities of American newsmen in China during my visit, allowing broader access to information and more extensive travel.

I have been here for five weeks, about two weeks longer than Tillman Durdin, also of The New York Times, who left on May 6 after becoming the first American newspaper reporter to visit China since the Communist take-over in 1949.

While it is easier in many respects for reporters and photographers to work in China than in the Soviet Union, the rules governing the foreign press remain far more restrictive than in Western countries.

Demonstrating the more liberal trend, Premier Chou En-lai received William Attwood, publisher of Newsday; Robert Keatley, reporter for The Wall Street Journal, and this correspondent and their wives for a dinner interview. It was the first time in 25 years that he had met American newsmen on such an occasion. The event was reported by the Peking radio and Jenmin Jih Pao, official organ of the Chinese Communist party.

Mr. Attwood spent two weeks in Peking at the invitation of Prince Norodom Sihanouk, deposed Chief of State of Cambodia, who is living there in exile. Mr. Keatley completed his fourth week on a journalist's visa today as I departed for Hong Kong from Canton.

Premier Chou and other officials indicated that American newsmen would be visiting periodically.

The press policy on Western newsmen is evolving slowly, but there is reason to believe that restrictions will be relaxed further, especially for correspondents stationed in Peking who have had little access to officials or opportunity for travel.

I traveled more than 5,000 miles by plane, train and car. The cities visited—in some instances the tours included their countryside as well—were Canton, Hangchow, Shanghai, Peking and Chengchow, and in Manchuria, the key industrial centers of Mukden and Anshan.

Mr. Keatley accompanied me on the trip to the northeast, the first made by a Western journalist in some years.

My wife, Audrey, a Canadian freelance photographer and writer, traveled with me during the latter part of her two-month stay in China. Virtually without restriction she took thousands of photographs, including some in industrial plants doing some defense work.

As for the restrictions, some provinces, such as Szechwan, Yunnan and Tibet in the west and the coastal provinces facing Taiwan, remain off limits to all foreigners.

There is no official press censorship, but outgoing messages are read in telegraph offices and on occasion officials will discreetly question specific ones on the ground of factual accuracy and imply that they would like corrections sent.

While Chinese officials tend to show off their best factories, communes and other enterprises, they do not represent the models visited as necessarily typical and often remark on how backward others are.

Visits to agricultural communes, factories, other enterprises and schools were prearranged and receptions were obviously rehearsed in some instances. Once on the grounds of any such establishment, I was generally able to interview anyone selected at random or visit any home. Requests for information elicited straight answers most of the time.

Yu Chung-ching, a 29-year-old London-educated interpreter for the China Travel Service, went with me when the services of an interpreter were required (I speak only a smattering of Chinese). According to every indication, Mr. Yu did a good job.

Central Government officials are difficult to see and national statistical information is often unavailable, but the uniformity in work methods, procedures and attitudes throughout the country permit a fairly full picture to be drawn through correlation of such information as was gathered.

Sightseeing from a car or wandering alone in a city allowed me to gauge the range of development.

Requests to the Information Department for visits to the Peking radio or to an army unit were not granted, but there always seemed to be other ways of getting at least some of the information needed.

When my plane made an unscheduled landing at the Changsha air force base with a bad engine no one got excited when I strolled about looking from a distance at refueling and training exercises involving fighter aircraft.

Hearing the Words in Person Makes a Difference

★

by Tillman Durdin

TIENTSIN, April 24—Little old Mrs. Wu Fung-ming tells how miserable life was in pre-Communist times and how satisfying it is today. . . . Directors of a factory that has been nationally publicized as a model describe how workers, technicians and cadres form a three-in-one combination to make improved new machinery . . . Revolutionary Committee members in a hospital portray treating the sick and the maimed as a manifestation of the class struggle and the conflict between the correct Maoist revolutionary line and the revisionist way that leads back to capitalism.

For a foreigner who has studied the People's Republic of China from the outside, listening to these tales inside China is like hearing an official report by Hsinhua, the Chinese press agency, only with animation and a question period added.

But the opportunity to hear the words in person, even on a carefully controlled tour of the country, does make a difference. One discovers that real people not only mouth the stock phrases and depict the stock situations described by official releases for the outside world, but actually live them from day to day and, moreover, can be pressed for details and amplifications. A whole society suddenly becomes human and more understandable.

The newsmen from the capitalist world who have been touring the People's Republic in connection with the visit here of foreign table tennis teams have been kept within close bounds by the presence of conducting officers and interpreters and no

private contacts with anyone have been possible. But they have
nevertheless imbibed much human detail about how life guided
by Mao thought works out in practice and, through queries,
have developed angles that have been broached only tangen-
tially in the Chinese press agency releases.

What then are the outstanding impressions?

Up high would have to come the effect of the sweeping pro-
letarianization and regimentation of society. Likewise the egalitarianism pushed to new limits by the Cultural Revolution.

Chinese today are a uniform mass, all workers of one kind
or another—even office hands have to do their stints of manual
labor—and with both men and women dressed in baggy pants
and lumpy jackets, they all look alike. And, incorporated as
they are in a system of directed group labor and social life,
they all say about the same things and act in the same way.

When an official told me the ideology of a worker was considered as important as his output and seniority in fixing his
wage, I asked what would happen if the best producer in a
plant said he did not believe in Mao thought.

"But that is impossible," he replied. "It couldn't happen. If
he did not believe in Mao thought he couldn't be a good
worker."

Chinese Communist egalitarianism is relative, of course. There
are differences in income but they are not wide, and under the
pressures of the Cultural Revolution against bureaucratic airs
or any display of individual status or ambition nobody wants to
reflect a higher income, even if he makes one. Chinese Communist society today is obviously one in which dissent or non-
conformity is out of the question.

So in the cities of Communist China I have visited things are
usually clean and neat but there is hardly a thought of bright
singularity, no display of individual affluence, no consumer
products, restaurants or places of amusement pitched to the
tastes of the well-to-do and, sadly, little evidence of the esthetic.
Chinese dress today is unattractive, Chinese product design is

undistinguished, and China's cities are ugly, with rectangular new buildings put up amid the crumbling, ugly old ones.

Obviously at this stage of development in the People's Republic, the toiling masses have little time or inclination for the artistic. Only in their ballets and new operas is there indication that traditional instincts for beauty still exist.

The regime and people, having emerged from the strains and turmoil of the Great Proletarian Cultural Revolution, are clearly in a more relaxed, contented mood today than for some time. In a commune outside Shanghai, surrounded by lush fields of grain, rape and vegetables, meals were visibly good, though somewhat lacking in protein foods. In factory communities, workers and their familes seem to eat and live modestly well.

How much discontent, how much disrupting factional rivalry there is in these circumstances did not show in the bland, regulated surface life on view. The extent of attention to and regard for Communist Party Chairman Mao Tse-tung overwhelms the newcomer, but foreigners long resident in the People's Republic say it was more in evidence a year to two ago than now.

After the Purges, Order and Stability

by Tillman Durdin

HONG KONG, May 10—Perhaps the most important message a visitor to China gets these days is that order and stability have returned to a society that was convulsed with the purges and factionalism of the Cultural Revolution about two years ago.

The country is back at work in a settled, regulated way, and the importance of this for a people as diligent, frugal and ingenious as the Chinese is enormous. Irrespective of political systems, progress is certain to be made.

For the writer, who returned to mainland China after an absence of twenty-five years, the last four of them spent studying the country from the distance of Hong Kong, not only the extent to which control and discipline have been restored but also the seeming general acceptance of the present-day Maoist way of life appeared even more extensive than the evidence had indicated.

There doubtless are deep dissatisfactions in sections of the population of 800 million, but the teeming, blue-clad throngs on the farms and in the cities I visited seemed cheerful and relatively at ease with their Government.

A sizable proportion seemed to be activists, including the youths singing and chanting as they did physical training marches through city streets and into the countryside, the workers and their families in busy suburban industrial communities, the omnipresent army and militiamen and the former poor peasant families now living as well as neighbors who used to live better.

175

The Chinese people are still poor, their ill-fitting clothing patched and worn, their cities drab and gray, but nine years of good harvests and, in the last two years, improved industrial output have given them a little better livelihood, and stabilized conditions have doubtless contributed to the brighter outlook that seems to prevail.

The stability has been achieved under a leadership that, one discovers, has most of the same faces as the old. "Less than 1 per cent of Communist party members were purged permanently during the Cultural Revolution," said a Foreign Ministry official in Peking.

Nonparty cadres also seemed to have survived to a great extent. In visiting small and large organizations from Canton through Shanghai and Tientsin to Peking, I found their controlling Revolutionary Committees usually made up of people who held leading positions in the same or similar organizations before the Cultural Revolution of 1966–69.

Many described vividly and with some embarrassment the denunciations to which they had been subjected by Maoist activists and the confessions they had had to make. Many were sent to the countryside or to factories for reindoctrination with hard labor. They professed to be changed men, but they were still around.

There was a conspicuous new factor in the picture compared with former times—the presence of military men, either regulars or militiamen, in every organization to see that proper Maoist loyalties and policies were observed.

Most of the same men and women who managed affairs before the Cultural Revolution were still doing so, but under the supervision of the military men through a new power structure of Revolutionary Committees and in conformity with refurbished Maoist policies.

The Cultural Revolution still goes on, officials emphasized, in constant mutual self-criticism and study of the thought of Chairman Mao Tse-tung, but it was also clear that there had been a relaxation of political pressures in home affairs as well as in foreign relations—the latter evident in the admission of American table tennis players and reporters.

The new stability and the new moderation apparently reflect a strengthening of the position of Premier Chou En-lai, whose close relationship with the chief of staff of the armed forces, Huang Yung-sheng, was remarked.

Yet, observers noted, that did not necessarily represent a loss of power by the 77-year-old Chairman Mao and his deputy, Lin Piao.

"Mao has relaxed pressures before," a foreign diplomat observed. "He is quite capable of doing it again. On the other hand, he is really beginning to show his age now and is possibly able to participate only in the big decisions."

A visit to the People's Republic of China also brings home the fact that a new generation is on the scene. Many oldsters may still be unhappy at the regimentation, drabness, leveling and conformity of life, the lack of intellectual freedom and the constant propagandizing, but members of the new generation have known nothing else and appear to take it all in stride.

Ambitious youths find ways of getting ahead and making careers within the system. But one gets the feeling that ambition, at least materialistic ambition, is not as active a force in the new Maoist Communism as in Western societies.

The constant group discussions, criticisms and self-examinations that are part of the Chinese system embody pressure from the less able and energetic against selfish aggrandizement, and that dampens ambition.

Moreover, the material rewards of getting ahead are not great. A senior worker in a factory, for example, makes about as much as a production manager, and a member of a Revolutionary Committee that runs a large rural commune gets nothing for committee duty, only the income from the regular job he continues to do—often that of a laborer.

Basic material security is as certain for the ordinary as the high-ranking—possibly more so since the latter are vulnerable to political hazards. Those able to work are assured adequate food through the ration system, housing at little or no cost generally goes with the job, and clothing of the everyday kind, which even high officials wear, is cheap.

Stable and somewhat more relaxed the present system may be, but one finds that it is still incomplete and uneven in application. The spokesman for a machine-building plant near Tientsin said its Revolutionary Committee was still experimenting with worker participation in management and had not finally settled the question of a fixed wage after eliminating bonuses for extra output paid before the Cultural Revolution but now condemned.

Another big industrial establishment near Peking, the Shihchingshan Steel Plant, did not have worker participation in management and had settled the bonus question by raising all wages 15 to 17 per cent.

The new Maoist educational system, with its increased emphasis on work-study and briefer schooling, is still not generally in operation. Even some Government ministries are not permanently staffed partly because many eligible officials are off getting re-education through manual labor at rural cadre schools, some of them remote from Peking.

Huang Hua, the new Ambassador to Canada, and his wife have just returned from protracted work-study in Hunan, where they spent much of their time laboring in the rice fields.

The assessment of what is going on in China presented here is based on a limited view of a vast country. The American and other newsmen admitted last month received no general backgrounding on domestic affairs from high officials and went as a group—usually accompanied by one of the foreign table tennis teams that were in China—to selected factories, communes, schools and exhibitions for inspection and discussion. There was no opportunity for talking with Chinese outside those encountered at officially arranged meetings.

As an American I was treated everywhere with consideration and cordiality. Occasionally I was introduced to worker groups as "an American friend who had been in Yenan," the base for the Chinese Communists in northwestern China, which I visited in 1946 and 1947. That always produced smiles and a crescendo of applause.

The places visited were for the most part showplaces, most of which had been depicted as examples to the nation by the official press service. Casual looks at similar establishments indicated that those inspected were not greatly different from others.

At producing institutions—communes and factories—workers and managers talked with candor and confidence, but at two places operated by high-level intellectuals, the strain such people labor under in a thought-controlled society was evidenced by tension and reticence.

At a Shanghai hospital that specializes in restoring severed hands and arms, the doctors were so effusive in giving all credit to the inspiration and leadership of Chairman Mao that they created the impression of protesting too much. At Tsinghua University in Peking, administrators, faculty members and Red Guards rushed through a presentation at which no questions were permitted, as if there was something to hide.

To me the China that Communism has made seems headed for another settled phase, possibly more outward-looking, with greater attention to economic growth and a consequent need for relations with the outside world.

A quotation from Mr. Mao seen these days in the hotels where foreigners stay says: "The Chinese people have high aspirations, they have ability and they will certainly catch up with and surpass advanced world levels in the not too distant future."

At Peking school for government officials, students present a program of revolutionary scenes.

Patriotic show at Canton airport. Poster shows Mao Tse-tung and Lin Piao.

The words of Chairman Mao are displayed prominently on a street in Canton.

行靠舵手 干革命靠毛泽东思想

Girl and her grandmother at worker's home in Peking. On wall, a poster of Mao.

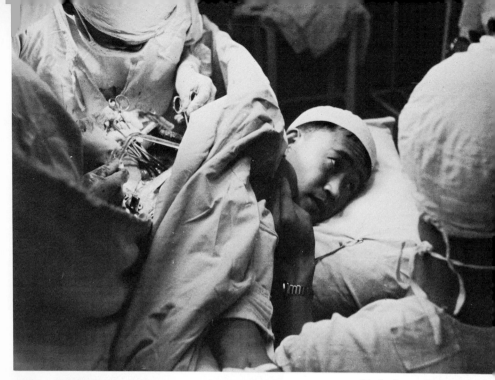

Technique of acupuncture the patient is fully awak while surgeons remove on lung and a rib. Local ar esthesia is provided by needle in the man's shou der.

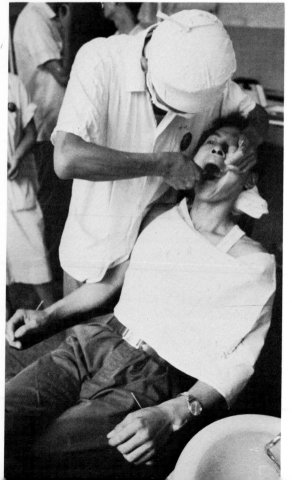

A dentist in Shanghai removes tooth. Needles in the patient's hands anesthetize region of jaws.

Folk and traditional orchestral instruments blend at concert in Peking.

Audience at opera performance in Peking. Subject of all musical works is patriotic.

The 2,500-year-old Great Wall, China's earliest architectural monument, winds 3,400 miles along country's western and northwestern borders.

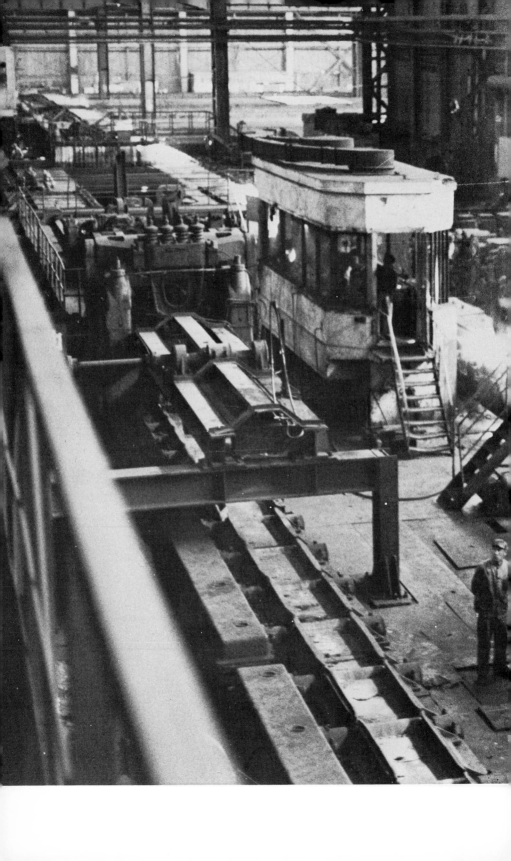

Iron and steel plant at Anshan. China is seeking to raise level of industrialization.

On a country road in the outskirts of Peking, a farmer leads his herd of goats.

Wheat farming in Sian. Agriculture remains the basis of China's economy.

At the Peking No. 3 cotton textile mill, over 60 per cent of the workers are women.

Women working at the alarm clock factory in Anshan.

An ore extractor at the
Chitashan strip mine,
which produces iron ore
for the Anshan steel works.

Men at work at a Shenyang plant that produces heavy machinery.

Anshan electricians repair high-tension wires while the power is on.

Shoppers at a department store in Canton. A salesman's abacus is on the counter.

At a Peking department store, the service is fast and the products are varied. The store compares well with shops in the U.S.

ldren's shop at
eking store.
e quality and
ntity of con-
er goods are
ng.

Ideological training begins at an early age as children memorize the writings of Mao. Shown below are youthful Red Guards.

Youngsters at a Peking school for deaf mutes wave the Little Red Book while they sing. Children have been cured with the aid of acupuncture.

Craftsmen paint screens and vases at a factory in Peking. Art works are manufactured for export.

Acrobats perform in a patriotic pageant in Sian.

马克思语录

我们的武器当然不
是批判的武器，但
现代的武器只能用
物质的力量来摧
毁，但是理论一经
掌握群众，也会变成物
质力量。

双水内冷汽轮发电机

125MW FULLY WATER-COOLED TURBOGENERATOR

Portraits of Marx, Engels, Lenin and Stalin decorate Shanghai industrial exhibit.

A soldier watches a visitor to Peking. The army is closely integrated into China's political and civilian life.

On the double, soldiers in Tientsin retrieve targets used in markmanship exhibition.

A truck carrying soldiers shares a Peking boulevard with civilians on bicycle.

Smog hangs over Shanghai, nation's principal industrial city. River at center, is the Whangpoo.

Shanghai harbor teems with vessels of all types. The port is China's largest.

Chou En-lai and James Reston, to whom he granted long interview.
(Photo by Sally Reston)

Cymbals clanging and banners waving, the people of Peking welcome
President Nicolae Ceausescu of Rumania. In the world of politics,
Rumania has maintained good relations with China.

提高警惕 保卫祖国

Canton poster exhorts people to be
alert and defend the motherland.

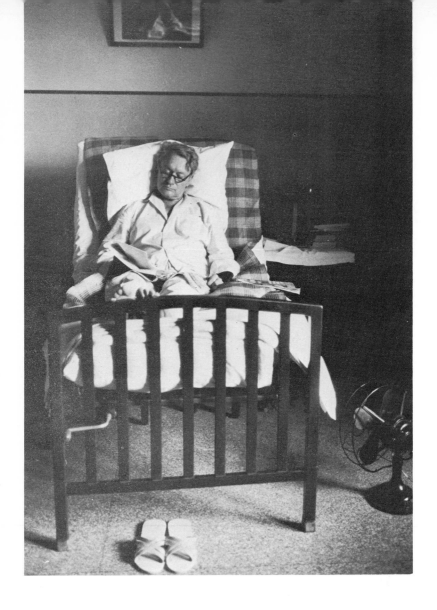

James Reston at the Anti-Imperialist Hospital in Peking,
where he underwent appendect-
omy with the aid of acupuncture.

Tillman Durdin about to enter China. He was the first American newsman to be admitted since the fifties.

Sally Reston, who traveled with her husband, took several of the photos that appear in this book.

Chester A. Ronning in Canton. Born in China in 1896, he served as Canadian diplomat from 1945 to 1951. He returned with his daughter, Mrs. Audrey Topping.

Seymour Topping at the Ching Tombs in Shenyang area.

Audrey Topping in Yenan.

CHAPTER THREE
The Everyday Life
of 'Maoist Man'

Wage Level Is an Unsettled Problem

by Tillman Durdin

PEKING, April 28—Wage levels appear to be an unsettled and controversial question in some sectors of the economy of the People's Republic of China.

The question is basic. The Peking Government is trying to pull up the level of China's development through a policy of rigorous self-reliance and without foreign aid of any kind except short-term commercial credit for some overseas purchases.

The Chinese assert with pride that the Government has neither external nor internal debt. A statement of economic policy last year surprisingly expressed approval in principle of acceptance of foreign aid without any strings, but nothing more has been said since then about the possibility of aid.

Peking's policy of self-reliance entails hard work, maximum possible productivity and wages kept at moderate levels. By these means the state-controlled system of farms and factories is made to yield as much capital as possible for reinvestment.

Foreign experts still feel that despite the undoubted growth in industrial and agricultural production in the People's Republic in the last two years, the country's ability to continue economic expansion purely through muscle power and its own capital accumulation has still to be demonstrated.

Be that as it may, the management of the Tientsin Heavy Machine-Building Factory visited last week by foreign newsmen reported that the wage level in the plant, which with 5,000 workers is one of the biggest in the country, was still a matter of debate between workers and management.

183

"We are still in the stage of struggle-criticism-transformation on this matter," Liu Wen-tao, the 44-year-old deputy chairman of the factory's Revolutionary Committee, said. Struggle-criticism-transformation is the phrase used to describe the discussions under leadership guidance that go on in the process of working out agreement within a group.

The wage question came up when Mr. Liu and others in the factory management were asked what had been done about the system of bonus incentives that prevailed for workers before the Cultural Revolution.

The Cultural Revolution attacked such incentive as contrary to the principle that persons should work out of devotion to revolution, the state, society and Communism and not for personal gain or advancement. Incentives were also criticized as causing rivalry and ill-feeling between workers.

More pay for extra output and overtime work appears to have been eliminated everywhere and it has been a fairly general policy to increase base pay to some extent to make up for the disappearance of incentive pay.

The machine plant management declined to say specifically what the problem was in the wage debate, but the wage level after elimination of incentive pay seemed to be the issue.

Present wage levels for workers at the plant were given as ranging from $21 to $42 a month. Wages were described as roughly the same as before the Cultural Revolution, but spokesmen failed to make clear just what the comparison was between present wages and the old wages plus incentive pay.

The machine plant is working out the wage situation in the context of a new system, based on concepts emphasized during the Cultural Revolution of greater participation in the operation of enterprises.

It was charged during the Cultural Revolution that "revisionist"-minded managers had authoritarian attitudes toward workers, placed emphasis on expertise and material incentives to get results, were aloof from the workers and simply gave orders instead of permitting worker participation in operations.

Mr. Liu and Kang Teh-ching, chief of production, explained that in the plant now there were 21 worker representatives on the factory's controlling Revolutionary Committee of 33 members and that 22 other members of the work force met as a committee about once a month for consultation with plant management on operations.

Aside from proffering advice on operational problems, the worker representatives have the responsibility of explaining the views of the mass of workers to the management and conveying management's decisions and policies to the workers, they said.

Mr. Liu said, however, that fixing wages was the prerogative of management, which abided by directives from a higher level. "Struggle-criticism-transformation" thus appears to be a discussion and criticism process whereby the work force comes to accept decisions made by controlling organs.

Mr. Liu maintained that workers were better off today than before because prices of many consumer items they use have been lowered while medical and other welfare services have been expanded and reduced in cost. Mr. Kang said that household income was greater now than before because more family members worked.

There are now no unions for workers. Unions previously used by the regime as a channel through which management and government dealt with workers were disbanded during the Cultural Revolution.

The only worker organizations that exist now are the consultation groups that meet with management, as in the machine tool plant, and congresses of worker representatives convened on local, provincial and national levels at widely separated intervals.

Mr. Liu and his associates insisted that worker enthusiasm was high in the plant, which makes mainly mining machinery, and that workers recently had voluntarily put in large amounts of overtime without extra pay during the difficult process of designing and producing a 6,000-ton hydraulic press without adequate steel furnaces and other equipment.

Mr. Liu said that worker initiative and innovations had played a great part in the successful fabrication of the press, which was shown to newsmen as it was squeezing a huge mass of hot steel into shape as a shaft in a power generator.

Mr. Liu stated that as a result of the policy that emerged from the Cultural Revolution of reducing bureaucracy and bureaucratic ways, the plant had sharply reduced its managerial personnel and staff.

He said that the plant previously had had a director, deputy director, 31 section chiefs and a staff of 500. Now, he said, it is run by the Revolutionary Committee in over-all charge of four groups responsible for production, political affairs, administration and logistics. The four groups have a total of 96 persons, Mr. Liu said, "and the factory operates much more efficiently now than before."

Welfare Plan ★
Assures Minimum
Living Standard

by Seymour Topping

PEKING, June 2—The Chinese Government has put into effect a welfare system designed to assure every family a minimum standard of living.

Since the reform of the wage structure during the Cultural Revolution, which began in 1966, new subsidies have become available to urban workers and peasants when their income is inadequate to feed their families.

Foreign observers have not recently seen any evidence of hunger in urban or rural areas of China they have visited.

The framework of the new wage structure and the welfare system became apparent during a series of interviews with senior officials of agricultural communes, factories and commercial enterprises in the regions of Peking, Shanghai, Hang-chow and Canton. The pattern is said to be uniform for the country, although the decreed changeover has not yet been completed in some areas.

The old incentive bonuses and overtime pay have been eliminated as having been an expression of the "revisionist thinking" of the purged chief of state, Liu Shao-chi. A new graduated scale of wages for urban workers has been substituted, with revolutionary criteria for determining how a worker should be classified.

Factories are grading all employes in eight categories ranging from 34 yuan to 108 yuan monthly, with apprentices earning from 18 to as much as 30 yuan. The value of the yuan,

187

according to the official Chinese exchange rate, is 2.4 to the dollar.

"We determine the category of a worker by his total contribution to the country, including length of service and development of skills," Chen Chang-yi, a member of the Revolutionary Committee that runs the Peking Experimental Chemical Works, said. What is described as the ideological ability of the worker is also taken into account.

Men and women receive equal pay.

A worker can move up in grade but he is not demoted. Skill tests for promotion are given each year by committees of workers. An apprentice can graduate to Grade 1 at 34 yuan after two to three years.

Under this system, a skilled worker with long experience may be earning more than his younger department head.

In visits to factories, it is difficult to get responsible officials to state their rank and responsibilities. Responding to Chairman Mao Tse-tung's dictum that intellectuals must integrate with the masses, senior administrators usually describe themselves as "ordinary workers."

The welfare system comes into play when a worker in a lower wage category has a large number of dependents and, with the common expenditure for food amounting to 10 yuan a person each month, finds his total outlay exceeding his income. Rent in state-owned apartments is only about 3 to 4 yuan a month.

There is no personal income tax in China. Government revenue comes from a 6 per cent tax levied annually on income of farm communes as a fee for land used and from profits accumulated by other state enterprises such as shops. Individual taxes are concealed in state-pegged prices of consumer goods.

In each region of the country, a minimum per-capita income has been fixed. Around Peking the cost-of-living scale is pegged at 12 to 14 yuan a person per month. When family income is below the per-capita minimum, the factory where the worker is employed is required to pay a subsidy that brings it up close to the general standard.

The subsidy system evidently is not overtaxed, because many families have more than one person working.

There is said to be virtually no unemployment in China although underemployment is reported in some areas. Since the Cultural Revolution, hundreds of thousands of surplus workers and their families as well as many students have been moved from urban areas into rural communes.

In the countryside the welfare system works somewhat differently.

Wages in communes are based upon the share of earnings of a production team. Each peasant is awarded work points for each day's labor according generally to one of four categories, established under criteria similar to those applicable for urban workers.

When a peasant, because of low income or because of physical incapacity, cannot feed his family from his earnings and the output of his small private vegetable plot, the commune assigns him a subsidy. The money comes from a welfare fund accumulated by a 2 per cent deduction taken annually from the total earnings of the commune.

Every peasant family is entitled to free medical attention, usually through membership in a medical collective with dues of 1 to 2 yuan a year. Children, like those in urban areas, are entitled to universal education, generally including access to the first three years of secondary school.

The state has established uniform social benefits for factory workers.

Each worker is guaranteed free medical service, but members of his family are entitled only to payment by the factory of 50 per cent of their medical costs.

In some factories, such as the Peking Experimental Chemical Works, and at the Shanghai Pungpo housing development, which serves a complex of 15 plants, the workers have founded cooperatives to pay the additional 50 per cent of the medical costs of family dependents. Each family gets complete coverage by contributing one-fifth of a yuan a month. This system seems to be spreading to most factories.

When a worker suffers an occupational accident or illness, the factory pays all medical costs and his full salary. Safety arrangements in Chinese workshops seem to be less comprehensive than in the West and there is probably a higher incidence of industrial accidents.

For other extended illnesses, workers get 60 per cent to full payment of their salary, according to length of service, during the first six months of the illness and thereafter 60 per cent. Subsidies are available to ease family hardships.

At the Peking No. 3 cotton textile mill, where 70 per cent of the 6,000 workers are women, excellent free nurseries and kindergartens are provided for children who cannot be left at home.

"In the old society we were fired if we got married or had a child, but here we get 56 to 72 days of paid maternity leave and special rest periods for the first seven months after returning to the job," Mrs. Chang Wen-lan, a 45-year-old worker, said.

Most large factories operate around the clock on three shifts, with each shift working eight hours including a half hour of rest added to the midshift break for lunch. Workers get one day a week off and seven days a year vacation, divided among the main festival holiday periods.

Two weeks a year are granted for a husband or wife, if separated, to visit the spouse, or for unmarried workers to visit parents who live at a considerable distance. A three-day holiday is granted for marriage.

The state stipulates retirement for women workers at the age of 50 and men at 60, at 70 per cent of regular salary. They may at the discretion of the factory continue on the job at full salary.

Most Chinese grandparents at retirement prefer to live with

one of their children in the traditional manner, caring for the
young grandchildren. The factory does permit them, if they prefer, to retain their apartments in its housing projects.

Birth Rate Is Cut
In New Society

by Tillman Durdin

SHANGHAI, April 21—Mrs. Hu Fang-tsu was emphatic about
it. "Children are a lot of trouble," she said. "Nobody wants
very many of them any more." The leader of a production team
in the Machiao commune in the countryside 18 miles west of
Shanghai, the 35-year-old Mrs. Hu has one child, and she and
her husband have no plans to add another.

Other couples in her team feel as they do, she said, and their
reasoning is incisive and practical.

Both husband and wife work in the fields or at other jobs
on the collective farm. Two very young children can be left at
nurseries during the day while the parents are at work but they
need home care and feeding and this is a burden.

And as children grow up in the society of the Machiao commune, there is progressively less and less interdependence between them and their parents. The children are taken into the

activities of schools and youth programs and by the age of 16 are on their own in the communes as self-supporting workers.

By the time they are teen-agers, the children have little need of their parents and the parents have little material need of their children, for the elderly in China today rely not on their offspring for support in their old age but on the organization to which they are attached.

Petite and attractive despite her garb of padded trousers and jacket of faded blue, Mrs. Hu gave her views on children and birth control in the clean, plain but neatly furnished upstairs bed-living room of her two-room home in an apartment building near the fields in which she works.

"The old idea that parents should have lots of children to honor and support them is finished," she said. "Most parents in this production team have one or two children. The largest family has only four."

Mrs. Hu's team forms a collective that is roughly the equivalent of the traditional Chinese village with its surrounding fields. Out of 248 persons in the team, 80 are married women, and Mrs. Hu said 20 had had sterility operations while others were taking birth-control pills or using contraceptive devices so they would have no more children.

At the commune hospital nearby, the doctor in charge said he not only was operating on women to make them sterile but was performing vasectomies on men at the rate of three a week.

The evidence provided at the Machiao commune, where a group of foreign newsmen visited today as part of a four-day stay at Shanghai, and at other institutions in the Shanghai area where the correspondents have asked questions about birth control, points to the probability that a steady decline is taking place in the birth and population growth rates in China.

The vice chairman of the commune, Wu Chiu-ling, with whom the newsmen talked, had no comparative figures from earlier years. But he said the present birth rate in the commune, which consists of 196 collective farms and 35,000 people, was

15 to 17 per 1,000. He had no figures on the death rate, so a population growth rate for the commune could not be calculated.

Factories and other establishments the newsmen have visited also report declining birth rates. The so-called extended Chinese family of former times seems to have virtually disappeared, replaced by just a man and wife with one, two or three children.

Officials queried here have no information on national population growth or the effectiveness of birth control on a nation-wide basis, and the lack of statistics in the Machiao commune would indicate that social organizations throughout the country are not recording very good population growth information for forwarding to a central authority.

Thus it seems doubtful that Peking has at present any very exact data on the rate of population increase. It is clear, however, that the central Government is encouraging birth control without making an intensive publicized campaign out of it.

The encouragement consists, for one thing, of constant pressure on the young not to marry before the age of approximately 28 for men and 26 for women. Additionally, birth-control pills and other contraceptive means are made available free. Vasectomies for men and sterilization for women can be had at nominal cost in hospitals.

China's population is usually estimated today at around 800 million. Peking itself has used a peak figure of 750 million.

The growth rate has for years been estimated at about 2 per cent annually, but it is possibly below this figure now.

Growth in China's enormous population has been one of the basic problems of the Communist Government. The increase has steadily curtailed the effects of economic expansion in improving the livelihood of the people.

Now it appears, as much because of factors stemming from the new way of life in China as because of the use of artificial contraception, that the birth rate and population growth rate are dropping appreciably.

Stores Give Customers A Better Deal

★

by Seymour Topping

PEKING, May 30—At the stocking counter of Shanghai No. 1 Department Store there had been scenes of indignation. Customers had put notes into a suggestion box protesting the poor quality and design of socks. Sympathetic salesgirls told how they had recorded the complaints of peasants.

Today at the counter, under a sign proclaiming "experimental types," there is a new line of cotton and rayon socks ordered from factories in keeping with the present emphasis in China on satisfying the consumer.

About 150,000 people each day throng through the five floors of Shanghai No. 1 Department Store looking at and buying an array of goods of greater volume and variety than has been available since the Communist take-over in 1949. After the stern years of the Cultural Revolution, colors are brighter and designs more varied.

There are transistor radios and small table television sets for sale but almost all goods are basic, functional consumer items that are usually simply made. There are virtually no goods that an American would classify as luxury items.

Most prices are high, depressing demand, but trade is still brisk.

Travelers report that similar goods and styles, varying according to regional needs, are available in urban centers throughout most of China. The Ministry of Commerce has imposed a uniform price system for the whole country, with only slight variations to take account of transportation costs.

In village stores, a much more limited selection of goods can be obtained. Some city department stores, such as Peking Commodity Store, take mail orders from peasants, provided payment is made in advance by postal money order.

On sale in the village store of Nanyen People's Commune, south of Peking, were cotton, synthetic and rayon cloth in 50 patterns, sandals, thermal jugs and other goods that one could buy in Canton at Nanfang Department Store.

All sales in department stores are for cash and there is no installment buying. There is also no advertising in China.

Goods in the Shanghai store are attractively displayed in showcases separated by wide aisles illuminated by fluorescent lighting. The Shanghai store, like the big Peking Commodity Store, would compare in appearance with some in the United States. The smaller Nanfang Department Store in Canton is rather dreary in appearance, as is the two-story Hankow shop, but the selection of goods is similar.

Service is excellent in the Shanghai and Peking stores, certainly faster and more efficient than in the GUM department store in Moscow and in many American shops. Salesgirls are taught in Communist party indoctrination sessions to be patient and to question peasants who come from the countryside on their needs and to advise them as to the best products.

The Shanghai store is open seven days a week, 8 A.M. to 9 P.M., and a special section is open from 6 P.M. to 8 A.M. to serve late-shift factory workers and peasants who bring their produce into the city in the early-morning hours.

Only a few items are rationed, notably inexpensive cotton cloth at six and a half meters a person each year. But there is no rationing of more expensive wool, silk, rayon and synthetic cloth.

The state, in effect, does exercise rationing through pricing, although the price structure has remained stable and there have been regular reductions in many categories of goods.

Drugs were slashed 50 per cent in price last year and plastic items, such as shoes and raincoats, went down 30 per cent.

The price rein on buying is illustrated by the problems of a typical customer, Chang Ming-yuen, who was selected at random by the writer for an interview.

Mr. Chang, who is 50 years old, is a veteran worker behind the meat counter of the food shop adjacent to the Shanghai department store.

Mr. Chang is fairly well off, since he has a monthly income of 120 yuan (about $50) of which he earns 70 and his wife about 50 as a factory worker. The family of six spends 60 yuan for food, rent for their three-room apartment is 3 yuan and Mr. Chang spends another 3 yuan on bus fares each month. Education and almost all of the family's medical costs are free and entertainment is cheap, leaving the family with about 45 yuan a month to spend on consumer items and to save, which Mr. Chang says he does.

When the Chang family goes to the Shanghai department store, they find that the cheapest shoes—those with cloth tops and rubber soles worn by many Chinese—cost 3.70 yuan. If Mr. Chang wanted, however, to buy black leather dress shoes, the cost would be 17 yuan.

An inexpensive blue-cotton tunic, which many Chinese wear over a shirt, costs 7 yuan, with trousers priced at 6 yuan. A woman's sweater is 10 yuan.

An alarm clock costs 15 yuan and a wristwatch 120 yuan. Transistor radios were cut 40 per cent in price last year because the Government wanted more people listening to its broadcasts. But the smallest, cheapest portable transistor receiving only medium wave was 31 yuan while a better make with additional shortwave band was 120 yuan.

With his wife working and his own salary level good, Mr. Chang is better off than the average Chinese. In the department store, salaries for the employes ranged from 40 to 90 yuan with the average 65.

Chu Sung-ling, a member of the Revolutionary Committee

that supervises the Shanghai store, gave a rare insight for foreigners into the operation of his enterprise.

In an interview, Mr. Chu said that there were 30,000 different items on sale in the Shanghai store, which before 1949 was the Ta Hsing store privately owned by the Sun company. Mr. Chu added that since 1966 there had been a 20 per cent increase in the variety of goods available and a 34 per cent increase in the volume. Only a handful of the items are foreign-made.

The store is manned in two shifts by 1,921 employes, who work an eight-hour day. In addition, they must spend an hour each day reading and discussing the works of Mao Tse-tung.

The store is under the administration of the municipal Department of Commerce, but operates with a great deal of autonomy.

Twice a year the store draws up a buying plan in coordination with state commerce officials. Demand is estimated, but if there are goods left in stock they can be returned to the central state distribution agency for shipment elsewhere.

Survey teams and sales personnel in the shop are used to explore consumer attitudes and to advise on the projected volume of sales and the type of goods wanted.

In addition to what is received from the central distribution center, the store may buy directly from factories and wholesale stores. It pays directly by check or cash, drawing for funds on its own bank deposits.

The state expects each department store to make a 7 per cent profit a year after all costs are accounted. Part of this profit is retained for a welfare fund for employes, but the bulk of it reverts to the state.

Industry Fails
To Blight 'Paradise'

by Seymour Topping

HANGCHOW, China, May 22—This lovely garden city embracing the ethereal West Lake has been transformed into a major industrial complex.

But Americans who visited Hangchow before the Communists took control of the China mainland in 1949 will find if they return that industrialization has not polluted what the Hangchow people call their "paradise on earth."

The central city with a population of 720,000 nestles among green, terraced hills. The people appear healthy. There are plenty of smiles.

The tree-lined streets are immaculate. Most of the population walk or ride bicycles. Only a few cars, trucks and buses nose among the pedestrians, horns honking.

Offices, buildings, shops and homes are neat and in a frugal manner extraordinarily well-maintained.

The factories, built since the Communist take-over, have been situated mainly in wooded suburbs with surrounding vegetation intensively cultivated as screening and to absorb fumes.

Some factory chimneys trail black smoke, but a program is being pressed for better control.

"We are trying to deal with pollution before it becomes a serious problem," Yang Shao-shen, a municipal official, explained.

"We are building special treatment facilities to convert waste water from factories into fertilizer for use on surrounding farms," he said. "One paper factory converted successfully after

198

the peasants indignantly protested that fish were dying from waste discharged. Now the peasants get fertilizer and the fish are back."

Situated in Hangchow is the Chentang truck plant, which assembles vehicles made from parts manufactured locally and shipped from elsewhere in the country. There are also iron and steel works and electronics, machine-tool and chemical plants as well as newly opened coal mines.

Hangchow remains a leading vacation mecca but no longer only for well-to-do Chinese and foreigners.

Today along the nine-mile shoreline of the West Lake where gondola-like native boats glide, there are secluded palatial homes that are believed to be the vacation retreats for top Peking officials. Chairman Mao Tse-tung is said to have a house beside the lake.

In the excellent Hangchow Hotel there are army officers and party and government officials who are traveling on vacation or on official missions. Occasionally a foreign delegation passes through and Western diplomats resident in Peking are sometimes granted permission to vacation here.

However, the mainstream of visitors consists of ordinary people. Thousands are bussed into Hangchow on organized tours. Family groups also travel here from nearby cities, some riding the comfortable double-decker passenger train from Shanghai.

The people look relaxed and there is more diversity and color in their dress than in Canton, although they are in the uniform costume of jackets or blouses over trousers.

The people stroll in the West Lake Park, and in the Hua Kang fish lagoon beside the pavilion of Calm Lake and Autumn Moon they feed the foot-long red carp that swarm to the surface for food.

The visitors lounge in pavilions of the Running Tiger Spring and sip the fragrant Lung Ching green tea of the region made with the mineral water of the spa.

Two great Buddhist shrines closed during the convulsions of

the Cultural Revolution from 1966 to 1968 have been refurbished and reopened as "historical relics" operated by the state.

Visitors swarm into the Six Harmony Pagoda, a russet-colored, 200-foot, 13-tiered tower built in the year 970, and the 1,700-year-old Ling Ying Temple with its magnificent gilded Buddhas.

There is no sign of the damage done to the Ling Ying Temple in 1966, when a mob of Red Guards, young ideological militants, attempted to destroy the structure, which was then a working Buddhist shrine. They were beaten off by a rival faction of Red Guards of Hangchow after some of the temple statuary had been burned.

Today Red Guards in columns of four still march in cadence through the parks, but now they are smiling, relaxed teen-agers who seem to be on exercise marches. The Red Guard groups, some of which wreaked the greatest, uncontrolled violence during the Cultural Revolution, have now been merged into one disciplined, ideological youth organization devoted to peaceful pursuits.

There are strikingly fewer propaganda posters about Hangchow, although occasionally columns of children or adults, two by two, pass by with their leaders, carrying red banners or portraits of Chairman Mao.

The scene in Hangchow is one of tranquillity and the people say, "Heaven above, Hangchow below."

In Peking, a
Subway Ride Is Fun

by Audrey Topping

PEKING, May 8—For two cents you can ride the entire 15 miles of the Peking subway from the Military Museum station in the outskirts to Peking Station and back. Every day, officials say, some 60,000 people take the ride just for the fun of it.

The fun consists of whizzing through the tunnels in a sparkling new train and looking at the 16 palatial stations, all built of different colored marble from Yunnan. No two stations are alike in lighting, construction and color—a white one, a red one, a pink one, a black one and a cream and green one, among others.

As the train passed through the stations young people learning to work on the subway stood by the elaborate marble pillars and waved their little red books of the sayings of Chairman Mao Tse-tung at the passengers. The passengers waved their red books back.

The subway is not yet open for general use. It was inaugurated on Oct. 1, 1969, and since then visitors from 60 countries on five continents have ridden on it. They were escorted down the moving stairway, which is switched on for them, served jasmine tea in china cups and given a briefing by the subway commandant before being whisked off.

The official said that "four million of our own masses have also ridden the subway and every day 60,000 people are allowed to go for a ride."

The subway was started on Sept. 1, 1965, "in accordance with Chairman Mao's policy of self-reliance." According to the

201

commandant, both Mr. Mao and Lin Piao, his deputy, showed great concern over the project, and the guiding principle was the chairman's statement that it should be "carefully designed and carefully constructed."

"There may be twists and turns in the building of the subway," he said, "but we will overcome and correct them."

The project took four years and three months, with army men, revolutionary cadres, technicians and 700 groups from 28 provinces and cities doing the work.

"In the building of the subway," the commandant said, "the workers, in accordance with Chairman Mao's instructions, displayed courage and studied Mao Tse-tung's thoughts to overcome the difficulties."

The trains, made in Changchun, have 60-seat cars that hold 180 people, the commandant said, adding that the longest trains have six cars. They travel at 50 miles an hour.

"At first we had all the lights red to signify that the East is red," he said, "but we did not realize that it would make it very dark, so we changed to white light."

"The sound is very loud and we are trying to cut the noise. There are also some wires on the walks and people can see them when they ride the train. This is not very comfortable for them."

Hsu Wen-chang, the motorman, is delighted with his job. He plays taped music and switches his lights off and on for the benefit of the passengers who turn up to look out the front window.

The interior of the subway was the only place in Peking where visitors were asked not to take photos.

Student Describes Her Life As a Peasant

by Audrey Topping

YENAN, China, June 18—Miss Chou Yu-fung, an attractive 21-year-old student from Peking, has been working as a peasant in the terraced fields of Yenan for the last two and a half years.

She is one of the hundreds of thousands of Chinese students, caught up in the convulsions of the Cultural Revolution, who in the years 1966 to 1969 were swept out of their classrooms and sent to villages to "reform themselves through labor."

"It was difficult at first," Miss Chou said. "The living standard in Peking is higher and just climbing the mountains here took the energy out of us. We couldn't tell a potato plant from a tomato plant."

Miss Chou and 11 other members of her class of 54 high-school students came to work in the Willow Grove Brigade of the Liu Ling Commune near Yenan. It was here in the caves of the Yenan Valley that the seeds of the Chinese Communist revolution were nurtured. Mao Tse-tung directed his armies from Yenan and also wrote his major theoretical and historical works in the cave dwellings.

Miss Chou lives in a similar cave dwelling and works with the peasants in the field.

Little is known of what has happened to the thousands of students sent to villages all over China. Miss Chou's story and an official account of the disposition of the 24,000 students transported to the Yenan region provide a clue as to what is being done with the students throughout the country.

Hsi Huai, vice chairman of the Yenan regional Revolutionary

Committee, said that of the 24,000 students, more than a hundred have joined the Communist party and about a thousand are members of the Communist Youth League.

He said that the young intellectuals serve, as well as learn from, the peasants. Seven thousand of them are working as scientists and 1,200 are teachers or barefoot doctors—those who are trained in first aid, sanitation and other basic health subjects. Three hundred have joined the People's Liberation Army, 1,400 have been transferred to industry, finance and trade where they are workers or staff members.

Two thousand four hundred have been assigned to supervise and work with 13,000 who work as peasants in the fields or do other manual labor.

Miss Chou and her fellow students looked strong and suntanned. They were finer-featured and had a different quality from that of the local peasants. Their long hair hung in thick braids. Like the rest of the students they get up each day at 6:30. They have half an hour to wash and eat before a study period from 7 to 8. At 8 they go to work, doing all the jobs that the peasants do.

Yesterday, they helped to construct a horizontal terrace, other days they weed in the fields, loosen the soil or participate in various harvesting jobs. Lunch is at 1 o'clock.

The main staple foods in Yenan are millet, corn and wheat. The students like to point out that Chairman Mao and his comrades all ate millet during their stay in Yenan. The students also eat fish or meat twice a day plus a variety of vegetables.

After lunch they rest till 3 o'clock and return to work until 6, when they return for the evening meal. In the evening they participate in performances from the well-known Peking Operas or create original shows. From 8 to 9 is a self-study period and then an hour of relaxation before 10 o'clock bedtime.

Some brigades have evening schools and their own broadcasting stations. In another they were given 1,800 mou, about 4.5 acres, of land to experiment with. According to Mr. Hsi, of the Revolutionary Committee, they grow kaoliang and produce ching chow wine.

When asked when she would return to the university, Miss Chou replied evasively: "My main purpose here is to receive re-education. We came determined to take roots and live here. If the country needs us elsewhere we will roll up our beds and go."

Only one student of the group in the Willow Grove Brigade was chosen to go back to the university this year. He was sent to Tsinghua in Peking.

Universities throughout China are still undergoing what is called a "criticism-struggle-transformation" stage. Those, like Tsinghua, that have opened are operating with reduced enrollment and faculty. There is a new emphasis in their curricula on practical rather than academic studies.

Unlike Miss Chou and her classmates who were completing a six-year course of high school, the new enrollees at Tsinghua will have finished only three years of study and then two years of manual labor in farm communes or factories before taking up their university courses.

Commune's 'Barefoot Doctor' Is a Farmer, Too ★

by Tillman Durdin

PEKING, April 30—Miss Chang Yu-jung, a "barefoot doctor" on a collective farm in the China-Korea Friendship Commune on the outskirts of Peking, does not wait for the sick to come to her but seeks them out and treats them in their homes.

Treatment is part of the medical service paid for by the collective—called a production team—and costs the individual only a part of his or her modest general input into collective funds plus an annual direct contribution of 40 cents.

China has been turning out large numbers of medical personnel with practical qualifications rather than with top-level college educations to treat the illnesses of peasants. These "barefoot doctors" work in the fields when they are not performing medical duties.

Along with two other barefoot doctors in the collective, the 23-year-old Miss Chang keeps in close touch with its 116 households and regularly makes the rounds of homes in which she learns individuals are ailing.

Miss Chang has had about a year of medical schooling over a period of three years and says she knows how to diagnose and treat most common illnesses and even how to set simple fractures and to stitch up cuts. If she thinks the illness is one she cannot deal with, she sends the patient to the commune hospital where university trained doctors are on duty.

When Miss Chang is not administering to the sick, she works in the fields like other members of the collective. She is credited with work points—the index to how much she will get of the

206

collective's earnings at the end of the year—equivalent to the number given to a full-time field worker. This comes to about $15 a month.

Miss Chang lives and works in a huge commune complex that takes in 24,000 acres of farmland and includes 120 village-centered production teams. The commune's croplands, dairy farms, piggeries, poultry farms, rice and flour mills, machine shops and other enterprises gross $20-million a year and last year sold 10,500 tons of wheat, rice and other grains to the state.

The China-Korea Friendship Commune, which is regularly shown to foreign visitors and is, therefore, probably one of the better communes in North China, is organized on three levels, like all the others that make up Communist China's system of agricultural production.

The commune headquarters exercises over-all supervision and runs a few major industrial undertakings, such as a farm-machinery plant, and grain, milk and cotton processing plants. Below the headquarters level are so-called brigades, nine in the case of the China-Korea Commune, that are an intermediate link with the basic production teams. The brigades run various small enterprises—dairies, animal-husbandry operations, fisheries and brick works.

The collective farms handle the growing of crops and dispose of them directly to the state, keeping some for their own use and for reserves. Proceeds in money and food are apportioned among the farm households, according to their work points.

Miss Chang lives with her parents and five brothers and sisters in a little four-room, tile-roofed house with a detached kitchen and storeroom. Five in the family earn work points. Three are children who attend school.

From their combined efforts, the family earns about $710 a year of which $340 pays for food, firewood and vegetables that the family gets from the collective. The family gets much of its food needs from a bit of private land it is permitted to till.

The Chang house is poorly but adequately furnished. It has a radio, a sewing machine, a new clock on the mantel. There is a new watch on Miss Chang's wrist that she insists is not hers but the family's because it was bought with their joint funds.

Family members were poorly but adequately dressed, Miss Chang in the padded trousers and jacket worn by women all over the People's Republic of China these days.

Miss Chang insisted they ate well and lived comfortably despite their modest means and enjoyed a good life.

"We have big meals with meat twice a week," she said "but we could afford meat or fish every day if we wanted it. Right now we are saving to build a new house and buy a bicycle."

Miss Chang has been engaged for more than a year but, obeying the Government injunction for late marriage—as a birth control measure—she does not plan to marry her fiancé, a Peking factory worker, until 1975.

As a barefoot doctor, Miss Chang dispenses birth control pills and urges the young people of her village to marry late. She said the people of her rural area, as seemingly in most of China, think small families are better these days than the traditional big Chinese family.

The commune has 140 barefoot doctors such as Miss Chang, some of them men, and 140 doctors with more formal medical schooling.

New Grains Increase Yields on Farms

by Tillman Durdin

HONG KONG, May 15—Improved varieties of grain are contributing substantially to China's "grow more food" campaign but officials at collective farms say that they have never heard of the development of "miracle" rice and wheat in the outside world. They say they rely on new strains developed in their own areas for higher yields.

Foreign newsmen visiting the Machiao commune, 20 miles outside Shanghai, last week were told by Wu Chiu-ling, 39-year-old vice-director of the commune's Revolutionary Committee, that 10 to 20 per cent of the annual increase in rice yields there was due to improved seed varieties.

When asked if the improved seeds had come from abroad, he replied they had not. He said that he had never heard of the new high-yield varieties of rice developed at the rice research institute in the Philippines financed by the United States.

"We develop our own improved strains," he said, "or we get new varieties by exchanging with other communes in the area."

Other commune leaders outside Peking and Canton questioned by newsmen gave the same reply. Their responses seemed to indicate that China has not brought in from abroad—or at least not openly—seeds of the new high-yield rice strains that have been making a green revolution in countries all over Asia.

The same situation seems to apply to wheat strains. Asked about "miracle" grains in the outside world, a commune official near Peking said that he had never heard of them and that improved wheat used on his commune was locally developed.

Annual increases in rice and wheat yields were reported at all the communes visited by newsmen. Mr. Wu of Machiao commune said rice yields there had risen by an average of 10 per cent annually and attributed this to the use of more fertilizer, better irrigation, better methods of cultivation and improved seeds.

"We still use more natural manure than chemical fertilizer," he said. "The proportion is 60 per cent for natural and 40 per cent for artificial fertilizer."

The Chinese have put a major effort in recent years into producing and importing more chemical fertilizers, but the evidence at Machiao and other communes is that they still rely mainly on animal and human excrement and other natural fertilizers.

According to Mr. Wu, unit production of rice in the rich farmlands of the Shanghai hinterland had risen to a very respectable level but was still below yields in Japan, Taiwan and other high-yield areas.

Last year, Mr. Wu said, rice yields at Machiao reached an average of 3,817 pounds a hectare—a hectare is 2.471 acres—with some fields producing 5,674 pounds a hectare. The latest statistical data available from Taiwan shows that the hectare yield there was 6,495 pounds in 1969. Chemical fertilizers are used extensively on Taiwan.

Mr. Wu reported that machinery was used extensively on the commune, but there was little evidence of it in the fields. Most of the work in progress was being done by hand in the traditional manner of the Chinese peasant.

Mr. Wu explained it was not the time of year for use of machinery in the fields and pointed out that many of the 106 tractors owned by the commune of 7,333 acres were being used for hauling loads along the roads. He said that all the rice, the principal crop of the commune, was irrigated now with electric pumps.

Increased yields were claimed for all crops—cotton, wheat

and vegetables in addition to rice. As a result, the cash income of the 35,000 people in the collective farms of the commune had risen steadily.

Factory Foreman
And Family Live Well

by Seymour Topping

PEKING, June 21—While touring the Peking Experimental Chemical Works, this reporter selected a worker to interview.

The worker, Chou Chieh-hua, 39 years old, is a muscular 5-foot-8, a pleasant looking man who was dressed in blue cap, tunic and trousers. He is foreman of a crew of ten men who install and repair machines. By going to night school, he has completed six years of secondary education, which helped him qualify for his job.

Mr. Chou earns 71 yuan ($28.40) a month, and works a six-day, 48-hour week. He and his family live well, and save money, because three others also work.

With two of his four children holding jobs and two in school, his wife recently became an apprentice in the factory at 18 yuan a month. A 19-year-old operates a lathe at the apprentice scale of 21 yuan and the 17-year-old is earning 17 yuan as an apprentice in a food processing plant.

The family lives half a mile from the factory in a sparsely furnished apartment that has two small bedrooms with tiny outside balconies, a kitchen and lavatory. For this they pay 7 yuan a month. Electricity for lighting and gas for cooking, central heating and hot water costs 1 yuan a month.

Their food costs about 10 yuan a person. At the end of the month the family has 59 yuan to buy consumer goods or to deposit in the people's bank at 4 per cent interest. Prices are high —a simple cotton tunic costs 6 yuan and a wristwatch about 110—and so they do not buy much.

The Chous eat pork or beef at least once a day. They usually have one meal a day in the clean, well-tended factory canteen. Mr. Chou has ulcers and is able to get the eggs and milk he requires.

The Chou family's life is built pretty much around the factory.

In the factory auditorium they attend showings of films, mostly propaganda pieces comparing the "bad old days" under Chiang Kai-shek and landlords with their present life. An amateur troupe puts on similar stage shows, mostly Peking Opera. At least half an hour and up to one hour a day is spent studying the works of Chairman Mao under the guidance of army propaganda teams.

Periodically, Mr. Chou is caught up in some special production drive. When the Peking Machine Tool Plant produced its first 2,500 kilowatt compressor, his crew worked 24 days and nights to install it in their factory.

Mr. Chou remembers the old days and says he is well off now. More than anything else, he is grateful to Chairman Mao for the opportunity to become a skilled worker.

His children also are reminded constantly how fortunate they are to be living now rather than in the capitalist days. With other Peking children, they go to the eastern wing of the Forbidden City to hear lectures and look at life-size

clay figures depicting cruelty of landlords and Nationalist soldiers.

Landlords are shown cheating peasants of their grain, beating them and dragging their daughters off to serfdom.

After the lecture, the children shout in unison: "Long Live
Chairman Mao!"

Economic Policy Stresses Local Self-Help

by Seymour Topping

PEKING, June 21—In the Mukden mini-tractor factory, all
the machines are painted either green or gray, revealing the
unique Chinese Communist approach to industrialization.

Green designates a piece of equipment that has been manufactured by the plant's own resources while gray means it has
been produced with state funds. Many, if not most, of the
smaller machines are painted green.

The plant, which was turning out water faucets in 1964 with
200 workers, now has more than 1,000 workers and factory
officials say it is producing about 450 12-horsepower tractors
monthly in a drive to modernize agriculture.

Since the start of the Cultural Revolution, heavy emphasis
has been placed on self-reliance, innovation and local self-sufficiency. This was the slogan on every farm visited and in fac-

tories ranging from small neighborhood workshops to large textile, steel, chemical and machine-tool plants.

In the·Soviet Union and other Communist countries of Europe, the emphasis is on economic centralization and specialization. In China Mao Tse-tung has opted for decentralization and local diversification. Each hsien, or county, has been given the target of becoming self-sufficient in food and light industrial products.

"See the country as a chessboard," each square self-sufficient but related, the people are told.

Peking's policy is not moving China dramatically and quickly into the ranks of the advanced industrial nations. In fact China has not yet fully entered the industrial age while the United States, Japan and some European countries are well into the postindustrial electronic era of automation and computerization.

Presumably at Chinese nuclear installations and in research institutes there are advanced computers. Those seen by this writer in factories were primitive models that, apart from a serial production model for operating lathes, seemed installed largely for training and experimentation.

Chinese officials, while showing off their agricultural communes and factories, tell you that in general the country remains backward economically and has a long way to go.

Agriculture, moreover, remains the foundation of the economy despite the drive to industrialize. Many imports needed to nurture the industrial base are financed by exports of such products as animal hides, soybeans, vegetable oils and canned fruit. Only recently have the Chinese begun to compete seriously with textiles and other light industrial products, largely in Asian and African markets.

The shortage of goods to export to industrial countries limits foreign exchange earnings and is a major factor in the relatively slow growth of heavy industry and explains the dependence on local efforts and innovation.

Nevertheless, the evidence of construction, the lush, well-tended fields, the markets full of food and consumer necessities and the energy exhibited everywhere add up to the impression that the basic needs of the people are being met and the foundation is being laid for a modern industrial country.

The policy of decentralization not only has compensated for inadequacy of the transport system but has given China the capacity to absorb a strong nuclear blow without suffering total paralysis.

The drive for local self-sufficiency can be illustrated by the industrial complex of Mukden, Anshan and Fushun in Manchuria.

In Anshan, the Chitashan open strip mine atop two mountains was opened last year and is producing four million tons of iron ore for the nearby iron and steel plant. The mines are being expanded so that production soon will be up to eight million tons. The ore is of a 30-per-cent grade and requires concentration before use in blast furnaces.

Previously Anshan drew on mines as far away as Hainan Island. The drive to tap low-grade iron-ore deposits nearby is bringing Anshan, Fushun, the coal-mining center, and Mukden, with its machine-tool, tractor and electrical equipment plants, closer to self-sufficiency.

Mukden, whose official Chinese name is Shenyang, has doubled in population in the last 20 years with about two million inhabitants in the city and another two million in the suburbs. With a short growing season of about 150 days, the region was dependent formerly on grain imports. Now it is close to self-sufficiency in grain with the introduction of rice fields and new techniques of intensive cultivation of wheat, corn, soybeans and vegetables.

Every agricultural commune, even if it used to grow specialty crops, is now seeking self-sufficiency in grain so as not to diminish central state reserves. At the West Lake tea commune near Hangchow, peasants recounted how for months they had fought back the swift waters of the Chientang River, building dikes and reclaiming land so that rice could be planted without diminishing the cultivation of tea, an important cash crop.

The central problem of the economy now seems within reach of a solution. Formerly the population was increasing at a rate —probably 15 million a year—that so consumed farm output that little was left for capital development or for export to pay for badly needed foreign machinery and raw materials.

Now agricultural production is increasing while the birth rate is dropping because of a policy of encouraging late marriage and such birth control measures as the pill and sterilization. Abortion is also legal if both man and wife approve.

Peasants no longer feel the need for several sons as security for their old age. The commune provides welfare funds where needed and a coffin at death. Families with two or three children seems to be the rule in the new generations.

While other foods seem plentiful, grain still is rationed in amounts adequate for the average family's needs.

According to Premier Chou En-lai, China's grain output in 1970 was a record 240 million metric tons, a figure that foreign experts traveling in the country and observing the bumper harvests tend to accept.

The country imported 5 million tons of wheat last year but this year has contracted for only 2.5 million tons from Canada, saving about $100-million in foreign exchange. The imports will compensate for higher-priced rice shipped abroad to bring in foreign exchange and to feed such aid beneficiaries as North Vietnam.

The upsurge in grain production is attributable to new water-management projects, more intense cultivation employing new techniques, greater use of fertilizer and mechanization and the incredible industry of the peasant.

The water-management projects completed with mass labor in every section of the country are a shield against the weather cycle, which in the past brought famine through drought or floods.

Many millions of trees have been planted in the countryside and in cities to guard against soil erosion and beautify the landscape.

In the countryside one sees peasant production teams marching out to work in the fields with a red banner fluttering at the head of the column. There are glimpses of army propaganda teams lecturing peasants beside paddy fields to spur them to greater efforts.

Army propaganda teams also have been trying to combat some dissatisfaction among the peasantry and tendencies toward the "capitalist road" that came under attack during the Cultural Revolution when Mr. Mao ousted former President Liu Shao-chi.

In the August First Commune near Mukden, San Kwang-ta, a tall, tough-looking party man who became chairman of the Revolutionary Committee a year ago, said serious ideological problems had developed in the grain-growing commune because of the "capitalist influence" of "the renegade Liu Shao-chi."

Mr. San asserted that the private plots that each peasant family of collective production teams is allowed, together with ownership of a house, had mushroomed in size. The plots, on which a pig and a few chickens also are kept, now have been cut back.

Free markets and speculation have also been ended, Mr. San said. Peasants now buy and sell their domestic side products such as handicrafts through a commune cooperative. Loans and savings deposits are made at a commune loan and credit cooperative at 4 per cent interest.

In factories there is heavy propaganda emphasis on a United States strategic ban on shipments of machinery to China and the abrupt termination of Soviet aid in 1960 as spurs to workers to build their own equipment. President Nixon's recent relaxation on trade has not been mentioned in the Chinese press.

Decentralization of the economy has paralleled changes in the structure of the national Government. Since the Cultural

Revolution, central government administrative personnel has been pared from 60,000 to about 10,000, according to Premier Chou. About 80 per cent of those removed, many of whom were linked to former President Liu, were sent to re-education schools. Thousands are still in these schools or in villages awaiting reassignment.

The Government's 90 departments have been consolidated into 26, each under a Revolutionary Committee made up of members of the army, which Mr. Mao regards as a "key component of the state," and of party and staff workers.

Throughout the country, responding to Mr. Mao's injunction to simplify the administrative structure, similar personnel cuts, often exceeding 50 per cent, have been made by local governments, factories, communes and other enterprises.

Mr. Mao seems to have boundless faith that through indoctrination the ordinary workers can be roused to increase production and through innovation renew the antiquated and makeshift character of much of the Chinese industrial plant. Each factory now keeps an official count of the number of innovations by workers.

In many factories army propaganda teams still grapple with resentments and dislocations caused by a decision taken in the Cultural Revolution to eliminate such material incentives as bonuses, payment for piecework and overtime pay.

Mass Efforts Achieve Great Feats

by Seymour Topping

PEKING, June 20—In China today one sees everywhere evidence of what people power—enormous numbers of men and women equipped with only primitive tools but all thinking alike and acting in concert—can accomplish.

Everywhere, the Maoist Man—a soldier, peasant or worker —is summoned on billboards to produce superhuman feats through combined effort.

At the August First Agricultural Commune south of Shenyang in the northeast, people tell an incredible story of how 50,000 peasants and soldiers labored 18 days and nights to dig a 30-mile canal that now irrigates their lands.

Across the broad Yangtze River near Nanking, there is a new two-level bridge, almost 10 miles long, which some foreign experts doubted could ever be built. It was completed in eight years with as many as 50,000 people working in a single day, carrying earth in baskets on their heads.

In a sanitarium, Mrs. Wang Yen-chu, a middle-aged seamstress who is recovering from a paralyzing illness of her leg joints, tells you with conviction that she now walks because first, according to Maoist precepts, she liberated her mind ideologically from any doubt that it could be done.

What kind of a society incubates this Maoist Man?

It is a world in which there is no pretense or tolerance of individualism or freedom in the Western context. Those few who have been exposed to foreign ideas have been re-educated or absorbed in the villages as peasants.

Illiteracy has been wiped out among the new generations, but they have no information about democracy or the West. Older generations retain no nostalgia for democracy because they had experienced it neither before nor after the Communist take-over in 1949.

Information about the world for virtually all Chinese comes from propaganda lectures, the controlled press or broadcasts of the central radio piped over loudspeakers into homes and public places.

Once a Chinese fully grasps Maoist doctrine, which he must recite from the nursery to the grave, he is considered ready to participate in "democratic centralism." This means he can take part in committee consultations on some decisions affecting his community, schools and job within the framework of directives of the Communist party. He has the right to criticize or appeal, bypassing every level of command up to the Central Committee headed by Mr. Mao if he feels his superior is violating the Maoist credo.

Women usually get equal treatment with men in Government and in the economy. Men factory workers can retire at the age of 60 with 70 per cent of their pay as a pension, while women retire at 55, or 50 if their job calls for hard labor. There is no stipulated retirement age on farms.

Garbed in loose-fitting tunics and trousers, the Chinese have a unisex look. Little sexuality is demonstrated. Premarital relations and sexual promiscuity are frowned upon, although marriage in the late twenties is encouraged by the state as a means of birth control and to heighten worker efficiency.

Boys and girls do their courting in parks, at theaters and in factory auditoriums while watching revolutionary Peking Operas and on mass organized hikes arranged for physical training and labor at distant farms.

To marry, a couple simply register at a municipal government office or farm commune center. There is no religious ceremony.

Freedom of religion is guaranteed under the state constitution, but virtually all places of worship were closed during the Cultural Revolution. In Peking, there is no active Christian church, only a mosque used by members of the diplomatic corps. Occasionally, one hears of meetings of small Christian congregations attended by older people in places where pre-1949 missionary influence persists.

Divorce is uncommon, but if both parties are in agreement, a marriage can be dissolved at a registry office. First, though, a social worker of a factory or commune usually will visit the couple to attempt a reconciliation.

After years of struggle against the habits of the old society, during which tensions developed between the generations, family life appears once more to have become close and intimate. The state demands more time and attention from the children, but it also encourages family ties for social and economic reasons.

The average city family has one combined living room and bedroom, but can often get another room if the grandparents move in. It is a custom for grandparents to take care of the children while both the husband and wife work. The state grants annual leaves so that the parents can be visited if they live at a distance. There are homes for the aged, but inmates usually have no children living nearby or are disabled.

Among the Chinese today there seems to be more of a feeling of kinship than in the old society. A road accident brings a swarm of helping bystanders. Before 1949, a beggar dying on the street or an injured person would often be shunned because to render aid would mean the acceptance of responsibility.

Crime does not seem to be a major problem, although the writer was not permitted to visit a people's court to get firsthand impressions.

A foreigner can leave his hotel room or parked car open with the certainty that his valuables will not be stolen. It is more probable than not that a camera lost in a park will be turned in to the lost and found and returned within a matter of hours.

The Chinese no longer accept tips and are meticulous about

returning change. Once a taxi driver knocked on my door, made profuse apologies and returned the overpayment of a bill worth less than a nickel that he had accepted the day before without realizing it had been stuck to another bill.

The sophisticated Chinese taste for beauty and grace in art finds little satisfaction in the Maoist society.

Such historical treasures of the imperial past as the Forbidden City and the Ming and Ching tombs are being restored and damage to some relics caused by rampaging Red Guards during the Cultural Revolution have been repaired. But in the countryside one still catches glimpses of stone figures that have been defaced.

Museums and art galleries, closed during the Cultural Revolution, are being rearranged, in keeping with Maoist precepts, prior to being reopened.

It was in the sensitive cultural area that Mr. Mao did his first open ideological sparring with Liu Shao-chi, the deposed Chief of State, and then signaled the onset of the Cultural Revolution. Mr. Mao's call for the sweeping away of remnants of the old society spurred uncontrolled extremist Red Guards to destroy art treasures held by elderly people and to deface Buddhist shrines and other historical landmarks.

In recent weeks, there has been some relaxation of restraints on the exhibition and sale of classical works. The Book of History, known as Shih Chi, and contemporary essays on classics by Kuo Mo-jo, have reappeared in the shops. In 1966, Mr. Kuo, now a member of the Government, said this book of essays should be burned.

In a railroad waiting room near Canton a traditional landscape by the painter Su Pei-hung, who died in the fifties, was on a wall that was occupied by a propaganda poster several weeks earlier. A few reproductions of classic paintings are being offered in Chinese shops other than the "Friendship Shops" where foreigners can buy originals at stiff prices.

Aside from these indications of greater tolerance of classics, the party insists that all art should serve the workers and peasants. Anything that smacks of association with foreign modern art has vanished. In its place are heavy figures and production scenes of the socialist realist school and heroic portraits of "socialist romanticism."

The rather conservative Soviet novelist Mikhail A. Sholokhov, who wrote "And Quiet Flows the Don," is denounced as a reactionary and Tchaikovsky as a "bourgeois idealist."

Nevertheless, the contemporary Yellow River Concerto, which is frequently played here, has romantic passages reminiscent of Tchaikovsky and Rachmaninoff.

Revolutionary Peking Operas are the backbone of virtually all theatrical production in the country. Directed by Chiang Ching, the militant wife of Mr. Mao and a leader of the Cultural Revolution, these operas turn mainly on the theme of the struggle between the People's Liberation Army, supported by the peasantry, against the wicked landlords, allied with the Chiang Kai-shek forces and the Japanese invaders in the pre-1949 period.

In Shenyang, the writer requested permission to visit the Conservatory of Music or the Academy of Art. He was told that the schools had been closed and their students sent to the countryside to work alongside the peasants while they underwent struggle, criticism and transformation.

In the center of Red Flag Circle in the heart of the largely Japanese-built section of the city, formerly Mukden, there towered a new statue of Mr. Mao, more than 30 feet high on a base more than 20 feet high. It was erected last year by students from the art academy who worked on it for two years under the supervision of a committee of workers and peasants.

Throughout the country, universities have been reopened. But most of their student bodies and faculties have been sharply reduced in size.

Instead of accepting applicants who have completed six years of secondary school, universities now admit many students who qualify by doing manual labor for two years after graduating from the three-year junior secondary course. Strong emphasis is now placed on practical rather than theoretical studies.

Thousands of students who were swept out of universities by the Cultural Revolution are still laboring in the countryside.

At the Nan Yuen Agricultural Commune south of Peking, Wang Wen-lung, vice chairman of the Revolutionary Committee, said some 150 intellectuals, students and former officials were doing manual work in the rice paddies. They included some who came originally from the area and others whom the peasants call "outsiders."

"It is difficult for them at first and it takes about half a year for them to become skilled in the fields," Mr. Wang said. "Some will settle down here with their families, others will go back to the cities and factories and some will be recommended to universities."

Some of the students have found life in the villages unbearable. Of the several hundred refugees who escape to Hong Kong each month, many are young people fleeing from duty in the villages.

The national academy of science and research institutes have reopened after having been reorganized and their staffs screened.

In a workshop of the Peking heavy electric machinery plant, the writer encountered Shu Tung-peng, a 30-year-old scientist of the Chemical Research Institute who had been there for a year. "I have been taking part in physical labor," he said, "but the workers often persuade me to do light jobs. They are re-educating me."

Isolation of   Dairen Slowly Ending

by James Reston

DAIREN, China, Aug. 14—The first thing you learn when you come to Manchuria is not to call it that. This rich industrial area, long the prize of war and struggle by Japan and Russia, is simply "Northeast China" to the Chinese, who now possess it in reasonable security and are developing it as fast as they can.

Dairen, the second port in China after Shanghai, is a fairly good symbol of how isolated China has been from the rest of the world and also of how this isolation is now coming to an end. Even in a metropolitan community of four million, it is news that an American correspondent has been allowed to come here for the first time in almost a generation.

Crowds gather in the streets just to observe this extraordinary phenomenon, and small children run indoors or seek the protection of their parents whenever the strange apparition appears. Yet Northeast China is obviously coming back into the world.

Along Dairen's modern waterfront these last few days were ships from Britain, Germany, Japan, the Soviet Union, Norway and Somalia. One dock was crowded with Chinese trucks being hoisted aboard a modern Chinese freighter for Dar es Salaam, and according to officials here, the commercial traffic is heavier than at any time since the Communists took over this country in 1949.

Dairen has a handsome setting at the southern tip of the Liaotung Peninsula, which juts out into the Yellow Sea. It has a vast,

225

well-protected, crescent-shaped harbor, fairly secure from typhoons, and has a backdrop of hills and an atmosphere quite different from most Chinese cities.

The evidence of Japanese occupation is still very apparent. The buildings are taller, more functional and less Chinese somehow than in other major Chinese communities. There is even a Victorian church on "Friendship Square" in the middle of the city, its green gate locked, its modest tower covered with a vast colored poster of Mao Tse-tung, and its churchyard almost invisible behind a large propaganda billboard.

Still, Dairen is obviously jumping with the Communist Government's drive for industrialization. It cannot compare with Shenyang, formerly Mukden, as a center of heavy industry or with Anshan, 75 miles north, which has the largest iron and steel complex in China; but it has a sizable electrical and locomotive industry, and if smoke is any indication of progress, it is on its way to acquiring all the advantages and disadvantages of the modern industrial world.

Officials here are naturally a little skeptical about Western reporters. In most places the Chinese people tend to vanish when you aim a camera at them, but on the whole officials have been generous about allowing the use of cameras and tape recorders, and even expediting film out of the country without questions.

But here in Dairen the regulations were a little more strict. Cameras inside or on narrowly confined subjects outside but no general views of the harbor or the city in general. This was no great handicap, since the factories were obviously more interested in the smoky atmosphere of production than anything else.

According to officials here, the Dairen harbor employed over 40,000 men during the Japanese occupation, but is now handling three times as much commercial traffic with a little over 10,000.

In 1970, officials say, Dairen harbor handled 50 per cent more goods than in the peak period before the Chinese Cultural

Revolution of 1966–69, and was 24 per cent above its official target for the first six months of 1971.

There is, of course, no way to make an objective check on these figures, but it is possible to confirm the official claim that the docks have been rebuilt and that modern freight handling equipment has been installed in the last few years.

Two things mark the official conversation in Northeast China: an obvious determination to increase production and improve the standard of life of the workers, and an intense anti-Japanese feeling that is even more noticeable here than in Peking or in the South.

Japan, of course, controlled Northeast China for forty years, more than half of this century so far, and many of the people a visitor is invited to meet have vivid and persuasive horror stories to tell about the suffering of the workers under the Japanese.

The main thing, however, is the obvious energy and activity of the people. One had been prepared for this in the agricultural South, and in the larger farms north of the Yangtze, but the Chinese workers are handling modern automated equipment in the vast steel-rolling mills at Anshan with the same enthusiasm and political zeal as the peasants in the agricultural communes farther south.

At Anshan, to keep the electrical supply going even during storms, they have developed a system of repairing high-tension wires without cutting off the power, even of using dynamite to fuse broken wires while workmen are actually handling circuits carrying up to 220,000 volts.

At least they put on a demonstration of the system, and for a man who is vaguely scared about changing a fuse, it was an impressive performance. So things are happening in what used to be called Manchuria, and if production is rising with the spirit of the officials, Northeast China will have a lot more to show to visitors in the coming years.

Canton and Peking: ★
Provincial
And Grandiose

by Tillman Durdin

PEKING, April 17—The transition in China from Canton to Peking is from provincial to metropolitan, from ordinary to grandiose.

Canton, the teeming capital of Kwangtung Province, has a population of three million and occupies a big place in the Chinese scheme of things as the marketplace of China's world trade, as a major port and as a main urban center of southeast China.

But Peking, with its seven million people, reflects the assurance that comes from leadership not only under communism but also under imperial rulers for centuries before the Maoist era.

The transition was made painlessly, almost leisurely, yesterday in a seven-hour flight, with a stop at Shanghai, in a British-built propjet Viscount of China's national airline.

The morning had been spent at the autumn Canton Fair, acclaimed by Chinese officials and by foreign traders as the biggest and best Canton fair ever.

The factory machinery, the farm tractors and harvesters, the clothing, the transistor radios, the sewing machines and the pots and pans all look sturdy and utilitarian if not distinctive. Some 3,000 foreign businessmen are swarming around the exhibits as if they had serious intentions of buying.

Over the years the fairs have become a unique example of how international business and the Chinese Communist way of doing things have managed to integrate.

The Chinese have excellent telephone connections between Canton and Hong Kong but no two-way Telex links. As a result, visiting businessmen are on the telephone from Canton to Hong Kong from early morning to late at night instructing agents to relay messages by Telex to the cities of the world about trade deals.

Many eat only snacks because they do not dare leave their hotel rooms for fear of missing out on a deal.

The fair, housed in one huge seven-story building and in a smaller five-story structure, contains a great deal of propaganda. One display shows the development of Communism in Russia and China, another depicts river conservation projects and a third the development of model communes.

The United States is a constant target of propaganda slogans. In the hotels and fair buildings, red banners proclaim, "People of the world unite to defeat the U.S. aggressors."

Other slogans quote denunciations of the U.S. "and its running dogs" made by Mao Tse-tung, the Communist party chairman. One says:

"It is the task of the people of the whole world to put an end to the aggression and suppression perpetrated by imperialism and chiefly U.S. imperialism."

The plane from Canton to Peking yesterday arrived late in Canton and left late. Seasoned travelers say that schedules are taken casually in China and passengers and pilots are permitted time at stops for leisurely meals. On yesterday's flight to Peking there was an hour's stopover at Shanghai.

Peking revealed itself in today's mild spring sunshine to be drab and gray like Canton but the people were somewhat better dressed and the whole spirit of the city seemed to reflect its importance and enduring quality.

Communist rule has eliminated the majestic medieval character of the ancient capital of the Mings and Chings. Gone are the city walls and most of their huge, high-roofed gates. They have been torn down to make way for broad avenues. Many of the city's old buildings have been replaced by barracklike structures, often with towers, in the Stalinesque style of Moscow.

The antique charm of old Peking is gone but somehow its people, despite the dowdy blue and green uniforms worn by both men and women, display a dignity and aplomb suited to a great capital.

Busy and purposeful, they swarm along the great broad streets on foot and on bicycles. Only a scattering of motor vehicles thread their way through them.

The visiting correspondent runs into problems. First he must register at the Foreign Ministry. He is issued a permit with which he can approach the telecommunications center, but there he finds that international credit cards are not recognized and that the filing of collect messages must await the arrival of a cable of guarantee from the addressee.

Careless phrasing of the messages of guarantee can bring disaster. One newly arrived correspondent today was given a stern lecture and told he was lucky he was not asked to leave when a message from his newspaper arrived addressed to "Peking, Republic of China" [the designation used by the regime on Taiwan] rather than "Peking, People's Republic of China."

But generally the goodwill shown toward the correspondents admitted with the American and other table-tennis teams continues to prevail and those presently in Peking were told they would be able to be in the city for this year's May Day celebrations.

China's Shiny Airports Await Planes

by Tillman Durdin

HONG KONG, May 11—Neat, well-furnished and shiny, the big international section of the Hungjao Air Terminal in Shanghai is mostly an empty showpiece.

Used by international air services only three times a week, the terminal, which this correspondent saw last week, symbolizes the near-isolation of China from world air traffic. However, its readiness for greater use may be a harbinger of future links that could result from the new Peking policy of opening doors to the outside world.

Similar big international terminals in Canton and Peking are also infrequently used. In fact, the only foreign airlines that fly into China are the Soviet Union's Aeroflot, the North Korean airline, Air France and Pakistan International Airlines. Peking's own Civil Aviation Administration of China runs international flights to Moscow, to Hanoi, to Rangoon, the capital of Burma, and to Pyongyang, North Korea.

Aeroflot has two flights a week to Peking, Pakistan International Airlines flies twice a week into Shanghai and Canton, Air France has one flight a week to Shanghai and the North Korean airline has once-a-week service to Shenyang and Peking. The Chinese airline flies twice a week to Hanoi, once a week to Pyongyang by way of Shenyang and once a week to Rangoon.

Both Air France and Pakistan International Airlines give the Chinese a chance to view American planes. Both fly Boeing 707's into China. Traffic on all the international flights to and from China is said to be light.

China's airline isolation from the areas to the east is most striking. The hundreds of Japanese, for example, who go to Peking annually have to fly almost 2,000 miles southwest from Japan to Hong Kong and, after an overnight stay, take a train to Canton where, if they are lucky, they can get a domestic Chinese flight the day after their arrival for the journey of nearly 1,000 miles northward to the capital.

If a jet air service existed between Osaka and Peking, the journey could be made in less than four hours.

The Pakistani airline and Air France have long sought to extend their Shanghai services on to Japan, but the Japanese Government will not permit this. The Japanese, who have no official diplomatic relations with China, want to make this link themselves, and one of the few levers they have for getting Peking to approve is to block any other international airline from operating a service from the Chinese mainland to Japan.

Canada has been seeking a service into China, but Peking has been noncommittal so far in responding to Canadian representatives. Canada might also face Japanese opposition if landings in Japan en route to and from China were planned.

Peking's dispatch of a civil aviation mission last year to Europe and other places seemed to indicate plans for extension of China's international air services, but there have been no definite signs that any new flights will start soon.

The Communist Government's domestic air services are also limited, though considerably more developed than the international services.

All the main cities are linked, but the frequency of service, even for the big coastal cities, is not great. There is, for example, only one nonstop flight each week from Shanghai to Canton. The daily flights operated on this route make two stops.

The Civil Aviation Administration of China still operates no pure jet aircraft. The mainstays of its fleet for longer flights are British Viscounts and Soviet Ilyushin-14's, both turbojet aircraft. The Chinese themselves manufacture a big single-engine biplane that is used for short hauls but build no larger transport planes.

Peking last year acquired four British-made three-jet Hawker-Siddeley Tridents from Pakistan, but these planes have not yet been put into service. When questioned, officials say that a training program for the crews that will fly and maintain the planes is still going on.

Actually, air travel does not appear to be very popular in China. Railway services are good and people generally seem to prefer the trains.

Rail fares were raised recently, and air travel is now cheaper than first-class train travel, but many planes still fly with empty seats.

Pilots on the Chinese planes wear no special uniform, not even distinctive caps. They dress in the same ill-fitting khaki trousers and jackets as military men.

Ground and cabin hostesses are helpful and courteous and especially single out foreigners to say, "Huan-yin, Huan-yin," which means "Welcome, welcome." They too have no special uniforms.

Facilities for instrument landings are meager, and if there is bad weather flights are simply delayed until visibility improves. Planes have Mao Tse-tung's slogans painted along the sides, but the loudspeakers that blared inside the cabins during the Cultural Revolution a few years ago have been turned off and sweet Chinese symphonic music has been substituted.

Oldest Civilization
Is Young and Vigorous

by James Reston

PEKING, July 27—The extraordinary thing about this oldest civilization in the world is that it seems so young. You do not have the feeling here—so depressing and oppressive in some other parts of the Orient—of weariness, sickness and death, of old men and women, spent before their time, struggling against hopeless odds.

To an American visitor China's most visible characteristics are the characteristics of youth: vigorous physical activity despite some serious health problems, a kind of lean muscular grace, relentless hard work, and an optimistic and even amiable outlook on the future.

In the vast expanses of the Soviet Union, you get the feeling that this is the way the world must have looked when it began, empty and untamed, all land and sky. China is not like that. It is alive with people. In the 1,500-mile train ride from Canton to Peking, my wife and I never once looked out the window and saw a vacant field, and the land is not untamed.

These people do not till the earth, they sculpture it, shape it with their own hands, bend and level it so that they can move the irrigating water from one level to another, not only on the level ground, but up into the lovely terraced hills.

There are some machines around, heavy trucks on the tree-lined two-laned main roads, some twelve- and fourteen-horsepower garden tractors in the fields, a plague of bicycles in the cities, but everywhere the scenes are intensely human and alive —but everywhere.

This sense of youthful activity is not only physical but mental. In the 21 years since the Communist take-over, the people have not had time to settle into any stable routine, and even when they seemed to be doing so in 1966, the leadership convulsed them into new and dramatic patterns of life with the Cultural Revolution. This has now passed through its violent phase when the young were encouraged to challenge the leaders of the bureaucracy and even some of the leaders of the Communist party, but it is far from over yet.

Accordingly, China is still in a highly active state of transformation where all workers, peasants, teachers, students and even technicians and other professionals are challenged daily to self-criticism and self-improvement in the performance of their tasks. Thus there is no time even for older men and women to settle down and relax. One is constantly reminded here of what American life must have been like on the frontier a century ago. The emphasis is on self-reliance and hard work, innovation and the spirit of cooperation in building something better and larger than anything they have known before.

Of course they have desperate problems in trying to mobilize and feed between 700- and 800-million people—nobody knows how many. They have a problem of snail fever, a killer parasitic disease, prevalent in the Yangtze Valley. They have a shortage of fertilizer and an obvious shortage of machines.

We drove over a hundred kilometers out of Canton to see a pioneer agricultural community at a place called Lo Tung. All the way out and back, we never saw a single passenger car other than our own. We did see some garden tractors in the rice paddies, but mainly the peasants were plowing the muddy fields behind water buffalo and of course planting the new rice seedlings by hand. On the way back to Canton, we came across a work brigade of what seemed to be over a thousand young men and women who were helping to build a section of highway in a gorge. So far as we could tell they had no equipment other than long-handled picks and shovels which they were using to dig the earth out of a hillside, and baskets which they carried on long poles to transfer the earth to the bed of the new road.

This was, of course, draft labor by city youngsters who were living in makeshift straw huts and cooking their own food, but they were treating it like an escape from the city and an outing in the countryside.

Visitors, of course, go where they are taken. On this particular trip we had to stop once at a police checkpoint beyond which foreigners are not allowed to go without a permit. Also, this was in the rich agricultural land of the south, which is quite different from many bleak areas in the west, and even here most of the houses we passed were poor by almost any standards except China's own in the past.

Accordingly, there is no way for a stranger to know whether China is likely to be the first major Communist country to solve its agricultural problems, but some things even a stranger can observe.

The people seem not only young but enthusiastic about their changing lives. There is no sense of intimidation in the relationship between the Revolutionary Committee leaders and the workers, and while the People's Liberation Army is undoubtedly the key to the future leadership of China, one is not really conscious of its pervasive influence.

Still there is a second paradox: China is not only an ancient country that acts young, but its youthful energy is sternly controlled by a Government of old men. This is a question very much on the mind of the leaders here, but that is another story.

New China:
'A Sink of Morality'

by James Reston

PEKING, July 29—The Hsinhua News Bulletin, a mimeo-
graphed collection of state information in English, is delivered
to your door at the Hsin Chiao Hotel here every morning with a
quotation from Chairman Mao Tse-tung printed in red at the
top of the first page.

Usually this is some brisk and waspish denunciation of the
wicked imperialists, but very often it is a McGuffy Reader moral
maxim: "We must learn the spirit of absolute selflessness." "Dili-
gence, frugality and modesty; remember these three." "The eight
points for attention are:

"(1) speak politely, (2) pay fairly for what you buy, (3) return everything you borrow, (4) pay for anything you damage,
(5) do not hit or swear at people, (6) do not damage crops,
(7) do not take liberties with women, and (8) do not ill-treat
captives."

Since you find the same sort of thing on each page of your calendar every morning, or printed on top of any notebook you
may buy, it is a bit of a shock to discover that your good Maoist
not only believes in struggle and revolution but in plain living
and high thinking. As somebody has said, "Communist China is
a sink of morality," and in their glorification of the noble yeo-
man and puritanical righteousness, officials here make Spiro Ag-
new sound positively permissive.

It would be unwise to mock or minimize this side of the Chinese Communist doctrine. They would be the first to deny that
there are any religious overtones to their propaganda and ideol-

ogy, but the similarities with the dogmatism of the Protestant ethic are not only unmistakable but unavoidable.

Chairman Mao is not only presented as the savior of the nation, but as the warrior poet and moral philosopher of a revivalist and evangelical movement, which has its own scriptural readings, its own Jerusalem [the Chingkang Mountains where Chairman Mao started his reformation in the wilderness], its own national revolutionary litany, its own heretics [Liu Shao-chi and Peng Teh-huai, for example], and even its own division of time and history [B.L. and A.L., before and after the Communist liberation in 1949].

Moreover, the influence of all this is pervasive. The education of a foreigner here illustrates the point and follows a simple pattern. It begins, whether you are taken to a model farm or table-tennis ball factory, in a common room dominated with a plaster or gilt bust of Chairman Mao. Here you are given cool wet towels, cups of delicious jasmine tea, and something like a military briefing on the purpose of the enterprise.

Here, says the chairman of the Revolutionary Committee, as the head man is invariably called whether he is the superintendent of a factory or the headmaster of a school, is what we do in this place.

Usually, he explains what was here before liberation, if anything, and it is a tale of unrelieved inefficiency and human misery, followed by an account of how, "with the help of Chairman Mao's teachings," the people began to cooperate with one another, increased production or learning as the case may be, and improved the general standard of life.

There then follows the inevitable disclaimer. The people have worked hard, they have been inventive and faithful, but they have not done as well as they might, not nearly as well as their comrades in the model industrial and agricultural communes, or even approached the goals they must meet if China is to become a modern industrialized nation.

After this, the visitor is invited to tour and inspect the work, and after the inspection is brought back to the common room for more cool towels and Pearl River orange squash and tea, and invited, even urged, to question and to criticize what he has seen.

No matter how often you go through this routine, you are seldom tempted to be casual or lighthearted about the experience. In the first place, there is something about these serious Revolutionary Committee chairmen that persuades you they are telling the truth, and secondly, the atmosphere of intelligent and purposeful work is impressive.

More important, it is clear that you are in the presence not merely of industrial or agricultural technicians but of true believers in the gospel according to Mao Tse-tung.

They don't only talk production but the Spartan philosophy of Chairman Mao, and it is fairly obvious that they believe the production will never be achieved without the philosophy.

All this, of course, raises many more questions than it answers. Can this philosophy of hard work, without the education of a modern technocratic and scientific élite, really deal with the vast complexities of organizing and administering an advanced industrial society? Maybe not, but that, say officials here, is a question for the future. The main thing is to get the purpose straight, to mobilize the people even if they have to move mountains with teaspoons, and to find a common philosophy which the people believe. And that they seem to be doing, ironically, by adopting many aspects of the old faiths the West has dropped along the way.

To the Visitor
Life Is a Paradox

by James Reston

PEKING, Aug. 3—The routine of life for an American visitor in China these days is full of paradox. For example, you live in an atmosphere of vicious and persistent anti-American propaganda, but are treated with unfailing personal courtesy and are free to cable your impressions without censorship from the lobby of your hotel.

There is not a word in the papers or on the radio here about the latest American moon landing, but you can call the desk at the Hsin Chiao Hotel for an excellent Chinese short-wave radio and listen to the conversations of the astronauts on the moon via the Voice of America and the B.B.C.

Officials here are obviously pleased about President Nixon's coming visit to Peking but his visit is not discussed in the press or on the radio, both of which relentlessly characterize the American Government as the "arch-criminal" of the world. The United States, they insist, has been "beaten black and blue" in Vietnam, but still goes on backing a "fascist clique" in Vietnam, and is reviving "Japanese militarism" and plotting new wars of aggression in Korea and the rest of Asia.

When you ask who writes these editorials in The Peking People's Daily and The Peking Review (a weekly published in English, Russian and many other languages) and ask to talk to them, you are told that your request will be "passed on." You are never told that any request is impossible. You are merely given the next day's schedule, which sometimes includes your requests but usually doesn't.

Still, things are obviously changing here, tactically and on the surface, at least. The Kissinger mission and the forthcoming visit of President Nixon are only the most dramatic evidence that the Chinese Government has decided to end its isolation from the rest of the world.

It sees Washington withdrawing from Vietnam, London joining a new Europe, Moscow and Washington talking about the control of strategic nuclear weapons, Japan emerging as a major industrial power, Moscow expanding its power in the Middle East and along the southern shore of the Mediterranean and building a navy for deployment in all the oceans of the world.

Peking obviously wants to be in on this new organization of the world beyond Vietnam, beyond the unification of Europe with Britain, beyond the present stalemate in the Middle East, and beyond the present talks on the control of nuclear strategic weapons.

So it is changing its attitudes and tactics. It is giving the diplomatic corps in Peking more leeway. It is allowing Western diplomats to travel more widely across China. It is inviting more journalists and scholars to come here. It is encouraging more nations to establish diplomatic relations with Peking, and for the moment, it is concentrating on getting into the United Nations.

Specifically, Peking is now negotiating with the British to establish embassies rather than lower-grade diplomatic missions in Peking and London. It has agreed to allow the Reuter News Agency of London to send off a full-time correspondent here, and it is now puzzling over the avalanche of appeals from Americans to visit or establish permanent offices in Peking. In a way, Peking's diplomacy with Mr. Kissinger and Mr. Nixon has outrun its capacity to deal with the practical problems of dealing with American scholars and the American press. The Foreign Ministry here now has over 300 requests from Americans and American institutions to come here.

These range from appeals for visas from Senator Edward Kennedy of Massachusetts, and Senator George McGovern of

South Dakota, which puzzle them, to requests from news agencies to establish permanent bureaus in Peking, and requests from the television networks to set up machinery for satellite broadcasts of the Nixon visit.

One has the impression that officials here don't quite know how they are to handle all these practical problems of their new diplomacy. They don't have enough Chinese-English translators on their staff to service so many visitors, and they seem a little vague about what the leaders of this Government want them to do with all these new requests.

So, for the time being, there is a dilemma between Peking's strategy and its tactics. Its policy remains the same—indeed Mr. Nixon's appeal to come here seems to have convinced Peking all the more that its policy has been right—and its more lenient attitudes and tactics seem designed merely to promote its policy of weakening American influence in this part of the world In short, Peking is ready for normalizing relations with Washington, but on its own terms: total American withdrawal from Vietnam and Taiwan, and, what seems to interest officials here even more than anything else, a weakening rather than a strengthening of Japanese power in the Pacific.

Army: A Work Force ★
And a Political Force

by James Reston

TIENTSIN, China, Aug. 5—You hear a lot about the Chinese theory of "people's war" and "protracted war" these days but what does it all mean?

Well, frankly, we don't know and the Chinese won't tell, but the 196th Infantry Division of the People's Liberation Army operates out of a flat agricultural plain at the village of Yang Chun, and for the first time since the Cultural Revolution of 1966–69, it is now open to inspection by invited guests. One thing is sure: That old country boy from Wisconsin, Secretary of Defense Melvin Laird, never saw a base like this. It does all the routine stuff, basic training, discipline, marksmanship, and particularly the techniques of guerrilla warfare, but in addition, it is a political school, a vast farm, producing its own fodder, a pharmaceutical factory, and a machine shop, making tools, spare parts, and repairing weapons and vehicles.

In short, it concentrates on political motivation, integration with the peasants and their work, simple weapons that can be carried quickly from one place to another, and self-reliance and self-sufficiency.

We were received at division headquarters by the deputy commander, Keng Yu-chi, who explained that the main purpose of his command was to help defend Peking. His division had been formed in 1937 during the early part of the anti-Japanese war, he said, and since that time "under the guidance of Chairman Mao," had killed 38,000 Japanese, Chiang Kai-shek "traitors"

243

and American imperialists in the Korean war. All this very politely.

His division, he explained, had three principles and three main tasks. The principles were to maintain unity between his officers and men, with each group teaching the other, to develop a common purpose between his division and the civilian population and to disintegrate the enemy, undefined.

His three main tasks, he continued, were to develop his division into a fighting force, a work force in the fields and factories, and a production and political force. His division numbered "over ten thousand men," plus their dependents who helped run the farms and factories, schools, and nurseries of his command.

He took us first to the barracks and club of Two Company of the 587th Regiment of the 196th Division. The club was a propaganda room with maps of the company's battles, photos of its heroes, exhibits of its captured weapons and citations, and a Ping-Pong table.

The barracks in the plain red brick buildings were immaculately clean with bare double-decker bunks fitted with mosquito netting, at the end of each row of beds were neatly lettered company "newspapers" composed of letters of gratitude to Chairman Mao. Each man had his battle roll on his bed for instant action, and automatic rifles, carbines and machine guns were racked neatly at a clear space beyond each double row of sixteen beds.

After a tour of the pig pens, rice paddies, and pharmaceutical sheds, we were shown how the pig bristles were used to make brushes to clean the rifle bores, taken to the machine shops and then given or offered a lunch of wine, mao tai (a clear distillation of sorghum and dynamite) and enough food to paralyze a regiment.

In the afternoon, the division produced a concert and series of propaganda skits, remarkably good and even amusing, after which we were taken to a vast artillery range where Two Company put on a demonstration of marksmanship by rifle, automatic and machine-gun fire, antiaircraft, mortar, antitank and rocket fire, and man-to-man combat and house-to-house guerrilla tactics. It was an impressive performance.

We were then invited to come back and discuss "the international situation." Asia, Africa, and Latin America, we were told, were fighting in unison against the American imperialists. Men, the deputy commander insisted, were more important than weapons. Any enemy invading China would be "drowned in oceans of people," he added, and did we have any comment?

We said we had come to China to report and not to argue and suggested that things were changing in the world and America was looking now to the future and to peace and understanding in the Pacific. This proved to be a disastrous gesture.

The past could not be forgotten, the deputy commander insisted. The main trend in the world was against the U.S. imperialists and all their running dogs. All nations wanted independence and liberation, all peoples wanted revolution and this was the irresistible trend of history.

China was friendly toward all peoples including the American people, he concluded, but imperialist and reactionary governments "never change," so the danger of a new world war still exists. Nixon, as he called the President, must get out of Taiwan and Vietnam and give China its rightful place in the United Nations.

He continued in this vein until an official of the Foreign Ministry intervened to say the sun was going down and we had to get back to Peking. The Chinese people and the American people were friends, he said, but the American Government was something else. It said it wanted to normalize relations with the People's Republic of China, but Secretary Rogers had suggested a two-China formula for the United Nations which was "a new brand with the same old stuff."

We went back to Peking a little sad thinking about memory. Maybe we have to learn to forget, we said as we left. How could we forget the past, the chief of staff asked—forget the Japanese, forget Korea, forget Taiwan? We would like to ask Nixon to think about that.

China Is
Building a New Nation ★

by James Reston

PEKING, Aug. 17—It is hard to see the Chinese people these days for the political billboards, but despite the ceaseless propaganda it is easy to understand why so many Americans have had such a crush on them for so long.

For they demonstrate, among other things, that the human animal can endure anything but hanging. History has dealt them a rotten hand. They have been poorly governed, savaged by nature, plundered and dismembered for centuries by scoundrels, foreign and domestic, yet they have not only survived but managed somehow to shinny up near the top of the greasy pole.

That is part of their appeal: they remind a doubting age of the immortality of the race, but there are other and simpler reasons why an American finds them so attractive, one of them being that they also remind us of our own simpler agrarian past before the complexities of surtaxes and wage and price controls.

Whatever you think of their political system, they are consciously engaged these days in the common life of rebuilding the nation and even in reconstructing themselves. This country is engaged in one vast cooperative barn-raising. They work at it night and day with a pride and persistence that are astonishing and they do it against a background of sights and sounds that tend to make Americans outrageously nostalgic and even sentimental.

For an example, they have plain old-fashioned steam engine railroad trains—what Tom Wicker would call the real thing—

with big red wheels and red cow catchers, and engines that pant
and snort in the station and run with a red glow through the
night, and dining cars where the cook comes back and negoti-
ates your dinner, and compartments with fans and lace anti-
macassars on the seats, and long lonely whistles that trouble
your sleep.

Also, it is something of a relief to visit a country where they
don't have so many things. The Chinese have few automobiles,
for example. A "service station" here is a place where neighbors
provide and deliver food or other necessities to the sick or to
working couples who have no time to shop before dinner.

The bicycle is the principal instrument of transportation in
the cities, and the dominant sound is not the automobile horn,
but the tinkling of thousands of bicycle bells in the twilight passage home. There are, I suppose, two kinds of countries, or
maybe it is only two different stages of development: One where
the people take a great many things for granted and the other
where the people take even the smallest necessities with gratitude. The Chinese are in the second category. They are always
telling you how much better things are now than they used to
be, and they are almost childlike in their wonder and thankful-
ness for small mercies.

Over a hundred years ago, Bret Harte wrote that he thought
he saw in the Chinese people "an abiding consciousness of deg-
radation, a secret pain of self-humiliation in the lines of the
mouth and eye . . . they seldom smile." He added, "and their
laughter is of such an extraordinary and sardonic nature—so
purely a mechanical spasm, quite independent of any mirthful
attribute—that to this day I am doubtful whether I ever saw a
Chinaman laugh."

He should have stuck around, for the corners of their mouths,
like the corners of the roofs on their buildings, now turn up in a
constant smile. Officials in Peking retain a noncommittal and
even skeptical reticence with foreigners, but such is the positive
reaction of most nonofficial Chinese that they usually seem to be

nodding their heads up and down in agreement before they have ever heard the translation of what you said.

There are, of course, some things on the other side. The glorification of Mao Tse-tung, though he undoubtedly deserves the credit for their present sense of unity and purpose, is more exaggerated than anything ever seen in the Soviet Union under Stalin, and though they are struggling out of the world of the abacus into the world of the computer, they show very little curiosity about the scientific revolution that is shaking the world, ask few questions about it, and concentrate on China's problems, China's progress and China's rights.

Still, leaving politics aside, which is hard to do in these parts, the people one meets seem remarkably simple, unspoiled, courteous and appealingly modest.

Both sexes dress in plain blue pants and usually in white shirts, which somehow they manage to keep remarkably clean in the oppressive heat. The women wear absolutely no makeup, and while they have produced the largest population of any nation in the world, they have somehow managed to conceal if not obliterate the female bosom, turning China into the flattest-chested nation on earth.

Compared to the hairy costume party of the West these days, all this seems rather tame, uniform and old-fashioned, but it has great beauty and charm. China is sort of a connecting link between a former period and the present generation. It is late in coming into the modern age, and that, paradoxically, with such an industrious and intelligent people, may be its great advantage.

CHAPTER FOUR
How China Is Governed

'Revolutionary Committees' Insure Discipline ★

by Seymour Topping

PEKING, June 1—At Peking's heavy electric machinery plant, Wei Ching-shen, the 50-year-old chairman of the Revolutionary Committee that runs the big factory, listened patiently as a young woman worker criticized his record.

Mr. Wei did not seem greatly perturbed by her unexpected outburst although he was being interviewed by an American reporter and top management officials of the factory, which employs 5,300, were also in the room.

The incident was revealing of the profound changes that have taken place since the eruption of the Cultural Revolution in management techniques and the style of operation of the Chinese Communist production system. Throughout the country, extending to the grassroots levels in farm communes, factories and other economic enterprises and schools, a new uniform structure of control and administration has been imposed.

Each economic unit and school is managed by a Revolutionary Committee that insures tight political control, ideological discipline and work methods in keeping with the Maoist philosophy.

Mr. Wei, a small, gentle-looking man wearing a plain gray cap and tunic, was flanked during the interview by Ma Kueitang, head of the 16-man army propaganda team, and Miss Yeh Ya-hua, 33, a design worker who voiced the criticism of the committee chairman.

The triumvirate, all members of the Revolutionary Committee, was typical of the prevalent "three-in-one combination" that

251

always includes management officials in responsible positions, representatives of the People's Liberation Army and workers or peasants.

When Mr. Wei was asked if he had been the director of the factory before establishment of its Revolutionary Committee on Feb. 14, 1968, Miss Yeh interrupted by saying: "Yes, he was formerly general secretary of the Communist party of the plant. He is now the same man physically but he has greatly changed since the Cultural Revolution."

Miss Yeh, a handsome, confident woman wearing braids and a worn olive-drab jacket over a gray blouse, glanced at Mr. Wei. As an aide took notes, the committee chairman confessed that before the Cultural Revolution his staff "had been divorced from production and the masses."

"We did not take part in manual labor and we had bureaucratic airs," he said.

In dress, it is difficult to distinguish Mr. Wei or any other senior manager from other workers in the plant. Possession of a wrist watch is sometimes an indication that a man or woman has a key job. Virtually everyone in the factory insists on describing himself or herself as "an ordinary worker."

The reception room in which the interview took place, the equivalent of the board room in the executive suite of an American corporation, was bare except for plain wooden chairs and a long narrow table on which jasmine tea and cigarettes were served. The walls were of unfinished white plaster but like the stone floor were scrubbed clean.

Mr. Wei said that the "pernicious revisionist influence of Liu Shao-chi," the former chief of state, had influenced the factory. Material incentives and rewards had been put in command and development of technology had been emphasized rather than production, he explained.

The chairman added that with the help of the workers and the army propaganda team, the factory had passed through a period of struggle and criticism and now was being run completely according to Maoist doctrine.

In early 1967 when Mao Tse-tung, the party chairman, was locked in a power struggle with Liu Shao-chi, he first issued his call for establishment of Revolutionary Committees.

"Proletarian revolutionaries, unite and seize power from the handful of party persons in power taking the capitalist road," Mr. Mao declared.

Unleashing millions of Red Guards—young militants—to smash the party and Government bureaucracy, which constituted Mr. Liu's power base, Mr. Mao sought control of the farm communes, factories and schools through Revolutionary Committees. The struggle and purge continued through 1969 and the "re-education" period is now in its final phase.

Hundreds of thousands of intellectuals, students, government and party officials and production managers are going through special schools where through manual labor and propaganda courses they are "integrated with the masses." Depending on the individual and how the school directors decide he is faring, a student may remain in the course anywhere from several months to several years.

To assure the most trustworthy framework of control, Chairman Mao has put the army, which he regards as the "main component of state," into the factories, communes and schools.

In some state establishments such as the Peking Experimental Chemical Works, an army representative has become chairman of the Revolutionary Committee and the former plant director has been relegated to a more junior post.

Mr. Ma, the uniformed 33-year-old head of the army propaganda team in the Peking electrical machinery factory, said his men had been there since June, 1967, to "safeguard and defend our red political power and to consolidate the dictatorship of the proletariat."

After factory sessions, members of the team go to the apartments of the workers who live in the housing complex nearby for further discussion with the families.

Mr. Ma said that his men spend one-third of their time in productive manual labor in the factory.

An infantry officer, Mr. Ma, like all army commanders, wears no identification of rank on his baggy olive-drab uniform with red collar epaulets.

He declared that he was ready to go to the front if "imperialists or revisionists impose aggression on our country." The term "imperialists" was an allusion to the United States while "revisionists" alludes to the Soviet Union.

The 20-member Revolutionary Committee, which has a standing committee of 10, nine of whom are members of the Communist party, has put into effect the Maoist precept: "Better troops and simpler administration." The factory's administrative staff has been reduced from 500 to about 200, Mr. Wei said.

Other enterprises visited in a number of Chinese cities reported similar cuts in their administrative personnel.

Touring the electrical factory, this writer saw propaganda posters everywhere stressing the central theme of self-reliance and innovation. In every workshop, workers proudly exhibit equipment, ranging from simple power-driven wheels that wrap generator coils to heavy presses and lathes, that had been designed and manufactured in the plant.

"The imperialists and revisionists have imposed a boycott on us and if we wait for the state to supply us, it would take too long," one shop foreman said. An intensive effort is being made through Maoist indoctrination to obtain a creative release of energy from the workers since such material incentives as pay bonuses have been eliminated.

The Army Holds The Balance of Power

by James Reston

SHANGHAI, Aug. 26—By all outward signs, China has a stable Government, based on the moral authority of Chairman Mao Tse-tung, the power of the People's Liberation Army and the experience and administrative skill of Premier Chou En-lai.

In Western terms, it is a dictatorship which allows and even encourages dissent within but not against the policies of the Government. They are frank to tell you there is no freedom of speech for ideological opponents of the regime even at Peking University, but for the time being this Government undoubtedly has the support of the vast majority of the Chinese people.

But what of the future, when the present leaders, now in their seventies, are gone? For over a century, the Chinese people have been compared to the bamboo tree: graceful, useful and supple, When the east wind blows they bend to the west, when the west wind blows, they bend to the east, when no wind blows they don't bend at all. So goes the legend.

Mao Tse-tung himself seems haunted by their pliability. As early as 1962, he was worrying about the possibility that the sons of the present generation would depart from his revolutionary faith. He got rid of Liu Shao-chi because he thought Liu was leading China back to capitalism. He launched the Cultural Revolution in the late sixties in the hope that the young and the army, even if they rebelled against the party establishment and disrupted the state apparatus, would prepetuate his revolution; and he chose his faithful military sidekick of the "Long March" days, Lin Piao, as his successor.

Not only that, but he had this line of succession written into the Constitution, and after the Cultural Revolution, which was best described by Lin Piao as "a civil war without guns," the balance of power in the Central Committee moved to the army.

Among the present members of this ruling body of the state, less than one-fifth of them were members before the Cultural Revolution, and military officers now account for 40 per cent of the total.

The most powerful rising figures, according to China watchers in the embassies in Peking—the Chinese themselves won't even discuss the subject—are Huang Yung-sheng, chief of the general staff of the army, who has recently been making some rather extreme anti-American speeches; Li Hsien-nien, Vice Premier under Chou En-lai, and Yao Wen-yuan, a member of the central Politburo and second secretary of the powerful Shanghai municipal committee.

Perhaps the most interesting question is the future relationship between the army leadership and the leadership of the party itself. Chairman Mao turned to the army at the most critical part of the Cultural Revolution when the masses were virtually provoked into rebelling against the party establishment. Since then there has undoubtedly been a powerful effort to integrate the leadership of these two factions—how successful this has been no outsider can know—but you don't have to be in China for long to feel the influence of the military officers.

Wherever you go in this country, whether to a factory, to a farm commune, to a hospital, or even to Peking University, you are introduced to the chairman or deputy chairman of "the Revolutionary Committee" who more often than not turns out to be a military officer in civilian clothes.

Even when we went out on the Yangtze River to see the Shanghai commercial shipping, we were turned over to the deputy chairman of the ship's Revolutionary Committee, though the crew of the ship numbered only four. These Revolutionary Committees are the effective governing apparatus right down to the rice roots of the countryside, and while it is hard to know just how much they are under the domination of the army, one has the impression that the decisive power of the future lies with these military officers, beginning with Lin Piao and Huang Yung-sheng.

It should be emphasized, however, that the Chinese Army is not a separate entity cut apart from the civilian life of the nation, as in other countries. It is not only actively engaged in the defense of the nation, and in the administration, education and propaganda of civilian enterprises, but is actually engaged, unit by unit, in farming and small industry.

In this sense, it is already much more closely integrated into the political and civilian life of China than would generally be supposed, and few observers here seem to believe there is any danger of the army breaking up into separate competing regional commands under any modern equivalent of the old China warlord struggles.

Oddly, most observers here think the legend of Mao Tse-tung will retain its influence for some years even after his death and might even be stronger in the first few years than it is now.

It is the wisdom and influence of Chou En-lai that most people here seem to worry about losing. For he was the unifying figure during the Cultural Revolution, and while Lin Piao will undoubtedly see that the legend of the chairman is perpetuated, nobody is quite clear about who could carry in the future the immense burdens now borne by the present Premier.

New Dogma, New Maoist Man

by Seymour Topping

PEKING, June 19—The doctrines of the Cultural Revolution have been translated into new Communist dogma. Under Mao Tse-tung that dogma has propelled China into a continuing revolution that is producing a new society and a new "Maoist Man."

Relative stability, prosperity and surface tranquillity have been restored with the end of the convulsive mass conflicts and great purge generated by the Cultural Revolution, which began in 1966 as a power struggle between Chairman Mao and Liu Shao-chi, then chief of state and since deposed amid charges that he had deviated from revolutionary principles.

Mr. Mao believes that he has interrupted an evolution that was turning China into a society on the Soviet model, characterized by a privileged bureaucracy and tendencies toward a rebirth of capitalism in industry and agriculture.

The gigantic Maoist thought-remolding program has profound implications not only for the 800 million Chinese but also for the world. It is producing a highly disciplined, ideologically militant population that is taught that Mr. Mao is the sole heir of Marx and Lenin and the interpreter and defender of their doctrine and that each Chinese must be committed to fostering a world Communist society.

Even so, underlying tensions persist in the party hierarchy and at the grass roots as the ideological struggle to resolve what Mr. Mao describes as "contradictions among ourselves" goes forward.

"We have won a great victory," the leader says, echoed by

his designated successor, Vice Chairman Lin Piao. "But the defeated class will still struggle. These people are still around and this class still exists. Therefore, we cannot speak of final victory, not even for decades."

In virtually every factory and on every agricultural commune toured by this reporter during a five-week visit, army propaganda teams originally sent three or four years ago were still struggling to root out what they regard as subversive thinking. All economic enterprises and schools were festooned with posters denouncing "the renegade traitor Liu Shao-chi," who took the capitalist path by encouraging money incentives.

"Material incentives corrode man's soul and make up a hotbed for creating individualism," said Tien Chi-ching, a party leader in Anshan, the big iron and steel center in the northeastern region.

To sustain what the Maoists consider to be ideological purity and progress toward the eventual classless society, a tighter nationwide system of ideological surveillance, purge and re-education has been instituted.

Government administrators and managers of economic enterprises have been locked into a "Revolutionary Committee" system of supervision under which their work is monitored by delegates of the army, the reconstituted Communist party and militant workers or peasants. Deviation from Maoist principles can land them in peasant villages or special schools, where they stay for several months to several years doing manual labor while undergoing ideological re-education.

An entire generation of students, young people attending secondary schools and universities when the Cultural Revolution began, have been ideologically screened, purged and re-educated. Hundreds of thousands have been sent to the villages to do manual labor under the surveillance of peasants and to be reindoctrinated, many without any hope of resuming their formal educations.

Hundreds of the so-called May 7 schools—the date appears

on a letter from Mr. Mao to Mr. Lin, who pioneered them—have been established throughout the country and members of the bureaucracy, intellectuals and technicians are being run through in rotation.

At a school in Peking's eastern suburbs there are such "students" as Ming Kuai-san, 38, a former deputy chief of the education division of the Cultural Bureau in Peking. He works as a laborer in a rice paddy while undergoing reindoctrination. Mrs. Hsu Ying, 26, a teacher, labors as a masonry worker. Tien Chi-chen, former vice chairman of now-disbanded trade unions in the eastern district of the capital, makes water pails in a school-run factory.

The ideological atmosphere is intense. For a westerner there is something frightening about the Peking regime's ability to summon as many as half a million people in a major city, red banners flying and drums beating, to shout tirelessly in unison and, given the slogan, welcome a friend or denounce an enemy.

There is no convincing evidence that Premier Chou En-lai's recent pragmatic gestures toward non-Communist states, including his Ping-Pong flirtation with the United States, represent any retreat from the underlying Maoist objective of world revolution.

There is also no evidence of an inclination at any level toward involvement in foreign military adventures. The prime emphasis in domestic propaganda is on consolidating the Cultural Revolution and building the economy.

During a tour of cities and countryside, in discussions with party and government officials, with managers of factories and farms, with professional men and women and ordinary peasants and workers, the writer gained the impression that Maoist principles were taking effective hold.

Apart from the influence of unending propaganda and organizational disciplines, the peasants and workers who make up the great bulk of the population are apparently favorable to the system because they believe they have a stake in it. Many members of this class say that their material living standards have never been better.

Ordinary Chinese carry themselves with a new dignity and respond to the exhortations of the party, which tells them. "You are the masters of the new society." The memory of foreign privilege—such as the restrictions in clubs and the old park sign in the Shanghai foreign concession saying "No dogs or Chinese" —have receded before new pride in China's unity and its status in the world.

The improvement in the physical condition of the people since the Communist take-over in 1949 is staggering.

Hordes of beggars and of the starving and diseased that once were familiar are gone. The people look healthy and are obviously adequately fed and clad although clothing is often worn and there is uniform dullness in blue and gray tunics over inevitable baggy pants.

As the hot June days settled on Peking a few bright long cotton skirts appeared and some of the girls fluffed their hair a bit instead of wearing it severely short or in tight braids.

The state assures each family a basic income sufficient to feed and house itself. Living standards are below those of Japan or Taiwan but seem uniformly adequate in the Asian context. The writer wandered unescorted down some back streets and village lanes without seeing sanitary conditions as bad as in New York ghettos.

Although tremendous improvements have been wrought by the Communists, the favorable contrast with the past is also attributable simply to a period of peace and unity.

Prior to the Communist victory China had been a victim of Japanese invasion and of civil war for 27 years. Brutal living conditions resulted from the constant turmoil as well as from the shortcomings of the Government of Generalissimo Chiang Kai-shek.

The great coastal cities look more drab than before largely because Western adornment and consumer goods have vanished and the bright lights have gone out. The cities are more typically Chinese, integrated closely with the economy of the interior rather than dependent on foreign luxury trade.

Chairman Mao, determined to reduce the gap in living standards between city and village, has had investment in new construction spread throughout the country. "In the interior most of our factory equipment is new," Premier Chou, day-to-day manager of government affairs, said.

With the notable exception of Peking, which has been spruced up for the role of a great world capital, the cities have lagged in housing construction. Old foreign and Chinese buildings have been painstakingly preserved but many still look scruffy.

Pressure on the cities has been eased by Peking's policy of moving surplus workers and ideological unreliables, particularly students, en masse into the countryside. Nearly a million from Shanghai alone have been shipped to the villages.

In the flight over central China, the new construction a visitor observes is mainly factories and central agricultural commune buildings. Otherwise the clusters of mud and brick houses with thatched and tile roofs that stand beside pampered fields—vivid green rice paddies in the south, then brown wheat beyond the Yellow River—look unchanged, though the landscape is gashed by great water-conservation projects.

The markets in towns and villages are full of food and there seems to be a plentiful supply of basic consumer goods, though high prices on more choice consumer items impose a form of indirect rationing.

The process of leveling up the living conditions of the masses has been accompanied by a leveling down of the status and material rewards of the political and managerial bureaucracy.

According to Government sources, monthly wages in urban areas range from 34 yuan to 108 yuan (about $14 to $75 at the going rate). In factories wages are fixed in eight grades according to skill, length of experience and ideological reliability. Only a relatively few technicians, managers and senior officials get salaries substantially higher than this scale.

The head of a mine in Anshan was earning 108, while a political chief of a big Shenyang machine-tool plant was getting 140. A master iron carver in Peking who had worked at his bench for 30 years was earning 100 yuan. In a Chengchow textile plant the chief engineer is paid 188 yuan while the head of the plant gets 166.

If a skilled worker has a wife holding a job, family income may exceed that of the head of a factory.

Specific titles—and elegant manners and fine dress—are frowned upon. A manager of a big enterprise, unless pressed, will identify himself solely as "a responsible member" of a Revolutionary Committee.

In Anshan a visitor was received by the head of a factory producing alarm clocks for export. He wore a brown tunic and dark trousers of slightly better texture than those of his workers.

An accompanying party official glanced at the factory chief, who had been through a rigorous course of criticism for ideological failings, and said that he had put on his best clothes to receive visitors. While the factory chief flushed and nodded, the party man said he would put on his working clothes as soon as the visitors left.

In Peking top Government and party officials live at secret locations, presumably in the fine state residences that can be seen around the capital. However, they all entertain in public buildings. They arrive at receptions in chauffeured cars that usually are several years old. In public there is no display of affluence and their dress is austere.

Mr. Mao has put the bureaucracy into a vise out of the conviction that the corruption of his society may begin with the emergence of new Mandarin classes. He is often suspicious of intellectuals and technicians, believing that only workers and peasants as a class can be fully trusted.

Foreign experts ask how long the members of the bureaucracy, who are required to perform periodic manual labor as part of the process of "integrating with the masses," can stand the situation.

Some of the experts say that many members of the bureaucracy are simply "bending like young bamboo" in the ideological wind; waiting for another change. With the most virulent phase of the Cultural Revolution over, a restoration of Mandarin attitudes is detected.

To allow Mr. Chou to get on with the business of pushing the country forward again economically and of coping with the imperatives of foreign policy, extreme leftist tendencies have been curbed.

Two Politburo members in the extremist faction, Chiang Ching, wife of Mr. Mao, and Kang Sheng, who had been concerned with security matters, seem to have lost some influence. A third, Chen Po-ta, formerly Mr. Mao's secretary, has not been seen publicly since August, 1970.

Although there has been some easing of pressures, Chairman Mao has not deviated from his fundamental line—egalitarianism and self-reliance, all in a spartan manner. Despite some rumble deep in Chinese society, Mr. Mao and his supporters are firmly in command as the Chinese Communist party prepares to celebrate the 50th anniversary of its founding on July 1.

Mr. Mao is 77 years old and is believed to be in failing health, but his disciples have already enshrined "the great helmsman" and his ideology in much the same way that Lenin lives in the Soviet pantheon. Mr. Mao's voluminous writings have become scripture not only for ideologues but also for peasants in their daily life.

However, the regime may have a problem of succession because virtually all the top leaders are in their sixties and seventies.

Mr. Lin, Mr. Mao's "close comrade in arms" who was designated his successor in the 1969 party constitution, is 63. Bouts of tuberculosis have left him in poor health. Mr. Chou, a tireless dynamo, is 73.

The rising star is Huang Yung-sheng, 64, army chief of staff and Politburo member. A tough disciplinarian who has been close to Mr. Lin, he was brought to Peking from Canton during the Cultural Revolution after he had crushed rampaging extremist Red Guards.

Presumably he would have the support of the army should Mr. Lin die. Army men already occupy powerful posts in every phase and on every stratum of economic and political life.

There is no reason to believe that Mr. Huang would deflect China from the course set by "the great helmsman."

Mao Is Seen ★
As Benefit
Even to Visitor

by Seymour Topping

HANGCHOW, China, May 22—From the moment a foreigner crosses into China, the personality of Mao Tse-tung pervades almost every waking hour.

Huge portraits, revolutionary songs piped into public places and constant references to the thoughts of "the great helmsman" in conversations with Chinese reveal how the Mao personality is shaping Chinese society.

There is evident belief that foreigners can be similarly influenced, and the thousands of foreigners who are now visiting the country are subjected to Maoist education.

Since the advent of Ping-Pong diplomacy and perhaps in anticipation of visits by Americans, the barrage of propaganda against "United States imperialists" has lessened. Some of the English-language anti-American posters have come down, although often their Chinese versions remain in place.

For thousands of overseas Chinese, most of them living in Southeast Asia, indoctrination begins as they walk across the bridge at Lo Wu near Hong Kong and enter mainland China.

Many of them are youngsters being sent by their parents on visits to ancestral villages to help them retain their identity and their links with the homeland. Dressed much like Western youngsters, some carrying Pan American flight bags, they don Mao buttons and are met by trained guides. In customs waiting rooms adorned with red banners and slogans, with revolutionary songs ringing in corridors, they dutifully applaud as they are welcomed in the name of Chairman Mao, the party and China.

In an adjoining room a group of Japanese visitors gets somewhat similar treatment.

According to Chang Teh-shen, vice chairman of the Revolutionary Committee in charge of the Canton Trade Fair, about 16,000 foreign businessmen and other overseas visitors came to the semiannual exhibition April 15 to May 15. No opportunity was lost during the fair, which had a record attendance, to impress foreigners with the thoughts of Chairman Mao. Among businessmen attending the fair were about 80 Canadians, 80 Britons and 1,500 Japanese, as well as a considerable number of West Germans and other Europeans.

Each exhibition room of the nine-story fair building was dominated by a huge portrait of Chairman Mao, and each counter of goods had blazoned above it Mao quotations and exhortations in praise of factory workers and farmers who had achieved production successes by using locally developed methods. The entire eighth floor of the fair building was given over to exhibits on the life and works of Chairman Mao.

In large new hotels, the only portraits of comparable size to those of Chairman Mao—who sometimes is shown standing with his Deputy, Lin Pao, at his side—were those of Stalin. It is the familiar Stalin portrait once seen everywhere in the Soviet Union but now, along with other tributes to the late Soviet leader, taken down by his Kremlin successors.

Businessmen report that two years ago, when the impact of the Cultural Revolution was stronger, they would sometimes be awakened early in their hotel rooms to hear Mao readings. Other selections were read to them during trade negotiations.

Leaving Canton at the new gleaming airport terminal, a traveler is greeted in a spacious but sparsely filled lobby by a massive white statue of Chairman Mao facing a great mural showing him standing before minority peoples in their traditional native garbs.

In the cavernous waiting room, eight girls dressed in green army tunics over blue trousers waved red flags and sang revolutionary songs in praise of Chairman Mao. They concluded their songs by shouting in English, "Long live Chairman Mao," and danced off stage waving their small red Mao books.

Before the writer boarded an Illyushin 18 of the Chinese civil airline for Hangchow—in the plane he would sit under a Maoist slogan declaring "People of the world unite and defeat the U.S. aggressors"—he spent a more pleasant moment examining exquisite calligraphy by Chairman Mao that covered the terminal wall.

It was one of the Chairman's poems, "Snow," which in English translation beside Chinese characters read:

This is the scene in that northern land;
A hundred leagues are sealed with ice,
A thousand leagues of whirling snow.
On either side of the Great Wall
One vastness is all you see.
From end to end of the Great River
The rushing torrent is frozen and lost.

The mountains dance like silver snakes.
The highlands roll like waxen elephants,
As if they sought to vie with heaven in their height;
And on a sunny day
You will see a red dress thrown over the white.
Enchantingly lovely!
Such great beauty like this in all our landscape has
  caused unnumbered heroes to bow in homage.
But alas these heroes! Chin Shih Huang and Han Wu
  Ti were rather lacking in culture;
Rather lacking in literary talent were the emperors
  Tang Tai Tsung and Sung Tai Tsu;
And Genghis Khan.
Beloved son of heaven for a day,
Only knew how to bend his bow at the golden eagle.
Now they are all past and gone:
To find men truly great and noble
We must look here in the present.

Mass Trial for Foreign Ministry Aide

by Seymour Topping

PEKING, June 20—A prominent Chinese diplomat accused of having been responsible for violence against foreign embassies committed during the Cultural Revolution has been imprisoned, according to reports circulating in Peking.

The diplomat, Yao Teng-shan, was a member of a revolutionary group that was in control of the Foreign Ministry in August, 1967, when the office of the British chargé d'affaires was burned and attacks were made on the Indonesian and Burmese embassies.

Mr. Yao, according to the reports, was taken June 11 to a mass trial in an indoor stadium in Peking, attended by 4,000 people, and denounced. He was said to have been accused of plotting in 1967 to do personal injury to Premier Chou En-lai and of holding Chen Yi, then Foreign Minister, as a prisoner for several days.

The mass denunciation has not been mentioned in the press. However, foreign diplomats have become aware of the trial through a number of Africans and Asians who said they had been invited to attend.

The extraordinary proceedings were seen as an effort to relieve the Government of responsibility for excesses committed during the most convulsive stage of the Cultural Revolution, which have been a source of embarrassment. Premier Chou, who is pursuing a new pragmatic foreign policy, has been at pains to portray China as a responsible member of the world community.

269

Peking is seeking to strengthen its diplomatic ties in its efforts to isolate the Chiang Kai-shek government on Taiwan and also to gain admission into the United Nations as the sole delegation of China. Recently diplomats of non-Communist governments have been shown new courtesies in Peking, such as being taken on more tours of the country. And in the last week army guards stationed at embassy gates have begun saluting chiefs of mission.

It was understood that Premier Chou had privately expressed his regrets to John D. Denson, the British chargé d'affaires, about the 1967 attack on the British office. Donald C. Hopson, who was then chargé d'affaires, was injured in scuffles with extremist Red Guards.

The way now seems open for an exchange of ambassadors between Britain and the People's Republic if London closes its consulate at Tamsui, in northern Taiwan, and gives full backing to United Nations membership for Peking. At present, the British and Chinese are represented in each other's capitals at the chargé d'affaires level.

In a further move to absolve the present Government of any responsibility for violations of diplomatic immunity during the Cultural Revolution, articles in the Chinese press in recent weeks have attacked leftist extremists as plotters against the Communist party and the Government.

In December, in a conversation with Edgar Snow, the American writer, Chairman Mao Tse-tung said he was not in control of the Foreign Ministry in 1967 and 1968.

Liu Shao-chi, the chief of state, was deposed in 1967 after Red Guards denounced him and his supporters in the Government and the party.

Mr. Yao became a leading member of an extreme leftist faction that took over the Foreign Ministry after he returned from Indonesia, where he had been chargé d'affaires.

According to some reports, Chen Yi, former Foreign Minister who disappeared for a number of years, attended the mass meeting. Mr. Chen, who is still a vice chairman of the influential military affairs commission of the party, showed up for the first time in many months at May Day celebrations this year. Chi Peng-fei, who is now identified as Acting Foreign Minister, was also said to have been present at the denunciation.

May Day
Hospitality
For Foreigners

by Tillman Durdin

PEKING, May 1—The new, more outgoing attitude of the People's Republic of China in foreign relations was reflected in May Day celebrations here today that were generally more relaxed than usual and showed special consideration for the larger-than-normal number of foreign visitors present for the occasion.

The Communist party Chairman, Mao Tse-tung, appeared at Tienanmen (the Gate of Heavenly Peace) Square for the annual May Day evening display but left after a few minutes.

He arrived and departed with his deputy, Lin Piao. The Chairman said a few words to Prince Norodom Sihanouk, whom Peking recognizes as Cambodian Chief of State and who was seated near Mr. Mao, then left without greeting others atop the gate as he sometimes has done in the past.

As has been the case for some years, Mr. Mao was accompanied by two nurses. The massed groups on the square below broke into wild cheering and chanted, "Mao Tse-tung wan sui!" (Long live Mao Tse-tung!) when he appeared. Bands broke into "The East Is Red" as he stood on the rostrum.

Neither Mr. Mao nor Mr. Lin has made a public appearance since late last year. All the members of the Communist party Politburo were atop the gate except for Chen Po-ta, Kang Sheng and Hsieh Fu-chih, who have not been seen in public for many months.

After Mr. Mao left, Premier Chou En-lai was the dominating figure on the gate and greeted and chatted with the many foreign representatives. These included Vietnamese, Koreans, a visiting Mali delegation and a number of prominent foreigners. There were no speeches. The regime's May Day remarks were confined to an editorial published jointly in two dailies, Jenmin Jih Pao, and Chiehfang Chun Pao, and the fortnightly magazine Hung Chi.

The display of dancing, singing, marching and revolutionary skits by the tens of thousands, mostly young people, in the vast square and its approaches was similar to the May Day shows of past years. Choruses, bands and orchestras filled the night with loud music as multicolored searchlights played over the crowd and beams of light crisscrossed above.

Buildings were festooned with lights and a fireworks display sprinkled the sky with sparkles and explosions of color for the second half of the two-hour program.

The evening show was the climax of a holiday round of festivities for Peking's millions of residents and tens of thousands of visitors.

Performances of music dramas, plays, political skits and music drew huge crowds to the grounds of the Summer Palace of the last Manchu ruler, the Dowager Empress Tzu Hsi, and other parks and entertainment places.

Foreign visitors and members of foreign diplomatic missions

were especially invited to the performances and were more numerous than usual. They were applauded as they entered and left the various performances. The crowds seemed to have been instructed to make a special show of welcome.

One group of Albanians and another of Japanese surprised and pleased the crowd by singing revolutionary Chinese songs. Security personnel showed great tolerance for foreign picture-takers. Many scenes that have been forbidden to photographers, such as military groups and certain parts of the city, were photographed freely for the first time in years.

The restraints and suspicions that grew to paranoid height during the Cultural Revolution seem to have melted considerably today.

The moderate mood of the day was reflected in the editorial that appeared in the three papers. It restated Peking's basic approach to international affairs and the ideological position of the Chinese Communists but made no direct attack on either the United States or the Soviet Union.

The central theme was support of the People's Republic of China for revolutionary struggles and Communist regimes and opposition to forces opposing them. But the editorial pointed out that Peking had "always persisted in striving for peaceful coexistence with countries having different social systems."

CHAPTER FIVE
The Children of Chairman Mao:
Education and Child-Rearing

Nursery Songs Denounce 'U.S. Aggressors'

by Tillman Durdin

SHANGHAI, April 20—The thought of Mao Tse-tung and Chinese national policy are integral elements of study and play, even for small children, at the Pengpu workers housing complex on the outskirts of Shanghai, foreign newsmen found on a visit to the complex this morning.

At a nursery, the journalists, who are on a tour of the Shanghai area, were entertained by 5-year-olds singing "We unite and struggle in Asia, Africa and Latin America; people join to defeat the U.S. aggressors and their running dogs."

Other songs hailed the leadership of Chairman Mao and denounced revisionists. One group of children did a dance in which they mimed bayonet lunges while singing the praises of the People's Liberation Army.

Another song and dance routine imitated a Tibetan dance and thanked the army for liberating Tibetans from slavery.

Teachers said that production themes, the struggle against capitalist tendencies and opposition to "Japanese reactionaries and American imperialists" were used as material for the children's lessons. The nursery, where 500 children from the age of a few months to 6 years are cared for, is an important aspect of a community of 15,000 people that seemed to provide a modestly comfortable life for its worker-members.

In a solid building with simple but adequate equipment, the nursery looks after the younger children of working couples. Some parents take their children home at night, others take them home only on the weekend.

After the age of 6, children in the housing complex begin attending regular school and living at home. But highly political and closely directed activities centered on the primary and secondary schools continue to take much of the children's time.

The Pengpu complex has 138 apartment buildings, and workshop, administrative and other buildings set amid farmlands and factories. It is typical of many housing developments that have been built together with industrial establishments around Shanghai with the idea of dispersing people and factories away from the congested main city.

The Pengpu complex has shops, recreational and other facilities that satisfy all ordinary needs and make it unnecessary for residents to seek these elsewhere. Even some small industries operate in the workshops.

The three-story apartment buildings of one-room, two-room and three-room units, with small balconies, are nondescript but solid and attractively set amidst trees and walkways. Residents can eat either at the messhalls in their factories, at home or in restaurants. Forty-three doctors and nurses provide a health service at nominal cost.

The men retire at 60 and the women at 50, at 70 per cent of regular pay, and continue living in the development. Rent for a one-bedroom apartment is $1.70 a month and for a two-bedroom home, $2.90. Water, gas and electricity are provided.

Mrs. Wu Fung-ming, a slight, erect widow of 58, gave a detailed account of the economics of life at Pengpu at a two-hour meeting with the newsmen.

Dressed in new, freshly pressed black trousers and high-necked jacket, Mrs. Wu looked much less than her age. Although retired for seven years, she reported, she has just taken a volunteer job in a nearby school.

She lives in a three-bedroom layout with two sons and their wives and four grandchildren. The eldest son, 38, makes $25 a month and the other, 34, earns $22 a month. The pay of their wives is roughly the same. With the $30-a-month pension of Mrs. Wu, the family has roughly $125 a month.

Mrs. Wu, who made it clear she runs the household finances, spends $45 monthly for food, which is in addition to the cost of meals eaten at factory messes, and $6.50 a month for rent. As an indication of clothing prices, her own costume was $4. Other prices were $54 for a radio, $25 for a sideboard and $25 for a bed.

"We have meat or fish every day and plenty of rice and vegetables and so live well but frugally," Mrs. Wu said. "We follow Chairman Mao's injunction to be thrifty and give as much to the state as possible, so we save $20 every month."

Mrs. Wu said that her youngest son, who was married and lived away from home, once argued that the family had enough money and ought to buy a television set but said that she had cited Chairman Mao's axiom about thrift and vetoed the proposal.

A party member, Mrs. Wu no longer needs to look at the party chairman's little red book. She made herself literate years ago by attending classes at the woolen mill where she worked, and she has learned by heart most of Mr. Mao's sayings and can even cite on which page of the red book they are to be found.

The bedroom, in which correspondents were received, had eight pictures of the Chairman on the walls and a small white bust of him on the radio.

Mrs. Wu said that the wives of the two sons living with her used birth-control pills regularly and the couples thought that two children each were enough. She said her youngest son and his wife did not have a child although they had been married for some time.

The family headed in matriarchical style by Mrs. Wu is not typical in size for the Pengpu complex. Reflecting the new preference in China for small families, the average in the complex is three members in a family. When families are larger, it is usually because a father or mother lives with a married couple.

Unlike some housing complexes, the Pengpu development does not have a separate home for old people.

Schools Retain Many ★
Conventional Subjects

by Tillman Durdin

CANTON, China, May 6—The changes that have been made in primary and secondary schooling in China do not appear to be as drastic as official publicity has depicted them.

A visit to one model middle school in Peking and questioning about lower-level education there and elsewhere show that much of the conventional teaching system remains.

At the Peking No. 2 Secondary School, for example, mathematics, languages, physics, chemistry, history, geography, physical education and public affairs—a kind of civics course—form a basic part of the curriculum just as these subjects did before the Cultural Revolution and just as they do in secondary schools in the West.

These courses are taught in so far as possible through use of maxims and philosophy of Mao Tse-tung, and, in addition, there are separate courses in political education, basic farming and revolutionary art and culture that have political indoctrination as their main objective. However, the teaching of basic general knowledge is obviously a major preoccupation of the school.

And discipline is back in vogue. A new student body of 1,500 boys and girls had replaced the youngsters who from late 1966 until late 1968 had no regular classes. During that period, pupils were free to rampage in and around Peking while hauling principal and teachers before "struggle" meetings at which they were denounced for so-called revisionist ideas and practices.

The former students have been sent off to work in the coun-

280

tryside or in factories, and their successors are obviously under firm control of the school authorities, who, oddly enough, include the same teachers as before. Now, however, military men stationed in the school see that things run properly.

Ma Yu-shan, who was principal of the school in 1966, no longer holds that post, which has been abolished, but is a member of the Revolutionary Committee that now runs the school. He gives the impression of still having a strong voice in school affairs.

This is not to say that broad changes have not been made. For one thing, the No. 2 Secondary School, as a junior middle school, has moved into studies formerly confined to senior middle schools.

This is in conformity with the new plan that provides for five years in primary school instead of the former six and for five years instead of six in junior and senior middle school. Under the new plan senior middle school graduates at the age of 15 and 16 go to work in factories or on farms for a couple of years and then, if found suitable, go on to a university for two to three years.

In addition the Maoist content of all studies, to say nothing of those courses especially designed to indoctrinate, is now all-embracing. In the two foreign languages taught in the school, French and English, lessons are made up of quotations from Chairman Mao.

"Unisons nous pour remporter des victoires encore plus grandes!" ("Let us unite to achieve even greater victories!") a French class repeats in unison after their teacher. Across the hall, a class in English declaims, "Be resolute! Fear no sacrifice and surmount every difficulty to win victory!"

The teacher in a Chinese language class uses a Mao poem extolling the heroism of the Chinese Red Army during the Long March that the Communist forces made in 1934–35 in their war against Kuomintang troops. In a geometry class, a Mao quotation on the wall advises students they "must deduce the rule from objective conditions, not merely to sum up but to guide actions."

The school is also more Maoist now in the way the students combine class studies with practical work. Each student must spend three hours a day for one month in a shop making metal and wooden chairs or performing the painstaking task of processing tiny disks into diodes for use in precision meters or transistor radios.

The school produces 30,000 diodes a month for electronics plants. The factories pay 12 cents per diode, but the money goes to the school, not the students.

Classes meet for 31 weeks. There are eight weeks of vacation during which there are periods of military training, four weeks spent learning work in a factory, four weeks spent learning work on a farm and a week of so-called summing up during which certain students are singled out for their class records and political understanding.

The new primary schools and senior middle schools follow a pattern similar to that of the No. 2 Secondary School, but officials acknowledge that the new schools at both primary and secondary levels are still experimental.

The new system has not been generally adopted yet in Peking, and in Shanghai officials questioned said that the city was still experimenting with the system.

One problem is trying to cram the material that formerly was covered in 12 years into 10 years. Another is that workers and peasants long past usual primary school age and without any schooling are now admitted to classes in which they study alongside much younger pupils. This involves disparities of learning speed and difficulties in the relationships of students.

Professor Praises the Cultural Revolution ★

by Tillman Durdin

PEKING, April 29—Prof. Chien Wei-chang, a researcher and lecturer at the California Institute of Technology from 1940 to 1946, says that he is a contented product of protracted and painful thought-remolding by students, workers and soldiers at Peking's Tsinghua University during the Cultural Revolution.

"Formerly I thought all I had to do was be a good scientist and hand down theory," Professor Chien said today. "But as a result of re-education and self-criticism I now know theory must be combined with production and one must follow the path of serving the people and integrating with workers and peasants.

"Formerly there was a great gap between me and the students," he continued, "but now I agree with them and feel like a new man."

Professor Chien spoke to a group of foreign newsmen who visited Tsinghua University for a look at the new system of higher education in the People's Republic, for which Tsinghua is serving as a pioneer and model.

Professor Chien was one of a group of teachers, administrators, students and military men who raced through an obviously well-rehearsed recital of their experiences during the Cultural Revolution and an explanation of how the new educational system works.

Following their presentation, during which no questions were permitted, they took newsmen to look at student dormitories, a mess hall and workshops. There students under the guidance of professors and veteran workers make trucks, complicated electronics components, machine tools and other equipment for factories associated with the university.

During the course of the tour, the newsmen drew Professor Chien and others into conversation to amplify information given in the briefing.

Tsinghua University is China's premier institution for engineering studies and had some 12,000 students before the Cultural Revolution. The university was founded early in this century and financed for many years with money paid by China to the United States as an indemnity for the Boxer Rebellion but returned for use in promoting Chinese higher education.

From late 1966 until late 1968, Tsinghua, like all other universities in the People's Republic, was in a state of turmoil. Classes were suspended as students became Chairman Mao Tsetung's spearhead in attacking individuals described as revisionists, bourgeois reactionaries and capitalist followers of the chief of state, Liu Shao-chi, who was purged from office early in the Cultural Revolution.

During this turmoil, most professors and high administrators at Tsinghua came under student attack.

They were charged with following a bourgeois and later a Soviet revisionist line in education, with aloofness from students and workers, with failing to integrate theory with practice, with making the higher educational process unnecessarily long and with spreading ideas that would lead the country to revisionism and eventually back to capitalism.

For two years many professors and administrators were intermittently brought before mass meetings to undergo criticism, confess the error of their ways and parade about wearing placards describing their deviations. A number were physically mistreated and many were sent to serve for long periods as workers in factories and on collective farms.

Ultimately the students split into factions and began to fight each other. Violence reached such a stage that Chairman Mao ordered worker-military detachments into Tsinghua and other schools to restore order.

Most students were sent to work on collective farms or in factories. Last year, when the army-worker teams had put university affairs in proper Maoist ideological order, classes resumed on a new basis: Workers, peasants and soldiers with years of practical experience and junior high school educations and above were brought into the higher educational institutions to start part study-part work programs. The new system called for two to three years of schooling that, in the case of technological establishments like Tsinghua, would stress practical applications of book knowledge.

Newsmen were told today that Tsinghua has 2,800 students with varying levels of lower education and 700 teachers and other staff members for studies in electricity, electronics, machine-building, chemical engineering and automotive engineering.

Tsinghua students, 20 per cent of them female, were said to spend 75 per cent of their time in classes studying technology, 10 per cent studying military affairs and working in agriculture and industry and 15 per cent in political studies centered on the thoughts of Chairman Mao.

Professor Chien, who said he had spent 1967 and 1968 being regularly "struggled" with at mass meetings and working in several different factories, praised the streamlining and elimination of unnecessary studies.

Speaking of himself, the rocketry specialist and professor of mechanics said that he was no longer called "Old Stubborn" by his students but was addressed as comrade. He added that he had no problem of discipline with students because he and they now "understood each other."

CHAPTER SIX
Science and Medicine

U.S. Biologists Tell
Of Scientific Gains

by Seymour Topping

SHANGHAI, May 23—Two American biologists who are completing a unique tour of Chinese Communist research establishments said today that they had become convinced that China had developed "a lot of important scientific information of which we are unaware."

The biologists are Dr. Arthur W. Galston, professor of biology at Yale University, and Dr. Ethan Signer, an associate professor of biology at Massachusetts Institute of Technology. Dr. Galston is a specialist in plant physiology and Dr. Signer in the genetics of bacterial viruses.

The two biologists, who are critics of the Vietnam war, are believed to be the first American scientists to visit this country in the last two decades and are certainly the first to be allowed into Chinese research establishments.

During their two-week visit they had a two-hour meeting with Premier Chou En-lai and visited the National Academy of Science in Peking and Peking University. They also toured Chung Shan University in Canton and Futan University in Shanghai. Dr. Galston said they had been given access to laboratories, libraries and conference rooms as well as to members of scientific staffs.

Interviewed in Shanghai before their departure for Canton and Hong Kong en route back to the United States, Dr. Signer said that the Chinese had provided "many indications they would look with favor on more exchanges of scientists."

Dr. Galston said that they had been given considerable data on Chinese advances in science.

The biologists said that in the field of genetics and the promotion of plant growth, for example, the Chinese had originated a method for mass-producing a substance known as gibberellin, which when sprayed on plants significantly increases crop yields. He said the substance was being produced on a large scale in communes, factories and at universities.

At Peking Hospital No. 3, one of the eight major hospitals in the capital, the two biologists witnessed and were allowed to photograph the use of acupuncture to anesthetize patients in four major operations.

Describing the Chinese-developed technique as "remarkable," Dr. Galston said they had observed tumors being removed while the patients remained fully conscious. In one operation, the woman at her request was shown an ovary cyst "as large as a baseball" immediately after it was removed from her body.

The method uses traditional acupuncture needles to probe at nerve points until the patient reports adequate numbness in that section of the body, enabling the operation to begin while the patient is conscious.

Electrical charges are used to keep the needles vibrating and to sustain the anesthetic effect.

Dr. Galston also said that they had become convinced that Western pharmacology had much to learn from traditional Chinese medicine.

The Americans reported that the National Academy of Science in Peking, which was closed during the Cultural Revolution of 1966–1968, had now been reorganized and was operating again. Officials at the academy told them that they would be delighted to send delegates to international scientific conferences but that they would refuse to attend any meeting attended by a representative of the Chinese Nationalists on Taiwan.

Dr. Signer said that on returning to the United States he and

Dr. Galston would stress that "more contacts with Chinese scientists would be of mutual benefit."

"We must also say" he continued, "that Chinese scientists admire us as the world leaders in science and they would be glad to accept advice and help if given in the right way. They would benefit from our technology tremendously."

The two scientists at first were apprehensive about the reception they might be given but were astounded when they were received with great warmth everywhere. The scientists applied for a Chinese visa during a 17-day visit to Hanoi, where they gave a series of lectures and seminars.

On arrival in China, Dr. Galston was welcomed by Dr. Loo Shih-wei, who returned to the mainland in about 1947 after completing his doctorate at California Institute of Technology in Pasadena while Dr. Galston was on the staff there. Dr. Loo is now at the Research Institute for plant physiology in Shanghai. He remained with the two scientists during their entire tour.

During their interview with Premier Chou, the two Americans were told by the Chinese leader that China was still a weak nation and had a tremendous job ahead to do at home.

Dr. Galston quoted him as having said that China had no desire to become a superpower or to post its soldiers abroad.

In Hanoi, Dr. Galston and Dr. Signer were received by Premier Pham Van Dong.

Dr. Galston said that the North Vietnamese were making important strides in education and public health. Despite the war, he said, the population was increasing at an annual rate of 2.8 per cent, or about 600,000 people a year. The two scientists said they found Hanoi calm, confident and determined to continue fighting till victory.

Doctors Explain ★
Limb-Saving Technique

by Tillman Durdin

SHANGHAI, April 22—Doctors at the No. 6 People's Hospital here say that they lead the world in reconnecting severed hands, arms and fingers.

"We have succeeded with dozens of cases," Dr. Chen Wei-tsung, the 42-year-old chief surgeon, told foreign newsmen taken to the hospital to learn about a technique that has been widely publicized around the world. "I have no reports that our achievements have been duplicated outside China."

Dr. Chen, a tall, round-faced man with long, slender fingers, and four other doctors told of the hospital's technique in the operations during a session that had more Maoist invocations than any the journalists had yet attended.

The newsmen are in Shanghai for a four-day stay as part of a look at China under Communism afforded by the recent Peking move permitting foreign correspondents to enter China in connection with visits by foreign table tennis teams.

Why the propaganda aspect was so prominent at the hospital was not clear. In his presentation, Dr. Chen spent almost half the time attributing accomplishments at the hospital to the correct revolutionary line of the Communist party Chairman, Mao Tse-tung; to the policy of going to the masses, repudiating revisionism and serving the people revitalized under the leadership of Chairman Mao during the Cultural Revolution, and to Chairman Mao's injunction to intellectuals to integrate with the working people in factories and on farms.

Dr. Chen is a member of the governing organ for Shanghai,

the Revolutionary Committee, which is headed by a Politburo member, Chang Chun-chiao. Dr. Chem is a 1954 graduate of Shanghai No. 2 Medical College.

Dr. Chen declined to be more specific about the number of fingers, hands and arms that his hospital had repaired than to say "dozens."

He said the No. 6 Hospital, a comprehensive establishment of medium size with 580 beds and 700 staff members housed in a former training institute for Christian missionaries, had pioneered the repair technique starting in 1963. He added that hospitals all over China had adopted the methods developed here.

Dr. Chen said the hospital had succeeded in successfully rejoining a hand to an arm 36 hours after it had been severed. Journalists were shown a farmer who was in an advanced stage of recovery. His hand had been sewn back 29 hours after it had been torn away.

A woman factory worker was produced who had lost four fingers in a factory accident. Doctors had been unable to sew back her little finger because of the smallness of its blood vessels, but the three other fingers had been rejoined and the woman shook hands all around with a vise-like grip.

Dr. Chen displayed needles and nylon thread used in rejoining severed blood vessels. They were almost invisible to the naked eye. He said they were made in Shanghai.

Dr. Chen said he had determined to try rejoining severed elements after he worked in factories to broaden his outlook after graduation from medical college.

"I determined to do something to serve the workers," he stated.

He reported "the law" of such mending was developed by experimenting with sewing severed blood vessels in rabbits' ears. He said the most important factors of success with humans was the rapid sewing together of blood vessels and the growing together of nerves.

Doctor Chen said the hospital has been "60 to 70 per cent

successful" in the restoration of full use of severed fingers, but he pointed out that restoration to full use always depended on how much crushing and mangling there had been.

He said it was possible to restore parts that had been severed for 70 to 80 hours if they had been kept refrigerated since severance.

Doctors at the hospital reported they had all done a year of "hsiafang," that is, going down to work among the peasants in the countryside, and acted in accordance with the policy that doctors should occasionally change work with nurses and lower personnel in the hospital.

"A doctor ought to know how to do other things in medicine besides his own specialty," one doctor said and the others agreed. "A doctor who has to depend on a nurse to give an injection lacks ability," he said.

Doctors at the hospital said that since the Cultural Revolution the old approach of the full-fledged doctors being superior to the rest of the staff and of keeping their knowledge to themselves had ended.

"They now share freely with the younger doctors and these are given the opportunity to put forward their views and do the main operations," a young doctor said. "Nurses are also given the opportunity to do some simple operations under the supervision of the doctors."

The doctors said medical hospitals in Shanghai had dropped unnecessary courses since the Cultural Revolution and now turned out graduates in three to four years, compared with four to six years in the past.

They said, for example, that mathematics had been eliminated as a course at medical colleges. They stated that if it was felt that math was needed for research purposes, selected students could return to learn it after graduation and a period of practical work.

They said efforts in the Chinese medical service were directed at turning out large numbers of medical personnel with practical qualifications rather than with the top-level education of college graduates. They said the hospital and medical schools now concentrated on producing a large number of these practical medical workers such as "barefoot" doctors who work in the fields while treating the peasants for illnesses.

Footnote

Surgeons at the Massachusetts General Hospital in Boston successfully reconnected a severed human limb in 1962, one year before Dr. Chen said Shanghai doctors had performed similar operations.

When the Boston surgeons reconnected the severed right arm of 12-year-old Everett Knowles Jr. nine years ago, the operation was reported widely in the world press. The case was reported in the Journal of the American Medical Association in 1964.

The youth's reconnected arm still functions, said Dr. William H. Harris, one of the surgeons involved, in a telephone interview from Boston last night.

Since that operation, Dr. Harris said that Massachusetts General Hospital surgeons had reconnected severed limbs for five other patients. The last such operation was performed three years ago.

The cost of this kind of surgery varies. In one instance, Dr. Harris said, a patient's bill was $11,000 for a series of operations that involved reconnecting a limb, later repairing tendons and nerves and finally some skin grafts.

Tientsin Doctor ★
Says His Needles
Cure Many Ills

by Tillman Durdin

TIENTSIN, China, April 24—The husky young woman, a weaver at the No. 1 Tientsin Carpet Factory, lay watching placidly as Dr. Nyi Fu-jung pulled 12 acupunture needles from her stomach, left leg and knee joint.

"I feel much better," she said as she got up from the bed and rearranged her padded trousers and jacket. "It didn't hurt at all."

She had just undergone treatment for a stomach-ache in the factory clinic and Dr. Nyi was showing her off as living evidence of the effectiveness of the acupuncture therapy he uses extensively as a member of the clinic's medical staff.

The woman weaver, it developed, would normally have taken medicine for her stomach-ache, but she wanted quick relief and so asked for acupuncture instead.

Her request reflected the widespread present-day popularity of a medical technique practiced in China for more than 1,000 years and in recent years emphasized more strongly than ever by the Chinese Communist Government.

The 49-year-old Dr. Nyi, who became an acupuncturist 20 years ago after taking a one-year course in a technical school for doctors, turned out to be a strong defender of needle therapy not only for stomach pains and diseases but for arthritis, headaches, paralysis, rheumatism, heart palpitations, ailments of the nose and eyes, nervous disorders, mental illness and even blindness.

"Yes, certainly," he replied when asked if he could cure a hangover.

He also said that acupuncturists were experimenting with

ways to prevent pregnancy and contribute to birth control in China, but he said that techniques in this field had not yet been perfected.

Dr. Nyi exemplified the wide development and use of acupuncture in the Chinese People's Republic, particularly since the Great Proletarian Cultural Revolution. There are more practitioners of the ancient technique than of Western-style medicine and great claims have been made as to its effectiveness in curing the blind, the deaf, the lame and sufferers from many less serious afflictions.

Institutes have been established to study the scientific basis for its effectiveness and to develop it further.

Visiting newsmen were told at a pharmaceutical exhibition in Shanghai that many new points on the body had been found where needles could be inserted with therapeutic effect and had been added to the old points, already running into the scores.

Dr. Nyi said that the effectiveness of acupuncture resulted from a stimulation of the nerves.

Doctors in China trained in Western-type medicine are reported not to be depreciating acupuncture any longer, as they did in the past, and practitioners of Western medicine and acupuncture cooperate to use both systems to best effect.

Since acupuncture requires less training than Western medicine, China's millions of new short-course "barefoot" doctors use acupuncture extensively.

Dr. Nyi, a stocky, athletic man who wore a white smock, conceded that more of the 1,200 workers at the factory took medicine than resorted to acupuncture, but he said acupuncture was "very popular." He did not say whether cures were permanent or indicate in how many cases he had experienced failure.

The clinic for the factory, which makes the thick, colorful traditional style Tientsin woolen carpets, has a staff of two Chinese-style and two Western-style doctors and four nurses. They work in a big, rambling, crudely but neatly furnished one-story brick building devoted mainly to rooms where babies of working mothers, who make up almost half the factory personnel, are brought for daytime care.

The head nurse, Sung Ai-wu, said that 60 per cent of the married women at the factory took birth control pills that she said had been developed in China and were different from any used abroad. She could not give the chemical formula but said that the pills were a composition of norlutine.

She stated that women took the norlutine pills for 22 days every month and that the pills, like all other medicines and treatment at the clinic, were free to the factory's workers. She said that the pills had been in use since 1966.

Acupuncture Aids Deaf Children

by Audrey Topping

PEKING, June 21—Yeh Nu-hsu, 16 years old, looks like a typical Peking teen-ager. She is bright-eyed and alert but speaks haltingly. "Until one year and a half ago," she said, "I was deaf and mute."

Miss Yeh spoke at the Peking No. 3 School for deaf mutes, who are being treated by doctors with the ancient Chinese method of acupuncture—the puncturing of various nerve points with needles. Miss Yeh and her 14-year-old sister are among the 238 pupils at the school.

The doctors say they have been successful in 90 per cent of the cases where the affliction is a result of a childhood disease. In the last two years, according to the doctors, they have sent 11 completely cured children into ordinary schools, where they are treated as normal children.

There are three other schools for deaf mutes in Peking, and there are also said to be similar schools in every province.

Wang Chen-ying, a member of the school's propaganda team, said use of acupuncture to treat deafness was discovered in 1968 by an army medical team in northeast China. He said its members located the nerve points that affect hearing after repeated experiments on themselves.

Teams were then sent all over China to set up schools and introduce the new methods into existing schools.

Fang Shou-suan, an army doctor, said that if deafness can be cured, the students can be taught to speak. Language teaching is 70 per cent of the treatment, he said.

"Acupuncture spurs the nerve system and adjusts the hearing nerve." Dr. Fang says, "We use several points. The acupuncture points near the ears have quick but temporary effects while the points farther away, as in the arms and hands, have a slower but permanent effect."

This writer toured some of the classrooms. The students ranged from 8 to 22 years of age and are divided into classes of 12, according to their ages and abilities.

The rooms are airy with windows on two sides. A blackboard covers the front wall and a portrait of Chairman Mao Tse-tung and displays of his sayings are on the opposite wall.

A warm relationship was apparent between the students and teachers, who spoke of the importance of encouraging each child individually.

The classes are divided into four main categories. First are classes for the new students. Here they use finger language and charts to explain the treatment process in store for the children. In the second category they give the acupuncture treatments and test the hearing nerves for response. In the third, students are taught the basic sounds. Fourth are language classes where the students are taught to speak.

In both the third and fourth types of classes mathematics, science and history are taught and the students are encouraged to reply orally.

In the acupuncture room the teacher and an army medical aide inserted long needles near the ears and into the arms of the children. The insertion appeared to be painless. The needle is twisted by hand until the nerve is stimulated and the child utters a little cry.

Dr. Fang said the students first undergo a 10-day course of treatments and then rest for seven days.

"For the first course we have a special set of points," he said. "Then we check the progress report and another set, depending on the results, is plotted for the second course."

"On some students, the effect is quick, and we get good results in six months," he continued. "Most cases take about a year, and in some cases, where the deafness was caused by brain injury or inflammation, it is very difficult."

He added that the treatment was usually more effective on younger students but that he and his colleagues attempted to cure all ages.

Dr. Fang said they were still carrying out research and experiments in an attempt to achieve better results.

"If we can get the child to hear from a distance of 3 meters, we know it will be all right," he said. "We then carry on until the hearing reaches 20 meters. Then we stop acupuncture and concentrate on teaching them to speak."

Acupuncture ★
Used as Anesthetic
In Heart Surgery

by Audrey Topping

WUHAN, China, May 12—Dr. Chu Yu-kuang, a surgeon, had just spent 13 minutes removing a tumor from the throat of a 54-year-old woman. Seconds after the last suture was tied, she sat up and ate an orange. Then she put on her robe, thanked the doctor and walked out of the operating room. On the way she stopped to wave and smile at the amazed observers.

In an adjoining operating room, a 33-year-old woman was undergoing open-heart surgery. While the surgeon held her heart in his hand she was fully conscious. She drank some orange juice through a straw and smiled at the onlookers.

The only anesthetic used in both operations was Chinese acupuncture needles.

Acupuncture has been used in China to treat ailments for more than 1,000 years. Only recently, however, has it been used as an anesthetic for surgery.

We witnessed the operations through observation domes in Wuhan Hospital. Prof. Chu Fa-tzu, head of the surgical department, explained the procedures to a small group of Canadian visitors.

Acupuncturists had inserted the needles into the patients' wrists 20 minutes before Professor Chu explained that the needles had been inserted into the nerve centers controlling the areas concerned.

The tumor patient had two needles in each wrist while the heart patient had an additional one in each forearm. One acupuncturist at each wrist was constantly twisting the needles.

302

The patient informs the doctor when numbness sets in. It usually takes 20 to 30 minutes.

As the surgeon made an incision in the throat of the fully conscious woman, she never twitched. While Dr. Chu Yu-kuang proceeded with the removal of the tumor, the visitors watched preparations for the open-heart surgery.

Professor Chu said that the objective of the operation was to enlarge the valve between the left auricle and the left ventricle of the heart.

After the chest incision, the removal of a rib and some tissue, the heart was exposed. It seemed to be beating very fast. Oxygen was given to the patient. Professor Chu explained that after the opening of the chest the atmospheric pressure made the patient feel unwell. Gauze dipped in a Chinese herbal medicine was used to prevent bleeding.

The surgeon picked up the patient's beating heart and held it in his hand. An attendant walked into the room with orange sections in a glass bowl and offered them to the patient. She smiled and refused but took a sip of juice through a straw.

Asked to explain how acupuncture works, Professor Chu said: "It is very difficult to explain exactly what happens. There are about 500 nerve points in the body that we know we can use. We know the results we will get, but we cannot explain exactly why we get them."

Now, About My Operation in Peking

by James Reston

PEKING, July 25—There is something a little absurd about a man publishing an obituary notice on his own appendix, but for the last 10 days this correspondent has had a chance to learn a little about the professional and political direction of a major Chinese hospital from the inside, and this is a report on how I got there and what I found.

In brief summary, the facts are that with the assistance of 11 of the leading medical specialists in Peking, who were asked by Premier Chou En-lai to cooperate on the case, Prof. Wu Wei-jan of the Anti-Imperialist Hospital's surgical staff removed my appendix on July 17 after a normal injection of Xylocain and Benzocain, which anesthetized the middle of my body.

There were no complications, nausea or vomiting. I was conscious throughout, followed the instructions of Professor Wu as translated to me by Ma Yu-chen of the Chinese Foreign Ministry during the operation, and was back in my bedroom in the hospital in two and a half hours.

However, I was in considerable discomfort if not pain during the second night after the operation, and Li Chang-yuan, doctor of acupuncture at the hospital, with my approval, inserted three long, thin needles into the outer part of my right elbow and below my knees and manipulated them in order to stimulate the intestine and relieve the pressure and distension of the stomach.

That sent ripples of pain racing through my limbs and, at least, had the effect of diverting my attention from the distress in

304

my stomach. Meanwhile, Doctor Li lit two pieces of an herb called ai, which looked like the burning stumps of a broken cheap cigar, and held them close to my abdomen while occasionally twirling the needles into action.

All this took about 20 minutes, during which I remember thinking that it was rather a complicated way to get rid of gas on the stomach, but there was a noticeable relaxation of the pressure and distension within an hour and no recurrence of the problem thereafter.

I will return to the theory and controversy over this needle and of herbal medicine later. Meanwhile, a couple of disclaimers.

Judging from the cables reaching me here, recent reports and claims of remarkable cures of blindness, paralysis and mental disorders by acupuncture have apparently led to considerable speculation in America about great new medical breakthroughs in the field of traditional Chinese needle and herbal medicine. I do not know whether this speculation is justified, and am not qualified to judge.

On the other side, it has been suggested that maybe this whole accidental experience of mine, or at least the acupuncture part of it, was a journalistic trick to learn something about needle anesthesia. This is not only untrue but greatly overrates my gifts of imagination, courage and self-sacrifice. There are many things I will do for a good story, but getting slit open in the night or offering myself as an experimental porcupine is not among them.

Without a single shred of supporting medical evidence, I trace my attack of acute appendicitis to Henry A. Kissinger of the White House staff. He arrived in China on July 9. My wife and I arrived in South China the day before, just in time.

But when we reached Canton we were told by our official guide that there had been a change in our plans. We were to remain in the Canton area for two days and proceed by rail to Peking on the evening of the 10th, arriving in the capital on the morning of the 12th. We demurred and asked to fly to Peking at once, but we were told it was out of the question.

Three days later, at precisely 10:30 A.M., while I was describing to several Foreign Ministry officials at the Peking International Club the unquestionable advantages of my interviewing Chairman Mao Tse-tung, Premier Chou and every other prominent official I could think of, Chen Chu, the head of the ministry's information service, interrupted to say that he had "a little news item."

Mr. Kissinger had been in Peking from July 9 to July 11, he said, and it was now being announced here and in the United States that President Nixon would visit Peking before May.

At that precise moment, or so it now seems, the first stab of pain went through my groin. By evening I had a temperature of 103, and in my delirium I could see Mr. Kissinger floating across my bedroom ceiling grinning at me out of the corner of a hooded rickshaw.

The next day I checked into the Anti-Imperialist Hospital, a cluster of gray brick buildings with green-tiled roofs behind high walls in the middle of Peking.

The hospital had been established by the Rockefeller Foundation of New York in 1916 and supported by it, first as the Union Medical College in Peking and later as the Peking Union Medical College.

By coincidence I had had a letter before leaving New York from Dr. Oliver McCoy, president of the China Medical Board of New York, explaining that his organization had been responsible for building and running the hospital with Rockefeller money until it was nationalized by the Communist Government in January, 1951. Dr. McCoy said that if we should happen to notice "a large group of buildings with green-tiled roofs not far from the southeast corner of the Forbidden City, it might be interesting to inquire what those were." It is interesting indeed.

My wife and I were taken to Building No. 5, which is the

wing used to serve the Western diplomatic corps and their families. On the right of the entrance was a large sign quoting Chairman Mao (it was removed during our stay). "The time will not be far off," it said, "when all the aggressors and their running dogs in the world will be buried. There is certainly no escape for them."

We were taken at once by elevator to the third floor and installed in a suite of plain but comfortable rooms with large light-blue-bordered scrolls of Chairman Mao's poems on the walls and tall windows overlooking a garden filled with cedars. It was a blazing hot and humid evening, with the temperature at 95, but a revolving fan at least stirred the air. I stripped and went to bed.

A few minutes later the two doctors who had originally called on me at the Hsin Chiao Hotel came in and said they had arranged some tests. They were Prof. Li Pang-chi, a calm and kindly man who was the "responsible person" for the case, and Chu Yu, a visiting surgeon and lecturer at the Anti-Imperialist Hospital.

Professor Li, who understood and spoke a little English, explained that other doctors would examine me later and that there would be consultations about what was to be done.

A parade of nurses and technicians then slipped quietly into the room. They bathed me with warm towels. They checked everything I had that moved or ticked. They took blood out of the lobe of my ear. They took my temperature constantly, measured pulse and blood pressure and worried over a cardiogram showing a slightly irregular heartbeat. They were meticulous, calm and unfailingly gentle and cheerful.

An hour later the consultants summoned by Premier Chou arrived; surgeons, heart specialists, anesthetists, members of the hospital's Revolutionary Committee, or governing body. Each in turn listened to the offending heartbeat.

I felt like a beached white whale at a medical convention and was relieved when they finally retired for consultation and returned with the verdict: "Acute appendicitis. Should be operated on as soon as possible."

They sought my decision. It did not seem the time to ask for a raincheck.

Accordingly, at a little after 8:30 in the evening they rolled me through the dim, hot corridors to an air-conditioned operating theater and Dr. Wu Wei-jan, a remarkably bright and lively man with a quick intelligence and a compelling smile, took over. He bound me tightly but comfortably on the operating table, put a small iron stand with a towel over my head, so that I could look backward to the interpreter but not forward, and then pumped the area anesthetic by needle into my back.

Everything was roses after that. I was back in my room talking with my wife by 11. The doctors came by to reassure me that all had gone well and show me the nasty little garbage bag they had removed. They asked my interpreter, Chin Kuei-hua, to remain at the hospital, gave me an injection to relieve the pain and lit a little spiral of incense to perfume the room for the night.

Since then I have lived with the rhythm of what must be the quietest city hospital in the world, constantly regaining strength and acquiring an intense curiosity about the politics and medical philosophy of the doctors in attendance.

They insist that the two cannot be separated and they are quite frank in saying that the sole purpose of their profession since the Cultural Revolution of 1966–1969 is to serve all the people of China, 80 per cent of whom live on the land.

For this purpose medical education and medical procedures have been transformed. The doctors at the Anti-Imperialist Hospital make an average of about 150 yuan, or $65, a month and take their turn for six months or more, training barefoot doctors in rural farm and industrial communes. The aim is to prepare a medical army of young men and women for public-health service all over the People's Republic as fast as possible. Their training begins with political indoctrination in the thoughts of Chairman Mao.

309 JAMES RESTON

The Anti-Imperialist Hospital is run by a four-man Revolutionary Committee—Tung Teo, chairman, and his deputies, Huang Chung-li, Shen Pao-hung and Tsui Ching-yi—two of whom are qualified physicians and two of whom are not.

They meet with the professional staff of the hospital constantly for discussion of the philosophy of Chairman Mao and for common criticism of each other and their work, and they discuss the procedures with the zeal of religious fanatics, constantly repeating, as in a litany, the need to improve their work and their moral purpose in the service of the state.

To understand the urgency of China's medical problem and its emphasis on the quantity rather than the quality of medical training, it is necessary to understand the problem's scope. Edgar Snow quotes Dr. William Chen, a senior surgeon of the United States Public Health Service, as saying that before the Communists took over this country in 1949, four million people died every year from infectious and parasitic diseases and that 84 per cent of the population in the rural areas were incapable of paying for private medical care even when it was available from the 12,000 scientifically trained doctors.

That helps explain the current emphasis on rapid expansion of the medical corps and the determination of the Government to increase the use of herbal medicine and acupuncture.

Dr. Li Chang-yuan, who used needle and herbal medicine on me, did not go to medical college. He is 36 years old and learned his craft as an apprentice to a veteran acupuncturist here at the hospital. Like most young apprentices in this field, thousands of whom are being trained, he practiced for years with the needles on his own body. "It is better to wound yourself a thousand times than to do a single harm to another person," he said solemnly.

The other doctors watched him manipulate the needles in my body and then circle his burning herbs over my abdomen with obvious respect. Prof. Li Pang-chi said later that he had not been a believer in the use of acupuncture techniques "but a fact is a fact—there are many things they can do."

Prof. Chen Hsien-jiu of the surgery department of the hospital said that he had studied the effects of acupuncture in overcoming post-operative constipation by putting barium in a patient's stomach and observing on a fluoroscope how needle manipulation in the limbs produced movement and relief in the intestines.

Even the advocates of Western medicine believe that necessity has forced innovation and effective development of traditional techniques.

Mr. Snow quotes Dr. Hsu Hung-tu, a former deputy director of the hospital, as saying: "Diseases have inner and outer causes. The higher nervous system of the brain affects the general physiology."

Professor Li said that despite his reservations he had come to believe in the theory that the body is an organic unity, that illness can be caused by imbalances between organs and that stimulation from acupuncture can help restore balance by removing the causes of congestion or antagonism.

The controlled Chinese press is reporting on cases that go well beyond the relief of pain in the gastrointestinal tract and illnesses of the nervous system or those of neurological origin. It is reporting not only successes in treating paralysis and arthritis but spectacular results in curing blindness and deafness.

While I have no way of knowing the validity of the reports, the faith even of the professionally qualified doctors at the Anti-Imperialist Hospital is impressive. Maoism itself has obviously become an infectious disease, even among many of the well-educated urban citizens who had a hard time during the Cultural Revolution.

"We are just at the beginning of all this," Professor Li said as he prepared to unstitch me and set me free. "We have gone through great changes in this hospital. We are now treating between 2,500 and 3,000 patients here every day—over a hundred of them by acupuncture for everything from severe headaches to arthritis—and we are learning more about the possibilities all the time."

I leave with a sense of gratitude and regret. Despite its name and all the bitter political slogans on the walls, the hospital is an intensely human and vibrant institution. It is not exactly what the Rockefeller Foundation had in mind when it created the Peking Union Medical College, but like everything else in China these days, it is on its way toward some different combination of the very old and the very new.

Mao's Poem Urges Drive on Snail Fever

by Sally Reston

PEKING, July 29—Snail fever, a parasitic disease related to the use of human excrement as fertilizer, is China's most serious health problem, according to doctors in Peking's Anti-Imperialist Hospital.

Known as schistosomiasis, the disease has killed untold thousands. It rages the entire length of the Yangtze and its tributaries, sometimes wiping out entire villages.

So widespread is the disease that Chairman Mao Tse-tung

has written a poem on the subject and called upon the people to mount an attack against it.

Snails living along the banks of the creeks, ditches and canals are the hosts for the parasites, which start in human excrement. Working in rice paddies and other irrigated fields, peasants pick up the parasites through their skin. For a short period they run a high fever, and this is followed by enlargement of the spleen, fluid in the stomach, and finally cirrhosis of the liver.

Antimony can cure the disease, but only in the brief period of initial fever. Prevention is being tried—teams of young people spray the banks of waterways to kill the snails.

Unfortunately, children are the most frequent victims and carriers of the disease because they like to play in the water—especially this summer when China has been sweltering in its worst heat wave in 16 years.

Domestic animals also die of snail fever because excrement is used as fertilizer for crops that the animals eat.

At a large commune north of Peking that supplies the city with vegetables, poultry and milk, the chairman of the Revolutionary Committee explained the use of wastes at his project.

The city of Peking delivers to him 2,000 tons of human excrement a year, which is processed into pellets for field fertilizer. Sewage water from Peking is piped into the commune reservoir for distribution through the irrigation ditches. There is no problem, however, with snail fever this far north of the Yangtze. The citizens of Peking look remarkably strong and healthy.

Eradication of the disease in the Yangtze Valley is complicated because there "it is a question of control of all sewage," Dr. Li Pang-chi, one of Peking's leading physicians, explained. "Human excrement must be sterilized before use for fertilizer."

Nevertheless, several country districts have managed to rid themselves of the scourge by storing the excrement, covering it with mud and allowing it to ferment long enough to kill all the parasites.

Chairman Mao took note of this success and wrote about the problem; "after reading in The People's Daily of how schistosomiasis was wiped out in Yukiang County, so many fancies crossed my mind that I could not sleep. In the warm morning breeze, as sunlight fell on my window, I looked toward the distant southern sky and in my happiness wrote the following lines." Chairman Mao's poem, "Farewell to the God of Plague," refers to a famous physician, Hua To, and to two mythical emperors, Yao and Shun. The poem follows:

> *Green Streams, blue hills—but all to what avail?*
> *This tiny germ left even Hua To powerless;*
> *Weeds choked hundreds of villages, men wasted away;*
> *Thousands of households dwindled, phantoms sang*
>   *with glee.*
> *On earth I travel eighty thousand li a day,*
> *Ranging the sky I see myriad rivers.*
> *Should the cowherd ask tidings of the God of Plague,*
> *Say: Past joys and woe have vanished with the waves.*
>
> *The spring wind blows amid ten thousand willow*
>   *branches,*
> *Six hundred million in this sacred land all equal Yao*
>   *and Shun.*
> *Flowers falling like crimson rain swirl in waves at will,*
> *Green mountains turn to bridges at our wish;*
> *Gleaming mattocks fall on heaven-high peaks;*
> *Mighty arms move rivers, rock the earth.*
> *We ask the God of Plague: Where are you bound?*
> *Paper barges aflame and candlelight illuminate the*
>   *sky.*

Despite the seriousness, complexity and magnitude of snail fever, Peking doctors are hopeful about China's chances to control it. They point to their success in wiping out kala azar, another parasitic disease carried by flies.

Kala azar packed hospital wards and left "hundreds of thousands of peasants dead in the villages and fields," the doctors say. "Now," said Dr. Li, "we may see only one case in several years." Cholera, typhoid and typhus, the doctors say, have also been wiped out.

Faith in Mao Is Part of the Cure

by James Reston

SHANGHAI, Aug. 21—In the present delicate state of Chinese-American relations, one problem is that the few Americans permitted to visit here are not qualified to judge or even understand many of the things they are shown. China's use of needles instead of drugs as anesthetic in major surgery is only an illustration of the problem, but pending the day when experts are allowed to come back to China, the amateurs will have to report as best they can.

My wife and I spent four hours yesterday at the Hun Shan Hospital in the middle of Shanghai. This was formerly the Chinese Red Cross Hospital and is now the center of experimentation with acupuncture in Chinese brain surgery.

We were properly sterilized and not only allowed into the operating theater, but urged to talk to two patients while they were undergoing surgery for the removal of tumors of the brain.

They were anesthetized merely by the insertion of very thin three-inch stainless steel needles into the body—usually with one needle inserted into the web of flesh—or, as the Chinese surgeon called it, "the joined valley" between the thumb and forefinger—and they were not only perfectly conscious while their skulls were laid open before us but remarkably alert within half an hour after the operations.

The first patient was a 41-year-old worker from the Taching oil field named Wang. He kept up a conversation with Dr. Chiang Ta-chieh, his surgeon, while the doctor made the incision for the removal of a small tumor in the occipital-parietal lobes of the brain.

The second patient was a 54-year-old man named Chuan Liao, who had been suffering from epilepsy as a result of a rather large tumor in the frontal lobe of the brain. He seemed sensibly puzzled by being introduced to a couple of American strangers during his ordeal but was courteous and patient, and we listened to his comments while the tumor was removed and even watched him eat orange slices and ask for more while the operation was going on.

We were also shown a subtotal thyroidectomy on a 47-year-old woman, the excision of a cystic tumor of the submaxillary gland on a 13-year-old girl, who got up from the operating table and walked to her room, and a major operation for the removal of the tubercular right lung and one rib from a 24-year-old man named Chen Chien.

In some ways, the operation on Chen Chien seemed even more astonishing than the brain surgery. His only anesthetic was a single needle inserted in his right shoulder at an acupuncture point identified by the surgeon as Pi Ju. He lay on his stomach with a vast gaping hole in his back, through which you could see the gasping of the remaining lung, but was wholly conscious through the ordeal, talked quietly and coherently in answer to questions and, like the epileptic patient, ate fruit while receiving blood transfusions.

It is very hard for any nonprofessional to sort all this out. Even the Chinese doctors are divided about how acupuncture works and are actually arguing out different theories in the Chinese official journals.

The old traditional Chinese medical theory is that there is a "channel" in the body and that the critical acupuncture points are fixed by this channel. The modern Chinese doctors, who approached this whole subject with considerable skepticism, reject the traditional channel theory and are more inclined to believe in the theory that there are certain nerve centers that govern feeling and can be affected by needle penetration.

The interesting thing here, however, is that, while they cannot agree on the theory of how needle anesthesia works, they are increasingly convinced that it does work, and they are operating on the pragmatic evidence and not waiting for theoretical justifications.

One troubling diversion in all this for a visitor is that the impressive objective evidence of the medical uses of acupuncture is always mixed up here with subjective psychiatric and even ideological explanations.

For example, all the patients we saw on the operating table were clutching their little red books of Chairman Mao Tse-tung's philosophic and moral teachings. And the doctors and surgeons, after participating in the operations, were explaining that the success of this system depended importantly on trust between doctor and patient and on a common faith in "Mao Tse-tung thought."

Dr. Chu Hsi-chi, the "responsible person" at the Hun Shan Hospital, explained that he always had careful philosophic and ideological discussions with patients before their operations. Faith and trust were important to the success of the whole system, he said.

Aside from this, however, there is enough objective evidence of practical medical information in the use of acupuncture to justify exploration by somebody more scientific than newspaper reporters.

The Chinese Government is a long way from agreeing with the United States Government on international political questions, but it is fairly close to agreeing that there should be a much wider exchange of nongovernment personnel and non-security information. The doctors and public health officials here are clearly persuaded that needle anesthesia is effective, particularly on the upper part of the human body, and that it is cheaper, safer and less subject to postoperative complications.

Also, Chinese officials, like Chinese doctors, make a great deal of wanting to help the whole human family. So maybe the time has come to get some serious medical exchange going between Washington and Peking. Something is really going on here, and it is clearly too important to be left to newspaper reporters.

CHAPTER SEVEN

Culture After
the Cultural Revolution

Traditional Art
Turned Out for Export

by Audrey Topping

PEKING—Centuries-old traditional crafts and modern propagandistic art are produced side by side in the arts and crafts factory in Peking. The emphasis for export is on the traditional, while the propaganda is more for local consumption. Peking has long been noted and respected for making the highest quality art goods in China and when Chinese crafts are purchased anywhere in the world, the fact that an article was made in Peking serves to assure the quality and raise the price. The Peking factory is the only one in China that carries on all the traditional crafts. It produces lacquer-ware of all kinds, cloisonné, carvings in jade, quartz, soapstone and other stones, ivory carvings, inlaid screens and chests and intricately painted furniture.

These crafts have been produced in China for more than 30 centuries, but now some of the traditional crafts have new subjects.

"Before the Cultural Revolution," said the factory commissar, "the traitor Liu Shao-chi adopted a revisionist line and there was one in this factory, too." Mr. Liu is the former chief of state, now purged.

"The workers produced things about the emperors and they were in the service of bourgeois revisionists," the commissar said. "But the workers rose up, criticized the revisionist line and now we have art that reflects the life of the worker."

The best-known example of the new subjects is an ivory carving called "Ten Thousand Ships." It depicts the workers building ships and is carved out of one long tusk. Other carvings show recent construction such as the huge new bridge across the Yangtze River at Nanking. They also depict heroic peasants and soldiers.

The newly made cloisonné vases and bowls are brightly colored compared to old ones. "This reflects our new spirit," the commissar said.

At a short briefing before a tour of the factory, the gentle-looking commissar told of the misery of the artisans' lives before the "liberation."

"They were poor and ill-fed," he said. "Many were forced to leave their crafts. After the liberation, and under Chairman Mao's directive, the workers were organized into cooperatives.

"Now their political consciousness and status have been raised and they are masters. We use electricity instead of coal. The work is less but the production is more."

The factory has 820 workers, of whom a third are women. The group of foreign visitors was taken through the rather dimly lit rooms, each decorated with a large poster of Chairman Mao Tse-tung, where the workers sit at long tables. They work an eight-hour day and are required to rest their eyes for 10 minutes every two hours.

The monthly wages range from 30 yuan ($12.60) to 100 yuan ($42), according to the age and skill of the worker.

Wan Su-ming, an attractive middle-aged woman, has worked in the factory as an ivory carver for more than 10 years. She began as a paid apprentice and now earns 40 yuan a month. She and her husband, who also works, live in Peking.

One of the older workers in the factory is Chi Te-jen, 55, who has done ivory carving since 1938, 11 years before the Communists came to power in mainland China. He said that in the old days he never had had enough to eat and lived from hand to mouth, hoping someone would buy a carving.

"Now I make 100 yuan a month and have security," he said.

Artisans Produce Heroic Figures For Propaganda

by Tillman Durdin

CANTON—The traditional shapes and designs that over the centuries made Shekwan porcelain objects highly prized art have been discarded at the famous 800-year-old Shekwan kilns at Foshan, in southeast China, 20 miles outside Canton. Instead, the porcelain workers at Shekwan serve the cause of Communist China's revolution by making utilitarian dishes for peasant households and garishly colored statuettes of heroic figures that have emerged in Maoist propaganda in recent years. A product just designed at one Shekwan porcelain factory but not yet in production is a statuette 12 inches high showing three handsome, muscular American workers, two blacks and a white man, standing together with clenched fists and gazing defiantly ahead. One has a foot planted on a crate that reads "U S A" upside down on one side, and one holds high a plaque that says "on strike."

"We were inspired to design this by Chairman Mao's declaration supporting the struggle of the American Negro," a worker at the factory told foreign newsmen taken out to inspect the operations.

He was referring to a statement by Chairman Mao Tse-tung several years ago that lauded the demands of United States blacks for their rights and pledged Communist China's backing for their cause.

The group will be in production by the end of the month and on sale abroad, where much of the factory's products are

323

marketed. Chinese Communist retail outlets sell Shekwan figurines in Hong Kong and throughout Southeast Asia.

The American worker group will cost $2 in Communist stores. It will be available on shelves filled with other Shekwan figurines—likenesses of Yang Tse-jung, a hero in a popular Communist opera, of a labor hero, Lei Feng, of the brave soldier who died saving others from a wild horse, of buxom peasant girls and broad-shouldered peasant boys and of Norman Bethune, the Canadian doctor who died doing medical work in Chinese Communist territory during the Japanese war.

One standard product of the factory for some years has been a group of figurines called "Rent Collection Courtyard." Made from a Peking design, the figurines show peasants in the courtyard of a mean, miserly landlord before the revolution, being beaten and otherwise mistreated as the landlord extracts rental payments from them. Shao Cheng, chairman of the Revolutionary Committee of the Shekwan art potters factory, said more than 100 sets of "Rent Collection Courtyard" made in Shekwan were now on display in various places in China.

Before the Communist take-over of China, Shekwan was famous for its crackle glaze porcelain and its realistically designed statuettes showing mythological Buddhist and Taoist saints and depicting characters from such classical Chinese novels as "Dream of the Red Chamber."

Centuries ago Shekwan pottery was exported to Southeast Asian countries and today is highly prized when dug from buried sites in the Philippines, Indonesia and elsewhere.

The art pottery factory is only one of several in the Shekwan area. Others make dishes and big earthen jars.

Four years ago the art pottery factory had dropped everything else and was making busts of Chairman Mao by the thousands. Its shift away from that production may indicate that the Mao bust market has been fully supplied for the time being.

Popular Ballet Is Reminiscent of 'Uncle Tom's Cabin'

★

by Tillman Durdin

TIENTSIN, April 24—Take the story of "Uncle Tom's Cabin" and make it into a ballet with a Chinese setting and Chinese characters and you have roughly the equivalent of the most popular theater piece now playing in the People's Republic of China.

The ballet is called "The White-Haired Girl" and, as presented in Shanghai to a packed audience that included a visiting group of foreign journalists, it turned out to be entrancing entertainment.

The score, written in conventional Western form and played by a Western-style orchestra, is light and tuneful and the choreography and vigorous acting carry the simple story along so easily and convincingly that even a Westerner finds it easy to understand and enjoy.

The leading ballerina, Mao Hui-fang, executes no virtuoso leaps or turns but she dances with such grace and elegance as to be a sheer delight.

Her big scene is late in the ballet. In what must be a physically exhausting episode, she depicts the torment of a pursued girl who braves storms and wild beasts after fleeing bondage in the home of a lecherous landlord.

Lin Kuei-ming is less pleasing as the leading man. His dancing is adequate but his acting somewhat wooden.

The standard plot is prescribed by the propaganda focus of the ruling Communist regime in China. A landlord in pre-Communist times mistreats his tenants. When an old peasant, Yang

Pai-lao, tries to prevent him from seizing his daughter, he is beaten to death.

The daughter, Shih Erh, is taken but after a period in the landlord's home manages to escape. For years she eludes capture by living in desolate hills and coping with snow, storms and wild animals. During this period her hair turns white.

Meanwhile, Wang Ta-chuan, her young lover from her home village, has revolted against the old system that produced landlords and has joined the Communist Eighth Route Army. Wang's unit eventually discovers Shih Erh and everyone joins the Communist forces to fight for liberation as a great Maoist sun rises over the hills to herald a new day.

Needless to say, the evil landlord gets caught and two shots offstage indicate that he came to no good end.

The ballet is propaganda of the crudest and most direct kind but is presented so well that it makes just as good an artistic vehicle as most Western ballets with their fantasy themes. Both music and choreography are worked out to appear thoroughly natural for Chinese theater.

"The White-Haired Girl" is part of the limited staple fare that was given all the proper political messages and nuances during the Cultural Revolution and that now provides entertainment for the Chinese masses.

Besides "The White-Haired Girl," the presentation of which was developed by the Shanghai Ballet School, the fare consists of nine other works. There is one other ballet, five musical dramas in Peking Opera style and three purely musical numbers.

All the 10 staples were created long before the Cultural Revolution but underwent extensive revision under the supervision of Chiang Ching, the wife of Mao Tse-tung, the Communist party chairman, to make their propaganda message conform with the revolution's political line.

All the works seem immensely popular and one hears songs and other excerpts from them being sung or hummed almost everywhere. They are constantly being broadcast over radio and television.

There are, one finds, some lesser theatrical and musical works being performed around the country, but entertainment for the 800,000,000 people of China consists for the most part of the 10 big approved productions.

The stories are all simple depictions in Communist terms of the triumph of good over evil. The Communists are shown as flawlessly courageous and heroic, the opposition as cruel and treacherous.

The operas represent an attempt to modernize the old Peking Opera format and, for this writer at least, they are not nearly as successful as the ballets.

As hybrids, they lack the stylized piquancy of the old operas and yet fall short of being successful modern music dramas. Their tunes seem strained and artificial and, sung with ear-splitting amplification, they appear to seek impact by sheer volume rather than artistry.

Dinner With Chou Is A Gourmet's Delight

by Audrey Topping

PEKING, June 21—Dinner with Premier Chou En-lai is a gourmet delight. Even the table talk, centered on hard political issues, couldn't detract from the joy of eating numerous superbly prepared and served exotic dishes.

The dinner tonight was served in the Fukien Room of the Great Hall of the People, which stands in Peking's main Tienanmen Square, near the Gate of Heavenly Peace. The Premier looked trim and handsome in his gray, Chinese-style suit with a Mao button reading, "Serve the people." His 73 years seemed only to add to his worldly charm.

Mr. Chou escorted us past an elaborately painted Fukien lacquer screen to a round table set with blue and white porcelain, place cards, silver knives and forks, ivory chopsticks and glasses for beer, wine and mao tai, a Chinese liquor. A circle of tempting hors d'oeuvres awaited us.

The Premier said we would sit according to Chinese custom, with his guests opposite him at the round table. The dinner was given for three American journalists, William Attwood, publisher of Newsday; Robert Keatley, a reporter for The Wall Street Journal, and Seymour Topping, assistant managing editor of The New York Times, and their wives.

"This is also how we sat the last time you were here," Mr. Chou said to me. He was referring to the night last month when I attended a dinner given by the Premier for my father, Chester Ronning, a retired Canadian diplomat. That dinner took place in the Kiangsu Room.

Tonight, with much of the conversation revolving around the Taiwan problem, use of the reception hall dedicated to Fukien seemed appropriate since the coastal province lies across the strait from the Nationalist Chinese island.

"The last time," Mr. Chou recalled, "we especially made some dishes from Hupeh Province because it is the birthplace of Mr. Ronning." The food tonight was equally delicious.

The menu, stamped with a red and gold seal, was rather deceptive. The nine courses, hand-printed in English, told only half the story. It read:

Hors d'ouevre; silver agaric consommé. Sea cucumbers, abalone and meatballs. Chicken slices, shrimp and green peas. Shad. Mushrooms and lima beans. Bean purée. Pastries. Fruits.

The hors d'oeuvre included a sumptuous array of cold chicken slices with paprika, stuffed crab meat, tomatoes and cucumbers, ham, sliced pork, bean curd and cold string beans. There were untold side dishes of buns, stuffed dumplings and boiled rice.

The silver agaric consommé consisted of jelly-like seaweed floating in a cloudy broth. The sea cucumbers are rather slippery sea slugs and are reputed to be good for curing hardening of the arteries.

The chicken slices, shrimp and peas were steamed and delicately flavored with green peppers and ginger. The shad was served with sweet sour sauce with nuts. The bean purée was cold, thick and sweet, and pastries consisted of sweet ground soybeans dipped in sesame seeds and sandwiched in almond paste. Watermelon and bananas were offered last. All this was served with beer, sweet red wine and the Chinese liquor called mao tai, which is made of sorghum.

We drank the toasts in mao tai. "Can you all drink mao tai?" Mr. Chou asked.

"Oh, yes," Mr. Topping replied. "We believe when trade begins that this will be one of your more successful commodities sold in the United States."

"We probably won't be able to supply so much mao tai," the Premier said, laughing.

Mr. Chou recalled how mao tai was discovered in Kweichow Province during the Long March. He said that the water comes from the Mao Tai River and is particularly favorable for making liquor because it doesn't go to your head. When this was greeted by skeptical laughter he added that he had consumed a lot of foreign liquor and none could be compared to mao tai on this point.

"You can drink three glasses tonight and I guarantee nothing will happen," he said.

Others present at the dinner included Cheng Wen-chin, director of the West European and American Affairs Division of the Foreign Ministry; Peng Hua, head of the Ministry's Information Department; Ma Yu-chien, one of his deputies; Kao Chien-chung, protocol officer, and two interpreters, Miss Nancy Tang, who was born in New York, and Chi Chao-chu, a former Harvard student.

The Great Hall of the People is where Mr. Chou usually holds both private and official dinner parties.

For a building of its size it was put up in record time for China. The enormous stone and marble three-story structure was built in 10 months.

The building has three main sections. The middle part contains the Hall of Ten Thousand People, a huge auditorium for rallies, concerts and party congresses. The West Wing is a magnificent gold and white pillared banquet hall with a capacity of 5,000.

The East Wing contains over 28 large rooms named after the provinces and main centers of China. Each provincial room contains lavish carpets and examples of the finest scrolls, paintings, carvings and other artistic crafts available from the area.

Bamboo Curtain Has Lifted, Chopstick Wall Remains

by James Reston

PEKING, Aug. 2—China may have the answer to America's problem of over-eating and over-weight. Having unsuccessfully tried every slimming formula from Lenten repentance to Joe Alsop's drinking man's diet, I have switched to chopsticks and reached the scientific conclusion that it is impossible not to lose weight if you rely on these slippery implements.

It's hard to find a fat man in this country. The Chinese are lean and muscular. Some say this is because their staple diet is rice, others that they work hard in the countryside and walk or ride bicycles in the cities. But after a few days of desperate experimentation with chopsticks, my problem now is not how to lose weight but how to avoid starvation.

Chinese food is excellent and plentiful. It is tastefully served on high tables and can, in an emergency, be shoveled into position if the victim is sitting on a low chair, as he usually is. But eating Chinese food properly with chopsticks, which is to say delicately and in reasonable silence, is a challenge which defies the law of gravity and the ingenuity of most Americans.

I naturally started with the overlapping grip. This is supposed to give you good control, but in my case it seemed to put spin on the bamboo shoots. I got good distance but developed a wicked slice to the right. I then switched to the interlocking grip, without noticeable success and, in frustration, finally tried stabbing with the business end of the stick. But stabbing, you are firmly told, is cheating, so there you sit, like a blind dog in a meat house, eager but helpless.

The Chinese, of course, are sympathetic. Innumerable amused but compassionate waitresses, Foreign Ministry officials, and understanding strangers have given me lessons, and I have tried to follow their advice. I have practiced in secret with easy items like dried beef. I have studied the sayings of Chairman Mao, but so far neither finger gymnastics nor Communist philosophy has done much good.

The generosity of the Chinese only adds to the foreign amateur's problems. When you arrive at the table awash with tea, it is loaded with delicacies, all neatly cut up in small portions and each with its own name: Crispy things are called su, long things tiao, shredded things are si, cubes are ting, peeled food is jen, chopped food mo.

But outside of ham and meat balls, you usually can't tell a sea slug from a pickled mushroom, and your host usually loads a little of each into your bowl and leaves the rest of the exercise to you.

This gives you plenty of time to study and fiddle with your chopsticks. Most of them are about eight inches long, some made of bamboo or lacquered wood, bone, ebony or plastic. Some are round and good for hitting foul balls, but most, fortunately, are square so that occasionally you can pinch a morsel on the edges. This increases your imagination and appetite without, of course, satisfying your hunger.

Meanwhile, the Chinese all around you use their chopsticks with the agility of a lobster and add a little more food to your undiminished mound. As the evening passes, you wonder vaguely if magnetized chopsticks would work, but steel filings in your meat might be a problem. Finally you look around furtively for a slice of bread, but that is almost the only thing in the whole culinary world that is not available.

Fortunately, there are a few consolations. The meat-ball soup is good, and you can swallow it, meat balls and all. Also, you learn eventually to abandon all efforts at pinching the food between the greasy spears and, by lowering the angle, slide a little food on to the rails and gradually balance it into your mouth.

Even then, however, the main consolation of losing weight is not so readily available, for Chinese beer is very good indeed, and what else can a man consume under the circumstances?

APPENDIX

Eric Sevareid's
Interview With
James Reston

Following is the transcript of a television interview by Eric Sevareid with James and Sally Reston. It was broadcast by the Columbia Broadcasting System as a Special Report entitled "Reston on China" on August 31, 1971.

ERIC SEVAREID—Good evening. After more than 20 years of hostility, including one undeclared war in Korea, the United States and the Communist People's Republic of China are on speaking terms. It began this summer after a lot of behind-the-scenes work by President Nixon. From July 9th to 11th the President's man, Henry Kissinger talked in Peking for twenty hours with Premier Chou En-lai, and Mr. Nixon's forthcoming visit was announced. In Peking at the same time, but unaware of the secret Kissinger mission, was one of the Western world's most influential political journalists, James B. Reston of The New York Times. Mr. Reston heard of the Kissinger-Chou En-lai transaction and promptly collapsed with an attack of appendicitis. After his operation Reston talked with Chou for five hours. That interview provided as good an insight to the Chinese state of mind as we've had in many years.

James Reston was born in Clydebank, Scotland, son of a factory hand. He grew up in Ohio; attended the University of Ilinois where he occasionally studied, frequently played championship golf and married a campus beauty and scholar Sally

Fulton, the daughter of a distinguished Illinois judge. He was a press agent for the Cincinnati Reds; wrote sports for The Associated Press; joined The New York Times in London. He has won the Pulitzer Prize twice, so far. Reston is handy with a No. 2 iron, all thumbs with a fly rod and has been scooping his competitors with outrageous regularity for 30 years. This broadcast is the case of one reporter interviewing another, a bit awkward for both; we'll see how it comes out.

SEVAREID—Mr. and Mrs. James Reston are now in Tokyo and speaking from our studio there by satellite; we'll wecome them back or out, I don't know which is the proper phrase. Scotty and Sally, did you come out with relief or a little regret?

JAMES RESTON—Well, that . . . that . . . both in a way, Eric. We came out rather tired because we traveled about 7,000 miles by train and car. But yes, we came out with regret. Fascinating experience.

SEVAREID—Did you feel, what they call, cultural shock, when you hit Hong Kong, a modern city, after all those weeks in China?

RESTON—Well, it was just all that affluence, all those cars, all those girls in skirts, you know. I don't think for six weeks we saw a woman in skirts in China, except once in a while.

SEVAREID—Scotty, now that you've had two, three, four days to think back about all this, is there any one, over-all impression that really sticks to your ribs about it, that really has you puzzled and thinking?

RESTON—Well, it would only be an impression, Eric, but yes, you can't help but have, I think, one over-all impression, and that is the staggering thing that modern China is trying to do. They're not trying to merely, to revolutionize, people, and establish a sense of social conscience, but they're really trying to change the character of these people. The place is one vast school of moral philosophy. I think that's the main thing; whether they make it or not, it's a heroic attempt. I don't think anything in the Soviet revolution or even in our own compares in magnitude with trying to change a quarter of the human race. That really is the one thing that sticks in my mind more than anything else, I think.

SEVAREID—I want to come back to that a bit later, Scotty. You know, your operation in Peking, probably the most famous one now since Lyndon Johnson's gall bladder—you may have started a new medical fad over here. You've had so much publicity about this acupuncture business. Did you come to really believe in it? Did Sally? She saw a lot of it.

RESTON—Well, I think you'd better talk to the chairman of the Revolutionary Committee here on my right. She knows more about that than I do.

SEVAREID—Sally?

SALLY RESTON—Well, I'm not sure I do, actually, because Scotty is the one who had a little bit of it himself in the hospital, but it was to us a fantastic adventure in medicine really to watch, Eric. I suppose outside of the morning when they gave Scotty a little bit of acupuncture and some herbal medicine along with it, which was quite interesting, the most interesting operation that we saw was a man who was having his right lung and one rib removed for—because of tuberculosis, and the operation had been going on for two hours when we got there and his only anesthesia was one needle in the outer part of his shoulder. And we talked to him; we asked him where he worked; he said he worked for the main foodstuffs company; we asked him how old he was; he said he was 24. Meanwhile they let me go around on the other side of the operating table and I stood up on a stool and took some pictures into the cavity in his back and we could see the lung—the other lung—breathing at the same time that he was talking to the doctors and to us. Scotty saw him eating some oranges at the same time and the only anesthesia used was one needle.

SEVAREID—Did they have to have your permission before they stuck those needles in you?

RESTON—Oh yes, they asked me if I wanted to do it, and I'm just enough of a ham to try it. It's not at all painful, Eric. It tingles a bit, that's about all.

SEVAREID—Didn't bring any of those needles back, did you?

RESTON—No, no needles back.

SEVAREID—Perhaps you'd like to try it on your friends? Scotty, let me ask you a bit about your interview with Chou En-lai, which had quite an effect all around the world really. Were there conditions to it?

RESTON—I wrote Chou En-lai a letter and said there had been a lot of casual conversation about the relations between our two countries, and I felt that the time had come for a precedent; and would he agree to a taped interview, and then would he look at it and he could scrub it if he liked. Well, he agreed on that—that was the first condition. They put two others. One was that the tape could not be used on a program like this, that is to say, I couldn't turn him on and let you hear him, which is too bad. The other was that in the informal part of the dinner where Sally kept the record, there could be no use of the tape recorder; that was all. And during the interview itself, I think it's within the bounds of our agreement for me to say that there was one other sharp comment that he made about the Soviet Union and he said, "I think we had better take that out, because it might be misunderstood in Moscow. They might think I had another motive." But that's the only thing he took out.

SEVAREID—He didn't—did he rule out any questions in advance? I don't think you asked him about the occupation of Tibet, for example. Did that come up at all?

RESTON—About the what?

SEVAREID—About the occupation of Tibet.

RESTON—No, no. But the answer to both questions is no, Eric. There was no—nothing was ruled out as a subject for discussion at all. As a matter of fact I had written that my first impression in China was that it was a very, very old civilization but had the sense of youth about it. That all its characteristics were young; it was healthy; it was clean; it was vigorous. But that it was run by old men. And I thought ahead of time how am I going to get at this rather sensitive point that Mao Tse-tung is 76 and Chou En-lai himself is 73. Well, he relieved me of that embarrassment by saying he had read this and he wished to explain to me that they were old men, but the reason for that was that our revolution in America had gone on for a very short time. Therefore, Jefferson and the early Presidents were very young men, whereas these Communists had run for 28 years before they'd come to power, were then in middle age. He did not explain why they felt they had to go on for 21 more years, but I guess that's the old story that people don't like to give up power.

SEVAREID—Sally, you must have taken the notes on that fantastic dinner that was described in one of Scotty's dispatches. He never knows what he's eating unless it's pumpkin pie, according to my memory. But what about those toasts that were mentioned. You had toasts to what or to whom? Do you remember?

SALLY RESTON—The toasts?

SEVAREID—The toasts.

SALLY RESTON—Yes. Yes, we did have some toasts, but I don't remember them being particularly remarkable, to the friendship of our two countries. I can't remember. Scotty, can you remember what the toasts were?

RESTON—No. The toasts were not significant. The only thing that was significant was that they toasted us in something called mao lai—mao tai, yes. That is a combination of dynamite and—

(CROSSTALK)

RESTON—. . . Sorghum juice and dynamite, Eric. I don't recommend it to you, but anyway the only point is that Chou En-lai managed to make a very graceful toast and lift his glass without taking one single drop of that stuff. So he's an old dog; he knows what he's doing.

SEVAREID—What did you do?

RESTON—Oh I belted it back.

SEVAREID—Were you surprised about his extraordinarily intimate knowledge, or so it seemed to be, about affairs here? Apparently he even reads the full transcripts of presidential news conferences over there.

RESTON—Yes he does. He—I had a little different impression of—from most people who had seen him, Eric. I thought he was older than I expected him to be. He has the coolest eye and most penetrating way of looking at you of any man I think I've ever seen. But I did feel that he was showing his age. But intellectually he never missed a beat. He used every question that was put to him, of course, for his own purposes, but he always came back, no matter how much he wandered, he came back to the point of the question. And he does read. What he does not apparently do, is ever sleep. I don't know how he does it, but apparently the guy's up 18, 19 hours a day.

SEVAREID—Did you get the feeling, either one of you as you traveled around that they still have this kind of middle kingdom feeling that China is the middle place between heaven and the ordinary earth? That kind of built-in arrogance or smugness, whatever one should call it. Sally, did you?

SALLY RESTON—Yes I did, Eric. I tend to remember faces of people rather than generalizations. But one very interesting thing there to us: We met it the first time on the train from Canton to Peking, which is almost a two-day trip, and we got off the train and a little girl, three or four, ran out of the door at the station and she saw Scotty and she turned around in fear and ran back and grabbed her father's trouser leg and hid behind his leg.

SEVAREID—I think that's very natural.

SALLY RESTON—However, this happened over and over again to both of us and as we got farther and farther from Canton and Peking, where the Chinese people had not seen Westerners, the children show a certain amount of uneasiness when they see Westerners.

SEVAREID—But you ran into no manifestations of hatred toward you as Americans?

SALLY RESTON—No, no. Not at all. They were unfailingly kind. Very courteous.

SEVAREID—I'm sure you had a guide interpreter all the time. Did you have any sense that you were being followed by police, or anyone else?

RESTON—No, not at all.

SALLY RESTON—No.

RESTON—No surveillance of that kind, Eric, and no sense, as in Moscow, that your room is being bugged or your papers looked at, or anything like that. None at all.

SEVAREID—Do you get the feeling . . .

RESTON—There is—it is a startling thing to go into a country at our age and suddenly feel totally different, so that you are an object of curiosity. When we went to Dairen, for example, up in Manchuria, maybe as many as four—five hundred people would be at the entrance to the hotel when we would go out. And when we went away on the train, great crowds of people would gather around and look at us in a startled way.

SEVAREID—Was there any great public excitement that you could detect when the Nixon visit was announced?

RESTON—No, not a single, single word. They—we tried to find out—to get the reaction to all that, Eric, and it was very curious. Here in the press and radio, and in a dominant controlled press, they had been putting out quite violent anti-American propaganda, so that one day the Nixon Administration is presented, not in one day, but for years, as the enemy of the Chinese people. And the next day he is an acceptable guest. So we tried to find out—well, what do you think about that? Does this cause you any trouble or no trouble at all because it has been decided by the Government that if President Nixon wishes to come to Peking and wishes to talk about his sins of the past, or the sins of America, well, why not let him come? And even at Peking University where we talked for hours with faculty and some students, the idea of any contradiction between the propaganda and the invitation didn't trouble them at all. In fact they thought our questions about it were rather stupid.

SEVAREID—Did you get the feeling that they're dreadfully ignorant about the rest of the world?

RESTON—Yes. And in some ways, although they are asked and exhorted by Mao Tse-tung to let China learn from the West and other parts of the world, they were not only it seemed to me, ignorant, but—of the problems of the rest of the world, or the new scientific revolution which goes beyond the industrial revolution that they are seeking to achieve, but they seem to me to be rather lacking in curiosity about it all. They're trying to move really from the abacus into this world of the computer. But the thought that educational equality should be combined with the new techniques of science in order to move into that world didn't seem to them to be relevant to the discussion at all.

SEVAREID—I was astonished to read—I think in one of your articles—about somebody being operated on, a brain operation and clutching in his hand the thoughts of Mao Tse-tung. Did you get any impression that anybody is getting bored with that little book of parables which sound as if they all come from a Chinese fortune cookie to me? Do they really believe all that?

SALLY RESTON—Well, I think so. Once in a while, Eric, you see a little bit of this. I went to a hospital in Shanghai and photographed some acupuncture in dentistry. They use now acupuncture for the extraction of teeth, and so on. And they put two needles only into the joint between the thumb and the first finger. In Chinese the word means "joined valley," and they put a needle here and a needle here and then the patients wait for 15 minutes and then the dental surgeon comes along and pulls the teeth and they feel nothing, they tell me, at all during any part of this. Perhaps something rather like a mosquito bite they said, when the needles were put in. However, I was shown some operations for tumors on the jaw, for instance, and then I went through the wards afterwards to see these people, and perhaps once I remember coming to the door and as they saw me everybody picked up their little red books now. Perhaps that's an accident, I don't know whether there is cynicism about it or not; it's very difficult for me to tell. I did notice that once, however.

RESTON—I think . . .

SEVAREID—Excuse me . . .

SALLY RESTON—Yes.

SEVAREID—Sally, did all those Chinese women you saw working—did they seem to act like liberated women or people permanently enslaved in hard work?

SALLY RESTON—Well, they do work very hard. Especially in the countryside, Eric. The loads they carry is just unbelievable —the women. And of course I asked that question and so did Scotty all the way around and they maintain they are absolutely equal. When I said to them, what do the women do in the countryside, in the—the peasants in the villages, and in the communes—and what do the men do? Well, they said the women work in the fields and the men drive the carts and if their trucks are around, they do the driving. I did think a little bit about that. However, I do think they are very equal and liberated. There are a lot of services for the women in the cities. There are organizations that go out and do their shopping at the grocery store for them; bring everything home and cut it up and get it ready for just the last bit of frying for dinner; people who mend and sew; just leave your things at the little shop in the daytime. I saw a settlement in Shanghai—a little sewing shop there—where people can leave a shirt to be patched and pick it up in the evening, for maybe a penny or two. So that—and I'm told they are paid equally with the men. So I think perhaps it really does work.

RESTON—One or two little points in addition to what Sally says, Eric, they—of course the old habit of arranged marriages is out. And they are under some pressure where they were not to marry until 26 or 27. And one of the key questions about China, namely how can they raise their standard of life when their standard—when the ratio—the birth rate is going up as fast as it has been doing in the past, we had the impression very definitely that the propaganda had gotten over to the young men and women about this. There are an awful lot of children around, I've got to admit. Presumably sex has something to do with that. But I thought the education program on behalf of birth control was good. The women keep their own names in marriage. They can get married very quickly and very easily after a physical test and they can get divorced almost equally easily. Now we couldn't get any figures about that, but Sally, you might talk about the number of divided families that rather troubled us.

SALLY RESTON—Well, we met several people whose wives were working in one city, perhaps Peking, and the husband in Canton, or something of that sort. We never did really get quite to the bottom of that, but of course everybody is assigned to jobs; they all say we go according to the needs of the state, wherever we're assigned. But when we questioned officials about that, they say that if the husband and wife want to be in the same city together that they try very hard to arrange that. I don't think it happens a lot, but it does happen sometimes.

SEVAREID—Scotty, they seem to have made a kind of god out of Mao Tse-tung. What happens when he dies? Are they preparing people for that time?

RESTON—Well, yes they are Eric. As a matter of fact we saw some physical evidence of this just in the six, seven weeks when we were in there. In the first place, nothing that you and I have seen in Moscow compares with the number of statues; the number of quotations of Mao Tse-tung. They're everywhere. They're on the front of the railroad trains. They're on your calendar. They're on the menu when you have breakfast in the morning. The din and the optic noise of signs with Mao Tse-tung sayings are all over the place. No, it's not only that Eric, but when people explain to you how dreadful life was before and how things are getting better at the present time they always put in the

phrase "with the help of Mao Tse-tung's teachings." Now that's
the way it has been and the way very largely it still is. But things
are disappearing; the big plaster saints of Mao Tse-tung are
coming down; one disappeared in the Canton hotel between the
time when we arrived and when we went out. A vast picture of
him, a painting of him, in Hsin Chiao Hotel in Peking was taken
down while we were there. Whether that's getting ready for the
eventual loss of their—what can only be described as a saint,
which is what they have made out of him—I don't know, or
whether it's in anticipation of President Nixon's visit. I would
think the former not the latter.

SEVAREID—Do you think he's gotten to the point of senility
now and is merely a figurehead—or is really . . .

RESTON—I have no way of knowing. We got not one whisper or suggestion of that even in the diplomatic corps. But everybody did emphasize, Eric, that the really key figure on the day-
to-day running of the government really is Chou En-lai and not
Mao Tse-tung. In fact, nobody seems to know where he is.

SEVAREID—Did you pick up any hints or suggestions as to
the possible date of the President's visit there?

RESTON—No, we—we in our rather cynical way rather assumed that you would know more about that—that it might be
tied more to the political interest of the President than the con-
venience of Chou En-lai.

SEVAREID—Well, I think it's being kept very flexible here
now. Any—any talk at all about Chou En-lai perhaps coming
here later?

RESTON—I got the impression very definitely that—that he
would like to go to the West. He is a man who was in some ways
cultivated and educated in the West and I think he has a great
curiosity about it and my guess would be if we could resolve our
problem with—with him about the U.N. that he might very
well do it, but I'm not at all hopeful we're going to be able to
do that.

SEVAREID—Scotty, you wrote a good deal about his preoccupation with the past, the old grievances with us, the Japanese and so on. Did he indicate at any time the realization that had it not been for the United States' defeat of Japan and we had to do it almost single-handed, they might still be partly occupied by Japanese troops or that it was United States that arranged a U.N. seat for China? In fact, we got into World War II partly because we would—in great part because we would not accept the Japanese intentions toward China?

RESTON—Well, Eric, their historical memory is very selective, Eric. They're sore as a boil about the two-China proposal of the President, and yet they totally forget that it was the United States over the opposition of the Soviet Union and Britain and France that got China into the U.N. Security Council as one of the five permanent members in the first place.

SEVAREID—That's right.

RESTON—They've forgotten all about that. I tried to say, you know, one of the most appealing things to me about our own fellow countrymen is that we have no memory. We were struck at Pearl Harbor by the Japanese but have no hatred of the Japanese and the same is true of the Germans, that we are forward looking people. Oh, they wouldn't accept that at all. They said that's dreadful and they more or less gave us back the old saying that people who forget history are likely to have to relive all the agonies of the past. And they would go then into the wickedness of the Japanese and the danger of the million Soviet troops on their borders.

SEVAREID—I don't quite understand their long-range thinking about Japan. They have no major allies anywhere. Now they would like us out of Asia in many respects, no doubt. They're almost at swords' point with the Soviet Union. Why this fear and all this anti-Japanese propaganda? Aren't they going to need a friend somewhere, sometime?

RESTON—Well, they don't seem to show much interest in that. They're fussing with everybody, Washington, Moscow, the Common Market, and more than that, with Japan. They're not looking for friends. They've been humiliated, and they're quite frank in telling you that, that, well, it's all right for the President to come to Peking, but look, he's coming here to compromise. We're not looking for compromise, we're looking for rectification of your wrongdoing in the West in the past. You humiliated, you dismembered our country. You have troops all over the place, on our borders, and bombers that could hit every city in China. And we want you the hell out of there.

I think the real thing that they're worried about is that Japan, in spite of present economic difficulties, is bounding along here, its gross national product going up 12, 14 per cent a year, and going to have, as time goes on, enormous surpluses of capital to invest all through this part of the world. And they just believe that it is in the Japanese temperament that if they have economic power it will be followed by military expansion and militarism.

SEVAREID—Well, he sounds as though he expects Mr. Nixon to be making a pilgrimage to Canossa here, to come hat in hand, humbled. Is it to be a one-way street entirely? Is that what you make out of it?

RESTON—Well, I don't see—I think Sally is a little more hopeful than I am about what's going to be got out of that visit. There is one aspect of it: It may be that they are so worried about their isolation and also about those million Soviet troops on their border that maybe they figure it wouldn't be a bad idea to have a little better relations with Washington and not be fighting with everybody all at once. But nobody would admit that to us.

SEVAREID—Well, would it be fair to say, or did you have the feeling that they now assume we are definitely going out of Vietnam, that will be done and that our military presence in East Asia is now a question of secondary importance to them, a declining problem—that Japan and Russia are much more important?

RESTON—Well, I think—I think they are—they're more

worried about the—the million troops to the north of the Soviet Union and I think they do assume that those troops will be there long after the United States has pulled out of Vietnam. I think they do think we're getting out of that, but they're—they're very dubious about Taiwan. They think that—and I think with some justification—that what we would like there is to keep Taiwan in the U.N. and that by saying nice things and sending President Nixon to Peking, that maybe a year from now we would— they would let us have our diplomatic agent like Bergus, our Foreign Service officer in Cairo, or a trade mission. Frankly, I don't—I don't think that's in the cards. I think these—these are men in a hurry and there's a kind of a quick opening play here in China and the President has seen the opening, but I don't think he's—I don't think he's decided to go for that opening boldly enough to win over the support of China. I think as so many times in the past he's dealing with the politics of the problem and not with the problem and my guess would be that—that he's—he's going to have to listen to some rather rough language when he comes to Peking.

SEVAREID—Are you convinced now, Scotty, after all those conversations in Peking that this is basically an inward-looking country, that the idea of territorial expansion that we've heard so much about here, especially in Washington the last 20 years, is really all over, if it ever was very real, that they're in some ways like Russia in that respect?

RESTON—Well, that, of course, is the real question in my mind. Just before we left, Eric, when you were away during the Pentagon papers flap, Sally and I happened to be dining during the night that the Attorney General sent the telegram to The Times asking us not to print. We were dining alone that night with McNamara so the conversation naturally got around to the question, "Why did you want this study made in the first place?" "Well," he said, "I think that the real problem of those past years was that we were able to justify doing almost anything in Vietnam on the basis of one hypothesis: that our premises were wrong."

One of our premises was that China was expansionist and
that the very least we could expect out of that part of the world,
if we happened to get in deep trouble in Saigon, was that we'd
have the domino theory taking over countries all over Southeast Asia and East Asia. I got no impression that these people
are world-minded. They've got a revolutionary doctrine. They're
saying to the world, "Look how well we did. And if you would
just have a revolution like ours, fine, you will do well too." The
universality of their propaganda, their doctrine, their revolutionary doctrine, I think is probably nonsense, but they say that.
Primarily, however, they want the unity of their country, which
is to say Taiwan. They want—secondly, they want to educate,
revolutionize and feed 750 million people and bring about their
moral regeneration at the same time.

Well, you know, when you're trying to take on all that, plus
worrying about Russia and Japan at the same time, it's pretty
hard for me to believe that this is a people who'd want to worry
about what's going on in Guatemala or Bolivia this week.

SEVAREID—Does it strike you that the so-called "work
ethic," which is intensely developed there, is developing at the
very time when it seems to be declining, especially among
young people, in this country and Europe?

RESTON—Very definitely . . .

SEVAREID—Any cosmic comparisons you draw from that?
It's a little alarming, in a way.

RESTON—Well, you know, it's easier for me to talk about
that once we got home, because I don't like to throw off on our
own country from outside of it. But you can't escape it, Eric. We
come from a country now that has got enormous problems with
drugs and dope, with one faction in the country fighting against
another faction, and you go there and you find, though they in-
vented opium, that they have no drug problem, that they are
working like dogs. I can't tell you the way these people work.
And you can't help but be impressed with this.

Also in the process I think they do get—although it's not
popular these days—there is something to the old ethic, the old

work ethic. They are working hard. And I think they've got a sense of purpose and maybe even a sense of nationhood developing from it. You know, it's not necessarily a bad idea. Mao Tse-tung and the Attorney General and the Vice President of the United States would all seem to agree about the same point, on the elite. They are fighting, in China, the educated elite, and they're trying to get—they're trying to get their doctors, their professional people, their professors and everybody else to spend a certain amount of time with simple people.

SEVAREID—Did any of them ever speculate, among the intellectuals and the others you talked to, about the fact that the industrialization that they're heading for brings an awful lot of miseries with it, as we're now suffering here?

RESTON—Well, not much, Eric. They stick to the brief. They don't get into that sort of thing, although one wonders, naturally, how will they deal with the problems of affluence? After all, our people on the frontier dealt very well with the problems of adversity. Our problem is that we've just been led into temptation too much. Well, they're not led into much temptation. They work away for very, very small things, but they show a sense of gratitude. They don't take things for granted the way we tend to do.

SALLY RESTON—There's another thing about China, too, speaking of industrialization. All the way from Canton to Peking, which is 1,500 miles or so, we never looked out the train window without seeing human beings. And they are already so crowded on the east coast of China, where most of the population lives, it's hard to believe. For instance, it was pointed out to us that really many Chinese, if not the majority of them, are never out of earshot of another Chinese person in their whole lives. It's hard, I think, even for us in America, living in big cities, to believe that that is true.

SEVAREID—If you and your husband should go back to China, what did you not see this time that you'd like to go and see?

SALLY RESTON—Oh, I'd like to go west in China. I'd like to
see Sian and I'd like to see Chungking. I would love to see the
gorges of the Yangtze and the river there. But no one has been
allowed into Chungking and up the Yangtze in that region at
all. But I would love to see that some day. That's one or two of
the things I would love to see.

RESTON—We were not modest in our requests, Eric, as you
can probably imagine. We asked to see every place imaginable,
and everybody, from Mao Tse-tung to his wife, who is herself
a real factor in the Cultural Revolution—also, to be dead honest
about this whole conversation, I think people have to realize
really how restricted we were. And I don't mean this in a critical sense. Actually we were able to see more and talk to more
people than we expected we would. But nevertheless it is very
hard to draw conclusions from the people we did see, what we
did see, because we were always, of course, always under the
terrible handicap of not being able to hear what people say
passing in the street or to question in one's own language or to
understand the other person's language. All that's a great handicap. And we were not able to get at the officials who are dealing with trade, we were not able to get at Lin Piao. Particularly,
we were not, oddly enough, able really to get at the propaganda
apparatus. It's a fantastic apparatus, centered some place in the
Central Committee, with the primary voice of it being the People's Daily in Peking. And I said, "Look, we read this stuff and
I want to know who writes it. Where does it come from? Who is
the informing mind in the whole business?" Well, we didn't get
anywhere with that. The People's Daily editors did give us a
dinner when we left Peking. But they would not discuss this.
And even when I tried to explain that these are not newspapers,
in our sense, that we cannot understand the role of the press or
the role of the Army in your society, you could not really get
a conversation going on that because that, you see, is against
what they call democratic centralism, by which they mean that
you can have dissent or discussion within the policy, but you

cannot say, you know, "This is a crummy old policy. I think you ought to do it a different way." You can't even do that in the seminars at Peking University.

SEVAREID—This prevalence of military people in every kind of enterprise, including commercial enterprises, is this to try to weld the ordinary people and soldiers together? Is there an element of restraint and surveillance in this thing?

RESTON—Well, I think it's the former, Eric, frankly. You know, when we went there and found—wherever we would go we would find this military character in civilian clothes in the Revolutionary Committees, even at schools. We said we were very worried because—they said, "Well, why are you worried?" And I said, "Well, look, the history of the 20th century is a history of violence, most of it having been brought about by armies that took over the civil government, of Germany and Japan, and so on. Why should we not be worried about that?" They said, "Well, you just don't understand the Chinese Army. The Chinese Army is not separate. It is in the commercial business, it runs farms, it runs industries. And it's not the same thing. You've got it all wrong."

Now, maybe they're right about that. But one still has to feel rather anxious.

SEVAREID—Why is it necessary? Does it just mean that's a more disciplined group that they command from Peking a little more easily?

RESTON—I think so, yes. I don't think it's any more complicated than that, Eric.

SEVAREID—But you don't believe, do you, Scotty, that they're going to succeed, by social means, political means, of changing the nature of the human animal? It's been tried before.

RESTON—Well, you know, Eric, you don't need to ask me that question. I'm a Scotch Calvinist. I believe in redemption of the human spirit and the improvement of man. Maybe it's because I believe that or I want to believe it that I was struck by the tremendous effort to bring out what is best in man, what makes them good, what makes them cooperate with one another and be considerate and not beastly to one another. They are try-ing that. I am not—I have seen it tried in the Soviet Union, and it's a sad picture at the end.

SEVAREID—Scotty . . .

RESTON—But these people are not like the Russians. They are quite different.

SEVAREID—Even a Scotch Calvinist would agree with me that the greatest glories of human creation that have remained, almost the only great things that have remained, have to do with art, and that these all come from individuals. Committees have not created great literature, great anything.

RESTON—Well, this of course is true, Eric, and the oppres-sive nature of the direct state—you know, one of the great things about going abroad, I think, is to make you realize what you have at home. And it is true that at Peking University, for ex-ample, when you talk about what you have just mentioned, the glories of the individual mind, the free mind, that can range and question, and all the rest of it, to professors at the univer-sity, where, after all, free thought, which questioned the old Mandarin society, it started at Peking University, and now you find the professor saying, "Oh no, that is not right at all. That kind of education, that kind of thought, led to bourgeois propaganda." And when you say, "Well, why do you—why does anybody who differs with you, why does he have to be charac-terized as a renegade, why do you have to throw him out?" "Well," they say, "because he is a renegade. He goes against what the state wants." And that is sad.

And then the old professors sort of confess. They seem to feel they have to have confessionals about how wrong they were in the past when they believed in the subjective thought and this free mind that means so much to us.

SEVAREID—Scotty, in your conversation with Chou En-lai, or anybody, was there any reference at all to what must have been an enormous cost in human lives to install this revolution back in the late forties, early fifties?

RESTON—Well, only in the sense of their blaming it all on

American imperialism and Chiang Kai-shek and our arming of
Chiang Kai-shek. Objective discussion of the point of the loss
of human life, they profess to great interest in that in the war
in Vietnam and in the agonies and humiliations of China in the
past, all blamed on the West. But in terms of what their own
revolution cost them in human lives, they regard this as heroic.
This is what produced—you see, all power comes out of the
barrel of the gun, they say. And look at this great, noble society
that has been created as a result of the sacrifices of those men.
That's the only answer you get back on that.

SEVAREID—Scotty, this is a very hypothetical, perhaps use-
less, question. But now, thinking back, now that you've been
there and absorbed the atmosphere of their minds, and thinking
back to the last two or three, four years in Vietnam, do you have
any doubt that, had we invaded North Vietnam or put the Hanoi
Government in real danger of collapse, that they would have
come in, the Chinese?

RESTON—I don't know about putting the Hanoi Government in jeopardy, Eric, because they don't seem to me to be as
close to Hanoi as I thought they were when I first went there. But
imperiling their borders, certainly, without any doubt. Just as
they went across the Yalu in the Korean war, I have no doubt
that they would not let—they would not see an American army
standing in the Red River Valley. That I don't think they would
tolerate.

They draw a very, very clear distinction between what they
do beyond their borders, which is to say they send ideas and
indirect aid, at the most, but not men. But when they talk about
their own borders and any threat of dismemberment of their
state or threat to its security, as was the case in the first half of
this century, you always get the same phrase, "We will drown
any invader in a sea of humanity." And I have no doubt that
they would.

SALLY RESTON—Could I just say—go back to one question, Eric? Have we got a minute?

SEVAREID—Please do.

SALLY RESTON—When we got out, Eric, we went of course to Hong Kong, and there has been an upsurge in the number of young people this year who are swimming across Mirs Bay or Deep Bay, escaping from Kwangtung Province into Hong Kong. The figures now are some five or six hundred a month. They swim at night, hiking across the hills and the forests to get there, for maybe six or seven nights, hiding in the daytime and walking at night, and then making the long swim, ten hours at least, at night, to get to Hong Kong.

I talked to some of the people in Hong Kong who—actually the agency that deals with them. And it's the question of the individual I wanted to go back to. They're finding a very curious thing about these 25-year-olds who come in there, both men and women, young men and women, that they don't know how to maintain themselves independently. Everything has been done for them in China, their housing, their medical care, their education, their transportation. They don't have to queue up for anything. So that when they get into an independent society they really don't know quite how to operate. They're finding that they have to begin teaching these young people how to be an individual and on their own again. It's very, to me, interesting.

SEVAREID—Nobody's swimming the other way, to get into Communist China?

SALLY RESTON—I don't know, but there's a good deal of free traffic across the border, between Hong Kong and Canton. Apparently you can go in and see your family. We saw thousands going across the border, taking in things, all sorts of things, into China, laden with them. Apparently there is a great deal of traffic of Chinese back and forth across the border. Whether people go back and stay, I don't know.

RESTON—Anybody who is going the other way, Eric, they're all reporters.

SEVAREID—And there will be more, many more.

RESTON—Many more.

SEVAREID—Well, thank you both very, very much. I hope it hasn't tired you too much. You've had a long, hard trip.

RESTON—Thank you, Eric.

SEVAREID—It's getting late at night here and lunch time for you.

RESTON—Wonderful to hear your voice and we'll see you home soon.

Index